The Long Term Care Handbook

Jeff Sadler

NATIONAL UNDERWRITER.

The National Underwriter Co. • 505 Gest St. • Cincinnati, OH 45203-1716

ISBN: 0-87218-160-X

Printed in U. S. A.

DEDICATION

This book is dedicated to Gloria C. Sadler,
my first long term care insurance client.

ACKNOWLEDGEMENT

Books move toward their final form not only due to the author's own work, but largely through the assistance of others. I am indebted to the contributions of the following people: Eileen Mazur Abel, MSW, for the Doan story; Pam Dunlap for editorial suggestions; Robert E. Parr, CLU, RHU for his mother's story; Eileen Sadler for her patience and understanding during the writing of this book; Janet Strickland for an endless amount of resource material; and to the editors, Jaclyn Meder Ruzsa and Darlene K. Chandler, J.D., CLU, ChFC for their usual sound work on my behalf.

ABOUT THE AUTHOR

Jeff Sadler began his insurance career with Paul Revere Life Insurance Company in 1975 as an underwriter in the disability income brokerage division. He moved on to the sales department in 1977 working in disability income product development and marketing. In 1979, he transferred to the Fort Lauderdale-Miami brokerage field office where he was named national representative of the month in July, 1980.

In March, 1981, Jeff joined Monarch Life to further develop its national brokerage system and eventually to write its new disability income portfolio, "Advantage," introduced to the field in the spring of 1982. After the initial national training phase of this product introduction, he established a new brokerage sales office for Monarch in Orlando, Florida and quickly built it into the company's third largest office in 1983.

In April, 1984, Jeff teamed up with Financial Security Corporation of America to conduct national training and marketing seminars in the sale of disability income. He continues to work with several insurance carriers, authoring a disability income and a long term care portfolio in 1986 and 1987.

In June, 1989, he co-founded, with his father, Sadler Disability Services, Inc., specializing in national and international agent training, joint field work and product development in both the disability income and long term care markets. Sadler Disability Services also became a licensed continuing education provider and currently operates in seven states, writing and teaching courses in the health insurance field. Currently, Jeff is working with World Marketing Alliance in Atlanta, Georgia, training agents in the sale of disability income and long term care insurance.

He is the author of *Disability Income: The Sale, The Product, The Market*, the second edition which was published in June, 1995 by The National Underwriter Company. He has written articles for numerous industry and consumer publications and has been a featured speaker at many of the industry's national and regional sales conventions.

Jeff has won the 1987 Distinguished Service Award from the National Association of Health Underwriters and the 1990 Stanley Greenspun Memorial Health Insurance Person of the Year Award from the Gold Coast Association of Health Underwriters. He is a past president of the Florida Association of Health Underwriters, the Central Florida Association of Health Underwriters, and the Central Florida General Agents and Managers Association.

TABLE OF CONTENTS

INTRODUCTION

It is a Norman Rockwell image of the typical American family: three generations all gathered around the table for Sunday dinner. You can see the joy on the faces of the children, parents and grandparents. This has long been society's picture of the ideal family.

The 1990s bear little resemblance to this family image. Adult children and their parents do not live in the same neighborhood; often they do not live in the same state. The single-parent family has become as prevalent as its two-parent counterpart. Parenthood itself is occurring much later in life than in prior generations. In many instances, parents well into their fifties are still rearing children.

In assisting today's adult children with financial planning — including preparation for an aging parent's illness or injury — a certain theme is often repeated: disbelief that a parent can have medical problems that are usually long term. This skepticism is only natural. We think of our parents as powerful individuals who will always be there for us and are caught off guard by the realities of aging and illness.

Yet we must strive to overcome these feelings and help our clients (and ourselves) focus on the preparation needed to ensure that plans are in place to help pay for medical costs that slip between the cracks of our traditional third-party payors. Such plans often include the use of long term care insurance. The case of Karen Doan Parker and her 70-year-old mother, Betty Doan, clearly illustrates the importance of planning ahead.

THE DOAN FAMILY

Karen and Steve Parker have been married for 20 years. Karen, 41, is a third grade teacher and Steve is an electrical engineer. They live in Orlando, Florida with their three children: Kim, 13, James, 8, and Amy, 5. Karen's sister Julie, 43, lives nearby. Julie recently divorced Jim, her husband of 21 years, and has two children: Peter, 13, and Carly, 6. Karen and Julie's brother, Robert, 46, lives in San Diego, California with his wife

Pam. Traditionally, Robert "visits the folks" once a year, usually in the spring. The Doan family tree looks like this:

THE DOAN FAMILY

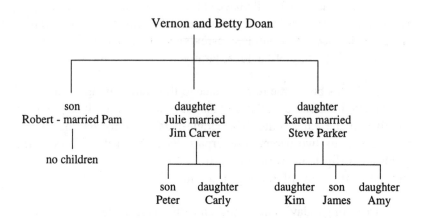

When Karen was a girl, she was very close to her mother and sister. During the girls' teen years, however, Julie and Mrs. Doan were always at odds with each other. It seemed they were constantly arguing. Julie resented Karen, whom she viewed as her mother's "favorite". The two sisters drifted apart.

After both were married, Karen and Julie once again developed a close relationship. They lived ten minutes apart and saw each other frequently. The two couples were often companions on Saturday nights out and their children played together. At least once a month they all gathered at their mother and father's house for Sunday dinner.

This pattern of family get-togethers continued even after the death of Karen's dad, but now it was up to Karen and Julie to host the Sunday family gathering. As their mother began to recover emotionally from her husband's death, Karen and Julie teamed up to provide the critical support to get through that difficult time.

Mrs. Doan and her husband had been married for 49 years when he died of a heart attack. While at first it was rough, the family was able to help Mrs. Doan as she made the transition to widowhood. Mrs. Doan joined a seniors' organization and continued to remain active in her church.

Karen and Julie continued to visit on a weekly basis, often inviting their mother out to dinner or a social event. Mr. Doan's life insurance had left Mrs. Doan comfortable financially. She had $62,000 in the bank and owned her own home. She often joked that "she was spending her grandchildren's inheritance." In the five years following Mr. Doan's death, Karen's husband, Steve, had taken care of his mother-in-law's financial arrangements, overseeing her investments and securities and helping with her taxes.

Over the past two years, the family's relationships have strained somewhat. Karen and Julie once again grew apart. Following her divorce, Julie returned to work as a paralegal in one of the city's most prestigious law firms. Her ex-husband, Jim, was recently made a partner in his company. He typically worked 12 hour days and rarely saw his kids. He continues to pay $1,000 a month in child support and Julie and the kids continue to live in their five bedroom, 3,000 square foot home. Julie and her children stopped coming regularly to Sunday dinners, which were now held exclusively at Karen's house.

One Wednesday morning while teaching reading to her third grade class, Karen received a summons from the principal assistant's office. Her mother had fallen while at the supermarket and was taken to Florida Hospital for treatment. Test results indicated that Mrs. Doan had broken her hip. The tests also revealed the presence of osteoporosis.

When Karen arrived at the hospital, she found her mother upset and in tears. Karen asked to see Mrs. Doan's doctor but was told he would not be back until the next morning. Steve called Julie and Robert to let them know of their mother's injury. Julie said she would try to get to the hospital after work. Robert asked Steve to "keep him posted."

Karen met with her mother's doctor the following morning. Dr. Ramon explained that her mother would require at least six months of skilled nursing rehabilitation care. She would also need to adhere to a special diet and exercise program and take calcium supplements to prevent further loss of bone. Should her hip fail to heal properly, the worst case scenario would result in the need for permanent home health care or placement in a nursing home.

Karen had promised her mother that under no circumstances would she ever have to go into a nursing home and if the need ever arose, she would see to her mother's care personally. Now, Karen was concerned about whether she would be able to provide the kind of care her mother needed and about the impact her illness would have on Steve and the kids.

With nowhere to turn, Karen sought advice from Mrs. Becker, the hospital's social worker and discharge planner. Because of the classification of Mrs. Doan's ailment, Medicare required that Mrs. Doan be discharged in 72 hours. Mrs. Becker assured Karen that she would help in any way to facilitate a smooth release for her mother from the hospital and discussed three options available:

1. Mrs. Doan returns home and receives 24-hour skilled nursing and skilled rehabilitative care;

2. Mrs. Doan stays at one of her children's house and receives private nursing care during the day for the next six months; or

3. Mrs. Doan is placed in a nursing home until fully recovered.

That evening Karen called Julie to discuss the alternatives. After hearing this, Julie tearfully confessed that with her job and the kids she couldn't take care of her mother. Karen, on the other hand, wanted to care for her mother but her three-bedroom house could not accommodate her, Steve and the children, and her mother. Karen told Julie that "If she had a house as big as Julie's, she'd gladly take Mom in." Naturally, this provoked both resentment and guilt in Julie, who responded angrily, saying, "You at least have a husband to help you out! I have to look after myself and the children. If I had someone to help me, I'd be able to have Mom come and stay with me, but it's too much by myself. If you can't get one of your children to give up their bed for a few months, then I suppose Mom will simply have to go into a nursing home." With that, Julie slammed down the phone.

Karen couldn't believe that Julie would even consider a nursing home as an alternative for her mother. She promised herself that she would investigate other options so that her mother would not have to go into a nursing home.

After talking with Karen, Julie decided to take matters into her own hands. Julie went to the hospital to explain to her mother why she couldn't stay with her and that Karen simply didn't have the room. Julie informed her mother that since she couldn't live with her or Karen and, obviously she couldn't live on her own, that a nursing home was the only solution.

Distraught, Mrs. Doan called her son Robert in California. She knew her son would not put up with the idea of his mother in a nursing home. She begged Robert, "Don't let them put me away!" He reassured her that it would never happen and hung up to call Karen.

Karen, blind-sided by Robert's call, could not calm her brother long enough to explain. She felt that Robert was unfair in blaming her. It was Julie that Robert should be talking to, not her. She assured Robert that she had no intention of putting their mother in a nursing home.

LONG TERM CARE: MORE THAN A FINANCIAL DECISION

As you can see from the Doan story, a parent's illness or disability can result in a number of emotions in a family. If you believe this to be an isolated situation, you're mistaken. The dynamics of families dealing with these circumstances are at the heart of what long term care is all about. An agent who works in this field should be prepared to balance the emotional and financial planning aspects of long term care.

Advanced preparation, for example, purchasing long term care insurance, would certainly have helped Mrs. Doan and her family. Each option involved both financial and emotional considerations and had to be sorted through in less than 72 hours.

This is the worst kind of pressure and many people put off thinking about what could happen in these types of situations until they are actually confronted with them. Unfortunately, decisions made based on emotions are often wrong decisions.

It is the agent's job to help people focus and plan ahead before these types of situations arise. By planning in advance for an injury or illness it will make the execution of the pre-determined arrangements a smooth process. That's what financial planning is all about.

Thinking both emotionally and financially, let's evaluate Mrs. Doan's options.

Option #1: Mrs. Doan Returns Home and Receives 24-hour Skilled Nursing and Skilled Rehabilitative Care

This seems like an ideal solution. Being in her home gives Mrs. Doan both the security and independence she desires without burdening any of her children. She feels loved by her family and not abandoned in a nursing home.

For Karen, this option allows her the peace of mind of knowing that she has lived up to her promise to her mother, without displacing her husband and kids. Best of all, Karen can visit without feeling guilty. This solution also creates the least amount of strain between her and her siblings.

Julie is also pleased by this choice. She can continue to balance her life between work and home with minimal disruption.

This option also appears to be good for Robert. Since his father died, Robert has felt that his mother tended to view him as a stand-in for his father. He resents his mother leaning on him and has difficulty saying no to his mother's requests.

This option clearly has a positive emotional impact on the Doan family.

With everyone in agreement, Karen makes several phone calls to arrange for 24-hour private nursing care for Mrs. Doan. With Mrs. Becker's help, she contacts several home health care agencies. Karen soon discovers that the cost of full-time skilled nursing care and physical therapy is expensive — with estimates ranging as high as $250 a day.

Realizing that her mother's savings of $62,000 would virtually disappear in less than a year. Karen decides to pursue other financial sources. In fact, she's sure that Medicare will cover these necessary medical services.

While part-time home health care is covered under Medicare, full-time skilled nursing care is not. Karen then turns to the Medicaid program as a solution.

Since Medicaid is a welfare program, Mrs. Doan, as a widow, would have to spend nearly all of her savings first before becoming eligible for any benefits. Thus, no money is available up-front to pay for the full-time skilled nursing care that is critical to her mother's recovery.

Karen's husband Steve, Mrs. Doan's financial adviser, points out that Mrs. Doan's Medicare supplement insurance policy does not offer additional reimbursement for home health care. Furthermore, Mrs. Doan does not own any type of long term care insurance.

Now, the ideal emotional option is not going to be financially feasible. Even after being successfully rehabilitated with full-time skilled nursing care, Mrs. Doan will have very little money left. And it is unlikely that her children will be in a position to help her financially in six months.

Option #2: Mrs. Doan Stays at One of Her Children's Houses and Receives Private Nursing Care During the Day for the Next Six Months

Because Mrs. Doan would be cared for by one of her children at night, it wouldn't be necessary for the family to contract for full-time home health services. Since her skilled nursing care will be part-time, the treatment is eligible for Medicare reimbursement. While there are some internal limits to the reimbursements, a normal recovery for Mrs. Doan would likely mean that the bulk of her expenses will be covered. Financially, this option seems to work.

However, where will Mrs. Doan go? Julie refuses to offer her home. Robert lives in California and Mrs. Doan does not want to leave Central Florida. So, this leaves Karen.

Karen knows both Julie and Robert would be thrilled by the decision to move their mother into her home. It would cost nothing and at the same time keep Mrs. Doan's savings intact and keep her out of a nursing home. Karen also knows that, given the choice, her mother would prefer to come to Karen's home. As much as Karen loves her mother and doesn't want her in a nursing home, she realizes that bringing her mother into an already cramped living space would place a tremendous emotional burden on her own family.

Moreover, there is no guaranteed time frame for her mother's recovery. What if the rehabilitation process takes longer than anticipated? How many more months will this makeshift arrangement have to last? How long can Karen keep up a work schedule during the day and take care of her mother at night?

While this option is financially sound for all concerned, it would be an emotional nightmare for Karen.

Option #3: Mrs. Doan is Placed in a Nursing Home Until Fully Recovered

Desperate now, Karen asks Mrs. Becker to check into nursing home placement for her mother. Within 24 hours, Mrs. Becker advises Karen that she has located a bed for Mrs. Doan. The nursing home is located in southwest Orlando, about 25 miles from Karen's house. While there are closer facilities, none had a skilled bed currently available nor had met Karen's requirements of a private room, weekly beauty shop, and excellent meals with a lovely dining room.

Emotionally, this is the hardest of the options. Financially, Karen anticipated that Medicare would cover most of the costs of her mother's six month nursing home placement. But the reality of it turns out to be quite different.

Medicare pays for *skilled* nursing care in a nursing home, but only on a limited basis. Medicare would pay some of the cost if:

1. the nursing home was Medicare-certified;

2. the doctor certified treatment; and

3. Mrs. Doan had at least a three-day hospital stay.

Medicare will pay for the first 20 days of skilled care in a nursing facility in a semi-private room. However, Karen requested and received a private room for her mother. Mrs. Doan will have to pay the difference between the cost of a semi-private room and the cost of a private room. After 20 days, Medicare continues to reimburse the costs of a semi-private room for an additional 80 days after Mrs. Doan makes a co-payment of $92 a day (1996 rules). Beyond this second period, there will be no further reimbursement from Medicare.

The cost for a private room in the nursing home facility is $125 a day. The semi-private room rate on which Medicare bases its reimbursements is $105/day. The payments break down as:

First 20 days:	Medicare:	$105/day x 20	=	$2,100
	Mrs. Doan:	$20/day x 20	=	$400
21st-100th day	Medicare:	$13/day x 80	=	$1,040
	Mrs. Doan:	$112/day x 80	=	$8,960
101-180 days	Medicare:	-0-		
	Mrs. Doan:	$125 x 80days	=	$10,000
Totals:	Medicare:	$3,140	(14% of costs)	
	Mrs. Doan:	$19,360	(86% of costs)	

Of course, if the rehabilitation does not go as planned, Mrs. Doan will have further expenditures of $125 a day for every additional day she stays in the nursing home.

Karen was led to believe that Medicare covered as much as six months of a nursing home stay. However, Mrs. Doan's Medicare Supplement policy will pay $92 co-payment in days 21 to 100, reducing Mrs. Doan's financial responsibility by $7,360. While this financial picture isn't nearly as bleak as the full-time home health care costs of Option #1, Mrs. Doan will spend $12,000 or more for this care. Combined with the bleak emotional and financial outlook of this option, it is no longer considered a possibility.

Karen realizes that the best option for everyone else (Option #2) is the most difficult option for her and her family *emotionally*. But she feels she has little choice. Her mother is to be discharged in the morning and the doctor and social worker need an answer.

BALANCING YOUR CLIENT'S EMOTIONAL AND FINANCIAL NEEDS

As an insurance and financial planner, you will be assisting your clients faced with situations like this if you haven't already. You must know how to address both the financial and emotional issues of long term care to be truly effective at marketing this type of product. Karen's choice is one many Americans are forced to make every week. We are slowly becoming a nation of "caregivers" because we are left with no other choice financially or emotionally.

The Doan family scenario suggests a number of issues that will be discussed throughout this book, such as:

- The emotional aspect of caregiving.

- The financial analysis of a family's net worth, liquid assets and discretionary income.

- How to determine who is a good candidate for long term care insurance.

- Family issues that surface during this critical and emotional time.

- The view of the person who will receive the care, who is often left out of the decision-making process.

- The role of government programs such as Medicare and Medicaid.

- The media coverage of long term care and how it shapes consumer thinking.

- The impact of the aging of America on all of us.

Long term care insurance can be one of the most important facets of pre-retirement estate planning. Today, thousands of people are seeing assets dwindle away as they struggle to meet the costs of the necessary long term care services.

You can help. Long term care is a market well worth pursuing since it will be one that continues to grow over the next two decades. This book can be your guide to future success.

Chapter 1

TODAY'S CHANGING DEMOGRAPHICS

In this age of information, there is plenty of data available that can be overwhelming and confusing. The information associated with the "graying of America" is no different.

- Since 1900, the percentage of all Americans over 65 has more than tripled (4.1% in 1900 to 12.7% in 1993). The most rapid increase is expected from 2010 to 2030 when the last of the baby boom generation reaches age 65.[1]

- The fastest growing segment of the elderly population consists of women over age 85.[2]

- The U.S. has more people over the age of 65 (33 million plus) than Canada has in its entire population (31 million).[3]

- About 70 percent of married people ages 51 to 61 have four-generation families — including elderly parents and children who've had children.[4]

- The over-age-50 population will grow by 74 percent in the next 30 years. Conversely, the under-age-50 population will achieve only a one percent growth.[5]

- The number of over-age-85 Americans projects to be 15.3 million by the year 2050.[6]

- There are currently 32 million members of AARP, the American Association of Retired Persons. Membership age begins at 50. Since baby boomers started turning 50 on January 1, 1996, AARP will gain a prospective new member every eight seconds for the following 18 years.[7]

WHAT DO THESE NUMBERS MEAN?

Obviously, this country is aging — rapidly. Advances in medical science and resulting longer life spans are well documented. No longer is it unusual for a person to live well into his 80's.

We are entering a new era for the elderly in this country. The image of a senior citizen as being frail, sick and dependent on others, is rapidly transforming into a more accurate picture of active, independent individuals who participate in many social and recreational activities, feel 15 years younger and have enough money set aside for the years ahead. The financial issue is the primary focal point for senior citizens today.

In an attempt to balance the budget, Washington has addressed two key issues — Medicare (health care for the elderly) and Medicaid (nursing home and long term care services). Discussion on how to deter the rise in Social Security benefits in anticipation of the swift aging of our population has yet to be accomplished due to the tremendous backlash from the senior population who not only count on benefit payments but also feel a certain entitlement to these benefits. How easy will it be to change the Social Security program when the senior population doubles?

Several years ago, a retired disability insurance agent contacted me to discuss the health industry. Retired for 23 years, he was a wealth of information on Social Security and reminisced about the wage freezes during World War II and other issues that he dealt with while selling disability income insurance. Inevitably, though, our conversation turned to his own health and the cost of home health care he requires at age 84. The financial worry, attributed to the high cost of medical care, was of great concern to him.

"What we dream will be a storybook retirement of foreign travel, great golf outings, and days spent lovingly dispensing aid to our children and grandchildren instead threatens to become the harrowing tale of a rapidly dwindling nest egg."[8] This idealistic view of retirement is shattered by the realization that financial concerns are still paramount for the aging population. The negative impact of financial and emotional concerns that the elderly experience is emphasized even more by the fact that in today's world a person lives longer.

THE CONSEQUENCES OF AGING

America is just beginning to see the effects of an aging population. On the one hand, it's wonderful that our children will know our parents. As a child, I only knew one of my grandparents and I still treasure her memory. She never missed listening to a Boston Red Sox baseball game on the radio. Her lifelong experiences taught me a lot and I was fortunate to have spent time with her.

It was my first exposure to a nursing home, where my "Nana" spent the last couple of years of her life. Seeing people in poor health, unable to care, feed or dress themselves was very traumatic. Yet, this is to be expected of longer life spans. Simply because one lives longer doesn't guarantee the quality of life. Our aging parents or relatives may live longer, but many will need our help both physically and financially.

In the April 9, 1992 edition of *USA Today* an article featured a story about role reversal between mother and daughter. The daughter who was 59 years old and the youngest of eight children, was now caring for her 93-year-old mother. The daughter, her own children now grown, made a conscious decision to move back to her mother's house to be a companion and caregiver to her mother. As it turned out, it wasn't how she had pictured it. "Taking care of a 93-year-old lady who's been independent all her life is really hard. I'm 59, and we're switching roles. In reality, I am her baby, but she's more or less my baby now."[9] Because of her mother's declining health, the time spent together was similar to that spent taking care of her own children when they were young.

Longer life spans also affect inheritances dramatically. As seniors live well into their 90's, their capital that was once intended to be passed on to the next generation will be consumed by the rising costs of health care. The income set aside for retirement purposes will have to come primarily from one's own resources.[10]

As the population ages, attention will be paid more to diseases that generally affect the elderly. Alzheimer's will garner the "lion's share" of attention especially now as the whole country watches how this illness affects former President Ronald Reagan. Alzheimer's today is responsible for a significant number of nursing home institutionalizations, the cost for which is being paid by private money or, when that runs out, Medicaid.

Today, more than four million older Americans depend on Medicaid for coverage of, among other health care concerns, nursing home and community based long term care.[11]

The consequences of aging can be poor health and/or poor finances. As insurance agents and financial planners we must help our clients prepare for the possibility of living a longer life. We must assist them in planning for their retirement years by helping to ensure some measure of financial security. We can help create resources that won't leave them or their future generations tapped-out if infirmity strikes.

GENERATIONS

Our first concern should be our own family. Regardless of what stage our own lives are in, we will doubtless be touched by the aging of America in some way or another. Look around you. How old are your parents? Grandparents? Children? Yourself? Are you prepared in the event a long term care situation arises similar to that of the Doan family depicted in the introduction?

Before we can do a proper job for our clients, we must first understand the consequences of aging in our own lives. When my father passed away in 1989, my mother quickly learned much about finances she didn't know before. Writing checks and balancing her accounts was new ground for her. She had read an article about long term care insurance and decided she wanted to know more about it. She bought a policy for herself in 1990 and is satisfied that she has taken a large step towards protecting her finances from most long term health problems that might arise.

Analyze your own family situation first. Who is close to retirement? Are they financially ready? How is their health? Is there a role for long term care insurance? This book will provide a greater insight in the chapters to follow on who are the best candidates for this product. There may be an important sale for you within your own family circle.

American Demographics magazine identified a group of individuals known as the "Post-War Cohorts". These individuals were born between 1928 and 1945, during the Depression and World War II. This group, about 41 million strong, went through tough times early on but survived to find peace and prosperity in the 1950's and beyond. They were security-conscious individuals who often sought out financial planning to ensure their preparedness for another cataclysmic-type event similar to what they had experienced.[12]

These individuals were ideal candidates for disability income insurance during their working years. Disability income protection provided replacement of a portion of their earnings if they were unable to work due to an injury or illness. The purchase of this product was in character as it provided financial security for themselves and their family with continued income despite not being able to work.

This group of people are now older and are currently between the ages of 51 and 68. Formerly ideal candidates for disability insurance, they are now ideal candidates to approach to discuss the consequences of aging. They will likely be the first group of people to uniformly benefit from the advances in medical science and can expect to live longer. Financial security is an issue and the threat of a long term illness jeopardizing their retirement is a danger they won't easily ignore.

If you have any clients in this age group, a discussion of the consequences of aging is in order.

Now factor in the aging "baby boomers". This generation, approximately 30 percent of the nation's population, is poised to completely change the way we think about the elderly. Boomers have a better lifestyle awareness, higher fitness levels and a more prudent consideration of both diet and health than any preceding generation.

There are 82 million people born between 1946 and 1965 whose parents are now getting older.[13] The boomers themselves are getting older. After all, this is the group that embraced the song "My Generation" by *The Who* as their anthem with lyrics like "I hope I die before I get old".

This group, now turning age 50, is hardened by the burden of credit card debt, raising young children and coping with aging parents all at the same time. Women today think nothing of having children at age 40 — the same age that their mothers had college age children. As a result, boomers will be facing college education costs and possibly parents needing long term care. Who could retire with those financial burdens?

Boomers are well educated, affluent and the healthiest generation in our nation's history. They have redefined marriage, education, work and family. Ultimately, this group will change the way in which the last third of life is lived and are prime candidates to talk to about the issues of aging and caregiving.[14]

Finally, the "X Generation" will have their own say about retirement. Surprisingly, unlike boomers, generation X'ers show sophistication about the intricacies of planning, saving and investing for retirement. Not only are they not counting on Social Security, they are convinced that they will be on their own for health care costs, too. They've watched boomers spend their money as fast as they can make it and know that ultimately this exacts a high price. According to a recent study by Kemper Financial Services, generation X'ers are willing to hold off on personal consumption and instead concentrate on saving for retirement.[15]

Long term care insurance, especially in an employer-sponsored setting, has a growing appeal to generation X'ers. Solidify tax consequences of the product and sales will further increase with this group. They have read much about the aging of America and will continue to be inundated with information on the importance of planning ahead.

OTHER ADULT LIFESTAGE EVENTS

The insurance industry is slowly awakening to the marketing potential of the "aging" of our country. Financial planning is critical in stretching the retirement dollar. A major reason for purchasing life insurance is to pay significant estate taxes and with the sophisticated life and annuity products on the market today, the insurance industry is in a good position to serve the needs of aging America.

However, there are a number of *key* adult lifestage events unique in our lives which are not being addressed. Situations unique to today's society fit squarely into the demographic changes happening around us. Ken Dychtwald, author of *The Age Wave*, a ground breaking book on the aging population, notes several significant events.

In the age group of over 50 years old, there are 6.6 million single men and 16.1 million single women, Dychtwald advises. Single mature women are a huge, untapped market and represent individuals interested in protecting their finances in the future.[16]

Another key event is caregiving. With one-third of all working adults already involved in some type of a caregiving environment, clearly this is an area of immediacy for many Americans. With the bulk of our nation's women having joined the workforce, caregiving responsibilities represent an overwhelming burden in addition to working all week. The need for some type of insurance protection that can pay for someone else to do the caregiving while the family member is working has become critical.

The "sandwich generation" is the term used for individuals who are typically female and who must raise children while caring for an aging relative. Delayed parenting has made this more of a reality and the financial setback accorded this type of arrangement can be devastating to the retirement hopes of the person caught in the middle.

Insurance companies and agents, in striving to assist individuals planning financially and emotionally, for the future, must be more aware of these types of trends.

THE PROSPECTIVE PAYMENT SYSTEM

The Medicare program, passed in 1965, was conceived as part of John F. Kennedy's campaign platform for the 1960 presidency and implemented during the Johnson administration. This program was to provide older Americans with some form of guaranteed health care, thus, preventing poorer older Americans from bankrupting themselves due to illness or injury.

The aging of our population has certainly taken Medicare to its breaking point. As more and more Americans qualified for "Part A" of Medicare at age 65, the resources set aside to fund the Medicare program began to deteriorate. Finally, in the early 1980s, faced with the increase in expenditures at an accelerating rate, Congress approved a prospective payment system designed to contain skyrocketing health care costs.

One feature of this system was the diagnostic-related groups (DRGs). Essentially, each medical condition treatable under Medicare was measured, on average, and a series of rules established identifying length and cost of each treatment. One outcome of the DRGs was to significantly curtail the amount of time spent in the hospital per condition with Medicare only paying for a stated number of days. If the hospital treated the patient in less than the time specified by Medicare, the institution would still be reimbursed for the number of days the DRG specified. If it took more time, the hospital was then expected to sustain the extra cost.

Most hospitals did not keep Medicare patients beyond the DRG-stated days. However, many patients were not well enough to leave the hospital. An interim stop-gap measure evolved whereby the patient would receive skilled, intermediate or custodial nursing care in a different setting, usually in a nursing home facility. As a result, an awareness of the cost of a nursing home stay grew quickly among senior citizens. During the first 18 months following the introduction of Medicare's Prospective Payment System, nursing home admissions increased by 40 percent.[17]

Many of these medical situations were short term but it did raise fears about the most significant loophole in the Medicare program — coverage for a long term or chronic illness. According to AARP, Medicare covers approximately seven percent of the average nursing home bill.[18]

Most older people have at least one chronic condition and many have multiple conditions. The conditions most frequent among the elderly in 1992 were:[19]

Chronic Conditions Per 100 Elderly

Arthritis	48
Hypertension	36
Heart Disease	32
Hearing impairments	32
Orthopedic impairments	19
Cataracts	17
Sinusitis	16
Diabetes	11
Visual impairments	9

The costs to treat long term chronic conditions can erode even the most substantial asset base. Traditionally, seniors have placed a lot of faith in the Medicare program, but their confidence in this government program has been eroded by their own nursing home experiences. The DRG program placed nursing homes center stage and created an even greater concern about the seniors' financial futures.

This concern is further exacerbated by a study done in 1992 by The Northwestern National Life Insurance Company on the growing impact of out-of-pocket medical costs on retirement income.[20]

The Northwestern National projections illustrated these dire results:

- A typical married couple who will retire in ten years and for whom one person at age 70 would need home health care will see assets depleted by the time they reach age 74.

- A middle-aged person who will retire in 2011 will see his or her nest egg completely diminished by health costs within one year of a nursing home stay at age 80.

The study indicated that approximately sixty percent of Americans think health care is the single biggest threat to a secure retirement. People associate health care costs with aging and how it will affect their retirement.

This, too, is an audience primed to talk with an insurance agent/ financial planner who can help them prepare properly for their retirement. The long term care market is one of the most exciting markets for an agent in terms of potential.

ONE LAST OPPORTUNITY

The insurance industry has the chance to take the lead in assisting people with their financial goals and dreams. The government does not want the complete burden to fall on them — witness the Medicare and Medicaid programs. Long term care insurance and pre-retirement financial planning can play a key role in assuring people that they will not only survive their retirement years, but will have every opportunity to enjoy them as well.

The American Association of Retired Persons (AARP) is an organization that offers benefits to its members not found elsewhere. One of the major benefits of AARP membership is that seniors are able to purchase long term care insurance. Recently, AARP ended the exclusive provider relationship they had with the Prudential Insurance Company.[21] Insurance companies began bidding for AARP's business in February,

1996. This has opened up a major market for long term care providers and the type and quality of the programs offered will be critical to how the insurance industry will be looked upon for its efforts to supply the aging public with long term care insurance.

This country will see a vast number of seniors in various stages of life — second or third careers and retirement. These individuals are determined to remain independent and active and are at the heart of the long term care insurance market.

CHAPTER NOTES

1. " The Senior Profile", *USA Today*, July 20, 1995, p. 3D.
2. Health Insurance Association of America, "Long Term Care Needs, Costs and Financing", 1992.
3. U.S. Census Bureau.
4. National Institute on Aging, 1994.
5. Ibid.
6. "Growing Old", *The Bradenton Herald*, October 22, 1995, p. 1.
7. "The Power of Cohorts", *American Demographics*, December, 1994, p. 22.
8. "The Truth About Retirement", *Fortune*, December 25, 1995, p. 192.
9. "How Families Will Cope With An Aging Population", *USA Today*, April 9, 1992, p. 11A.
10. "Why We Will Live Longer", *Fortune*, February 20, 1994, p. 66.
11. Florida Agency for Health Care Administration, Tallahassee, Florida.
12. "The Power of Cohorts", *American Demographics*, December, 1994, p. 22.
13. "Making A Catch in the D.I. Marketplace", *Best's Review*, November, 1993, p. 69.
14. "Here Come The Boomers", AARP Bulletin, December, 1995, p. 1.
15. "Generation Xers Are Wise In The Ways of Retirement", by David C. Jones, *The National Underwriter*, July 10, 1995, p. 10.
16. "Industry is Ignoring Key Adult Lifestage Events", *The National Underwriter*, November 1, 1993, p. 3.
17. Health Care Financing Administration data.
18. Health Care Financing Administration, 1994.
19. "A Profile of Older Americans", joint report by AARP, Administration on Aging and U.S. Census Bureau, 1994.
20. "Escalating Health Care Costs Cited", *USA Today*, November 14, 1991, p. A1.
21. "Pru Loses Exclusive Provider Status With AARP", *National Underwriter*, December 4, 1995, p. 4.

Chapter 2

THE EMOTIONAL BURDEN OF AGING

As insurance agents and financial planners we ask ourselves, what is long term care? What exactly does long term care cover? What do we hope to accomplish by addressing this need with our clients?

You will recall from the introduction, long term care decisions involve both emotional and financial issues. While we are used to designing programs to assist our clients financially, the planning of long term care also requires us to understand the emotional dynamics involved. Understanding the emotional implications of long term care will help us better communicate the importance of advanced planning to our clients.

What types of situations could our clients face?

LONG TERM CARE SCENARIOS

Scenario #1

A 51-year-old North Carolina man picked his mother up from the hospital in Charlotte. To avoid being charged for another day in the hospital, his parents were waiting for him in the hallway. His mother was suffering from a degenerative neurological disorder that had left her unable to walk or use her hands. He knew his father was not capable of taking care of his mother so it was decided that she would live with her son and his family.

Her son arranged and paid for home health aides to visit daily, took his mother regularly to the doctor's office and juggled his family weekend schedule around the tasks involved in caring for his mother. This arrangement proved to be a complete change of lifestyle for his entire family.[1]

Scenario #2

A woman lives and works in Washington, D.C. and was visiting her ailing mother in South Carolina. With her mother's health steadily declining, what was to be a "short leave of absence" turned out to be several weeks.

Unable to convince her mother to come stay with her in D.C., she returned to work. Although she calls her mother three or four times a day to check on her, she feels guilty and the inability to see her mother every day is emotionally devastating. Her worries over her mother's illness have caused concern over her own health, specifically her high blood pressure which her physician attributes to nerves. The most favorable solution isn't always the most logical or feasible solution. It isn't easy to simply leave a job and home and move back home when a parent or relative becomes ill.[2]

Scenario #3

A 45-year-old California man recalls that placing his 86-year-old mother in a nursing home was the most difficult thing he's ever had to do. Although his mother seems to have adjusted reasonably well, he still feels guilty. He visits twice a week and calls every day. His sister lives closer and visits three times a week. While their mother is doing fine, the emotional toll on them is high. The nursing home cost is about $45,000 a year and is paid from their mother's savings. The children realize their inheritance is being spent, but they want the best care available for their mother.[3]

Scenario #4

A man living in North Carolina moved his mother to a facility that accepted Medicaid. The nursing home was close to his house so he could visit every day and provide the kind of emotional support she needed. This arrangement seemed to go well for all involved until his niece in Florida intervened. She didn't want her great-aunt to be in a nursing home and if her uncle wouldn't take her into his own home, she would move her great-aunt to Florida to stay with her and her family.

So she moved her great-aunt to Florida. Even though he had no access to his mother, the son felt that she would be well taken care of in his niece's home rather than in the nursing home facility. It certainly had to be a better situation. Unfortunately, after two months, his niece realized she couldn't cope with the frail, elderly woman and arranged for her to move into a nursing home that was Medicaid certified in a nearby Florida town. The result of this emotional tug-of-war was the ultimate placement of his mother in a facility that was a nine hour drive for him.

Scenario #5

A 65-year-old Illinois man living alone in his own home was doing his normal Saturday morning grocery shopping. While transferring bags from a grocery cart into the trunk of his car, he lost his balance and fell breaking three fingers and fracturing his wrist. He has to wear a cast on his right hand for at least a month.[4]

At the beginning of the next month, his bills came due. He is right-handed and cannot write the checks so he lets the bills sit. He has a daughter living in New York but what can she do for him living out of state? He has enough groceries in the house to last a couple of weeks. His hand does not heal as quickly as he had hoped. Complicated by an old war injury, his current injury requires surgery. By this time, second notices have arrived and the next months' bills are due.

Although his daughter calls him periodically, he doesn't tell her of his difficulties. A month later, when his daughter visits for Thanksgiving, she is shocked to find her father has lost a significant amount of weight, dishes are piled up, bills past due still lay on his desk, the phone company has threatened to turn off the service and letters from the bank and electric company warn of a similar disaster. His hand is now healing, but the cast won't come off for another five or six weeks.

ROLE REVERSAL

Do these scenarios sound far-fetched? They are not. All of them are documented cases and are representative of thousands of similar situations across the country.

Very few people are prepared. The aging process carries with it an increased dependency, similar to that of a baby. Many elderly need assistance with eating, getting dressed and walking to name just a few activities. The patience one exercises with a child must apply in an even greater measure for an aging parent or relative.[5] A child has no expectations yet; an adult has already performed all of these functions capably for years and the loss of these simple abilities carries a heavy emotional price.

While the aging person copes with these adjustments, so too must their children. It is difficult to see your parents in a dependent role. After all, you were completely dependent on them as a child. This role reversal has a great impact on the lives of Americans everywhere. There is no rehearsal, no preparation. Longer life spans are something of a recent phenomenon and an aging parent or relative in his or her 80's is no longer the exception but the rule.

If you haven't been around your parents for some time, you may be surprised at the differences when you do see them again — changes that are not obvious from a regular phone call. The female baby boomer who has had a child at the age of 42 may look forward to bringing her new grandchild home to her parents only to discover that her parents don't have the patience for a young child any longer.

Individuals who put themselves in the role of caregiver may expect gratitude from the individuals they are taking care of and empathy from siblings who live a distance away. Very likely, they will receive neither. As one female caregiver laments, "I have brothers and sisters, but there's nobody here to help. They'll call and say what they think I should be doing, and at times I really get upset. They don't know what it's like. They're not here. They don't have to change her diaper. They don't have to give her a bath. They don't have to listen to the verbal abuse."[6]

Perhaps the greatest fear that an aging person has is the loss of independence. Think about it. Many of us treasure the control we have of our own time and space. Now, in a caregiving situation, *both* caregiver and caretaker lose that control. In life's role reversal this is the centerpiece of an aging America, the elderly need help doing all of the things they've done for themselves and their children must rearrange their own lives to care for their elderly relative. The emotional burden on both sides can further be magnified by any past resentments or family squabbles that are sure to surface with the responsibilities of caregiving.

Guilt is only one of the emotions that the children will feel when trying to make the emotional decision of what to do about their parents. A nursing home placement is likely to leave a permanent emotional scar that no amount of visitation can heal. Trying to maintain the delicate balance within one's own household while making room for a new "boarder" is often a lost cause. Family members know they will lose some of the caregiver's attention and resent having to give up time and space to an elderly relative.

Long distance caregivers battle different problems. Guilt is still the primary feeling combined with the inadequacy one feels when a situation is out of control. Hard as it is for the direct caregiver, the long distance caregiver will likely spend an inordinate amount of time on the phone to compensate for being away. The result is a similar loss of time for the caretaker's own immediate family. Add to that the common symptoms of loss of appetite and insomnia due to worrying, long distance caregiving exacts its own emotional toll.[7]

These are problems that we must help our clients work through. A long term care insurance product may help financially, but some of the emotional battering and the making of tough decisions will still be necessary. Recognizing these difficulties and playing a small, but important, role through advanced planning can make a world of difference when a long term care situation arises.

THE SANDWICH GENERATION

For the first time in history, an entire generation may find themselves "sandwiched" between caring for growing children and aging parents. A recent government study reveals that the average U.S. woman will spend 17 years raising children and 18 years caring for aging parents.[8] *Newsweek* coined the term "daughter tracker" describing this type of woman.

Despite some societal progress, the role of caregiving will still fall to women. Roughly 75 percent of all caregivers today are women.[9] Because women traditionally have longer life spans, the person that requires care is likely to be female. The combination of younger children and the fact that more females than ever before have joined the workforce, is bound to create emotional fireworks in the future.

The presence of younger children and aging parents is unique to the baby boomer generation. This group waited to have children and women giving birth in their 40's is quite common today. The unexpected consequence of this delayed parenting is that the raising of children is coincident to a need for assistance on the part of parents in their 70's and 80's.

Juggling a work schedule, having kids in school and day care and parents at home or in day care themselves (adult day care centers are a growing industry) requires an enormous amount of planning and organization. There will be days when you've promised an adult to take them shopping only to have to cancel because it conflicts with a PTA meeting. Or vice versa — you can't make it to your child's piano recital because your mother needs to go to the doctor's office.

But what's a sandwich generationer to do? The most traumatic decision to be made is deciding whether a parent will go into a nursing home or move in with you. There's no ducking the issue. It must be faced without regard to readiness. The key to a successful transition is to face the issues *before* something does happen.

It's easier said than done. When it comes to communicating about future planning and making decisions, neither child nor parent is exceptionally good at addressing the issues. Because both sides dread the possibility of illness that is associated with aging, it's easier to avoid the subject than to talk about it.

COMMUNICATION

Planning ahead of time requires good communication between parent and adult. There is no better time to do it than when everyone is healthy and putting the plans into action seems a long way off. Talking about long term care will elicit parent's wishes in this regard. The child may be surprised when parents say they'd prefer a nursing home facility to being dependent on their children. Without a discussion of long term care needs a parent would not ordinarily volunteer this information.

The ideal situation would be to have a parent taken care of by a home health care nurse or aide in his or her own home. Leaving parents in familiar surroundings rather than disrupting them with a move to an institution or another family member's home is a preferred arrangement for all concerned. If it can be done financially, it is likely to be the first choice. Medicare may or may not cover the expense, but a long term care insurance policy today would handle the majority of the costs.

Keep in mind that a person has to qualify for the policy and, as such, must apply for it before the necessity for long term care services arises. Unless there are early discussions about planning for this possibility, long term care insurance is unlikely to be an option considered. In the introduction to this book, the lack of advanced preparation meant Mrs. Doan didn't have, among other things, a long term care insurance policy to provide a possible solution in the event of a long term illness.

In addition to insurance, there are a variety of resources available to seniors which can be of help during a time of need. It's much easier to learn about these resources in advance of needing them. A listing can be compiled and kept in a safe place for consultation purposes when a long term care plan of action is put into effect. (A listing of resources appears in Chapter 16, The Agent's Checklist.)

Those "sandwiched" between children and a dependent adult need to realistically assess their abilities to handle both should it be needed. For someone who works, it would be impossible to do it all. Much as one may want to take on the entire burden, the "Superwoman" label will wear thin before too long. Communicating in advance about what can be done practically will be critical to organizing a plan that will actually work.

There will be arguments. Discussing parents' future situations only serves notice as to one's own eventual needs. Unless prior communication is done about possible long term care situations, the entire family will be placed in the position of having to make rash decisions at a most difficult and emotional time. Decisions made under these circumstances are usually not the best decisions.

The financial planner should know this. The same considerations — emotional and financial — used when planning in the event of a death should also be used in planning for long term care. Advanced planning is what our jobs are all about.

EMOTIONAL ASSISTANCE

A person should not feel he or she is battling this alone. In the scenarios outlined at the beginning of this chapter, individuals seemed to be making decisions entirely on their own but were unsure if they were doing the right thing. This concern created feelings of guilt, leading to their own health complications.

In example #5, the man could have avoided angering creditors by assigning his daughter durable power of attorney which gives her the ability to pay his bills until his injury has healed. (Durable power of attorney is explored more thoroughly in Chapter 7, The Need For Financial Planning.)

The long distance caregiver from Washington, D.C. in example #2 may have felt better about the situation if she was able to interview and hire a geriatric case manager in the weeks she spent in South Carolina with her mother. A geriatric case manager may be the solution even if the caregiver is only a few miles away especially since so many couples today are dual income earners and can't afford the time away from work to care for an elderly parent.

These case managers are licensed professionals and include social workers, nurses, gerontologists and others who can provide an assessment of the long term care situation and develop a plan to meet the needs of the person needing assistance. It may be easier for an unbiased third party to come in and help bridge the communication gap between the parent and child. If nothing else, one doesn't have to communicate the difficult choices alone.[10]

These managers can handle every aspect of an aging adult's care from interviewing and hiring household help, paying the bills and managing the financial accounts, arranging transportation as needed and calling on community resources that might be otherwise unknown to the children.

Geriatric case managers charge fees for their services ranging from an initial assessment charge of $500 up to $3000 or more and a monthly fee for ongoing services.[11] They are the child's "eyes and ears" when the child can't be there. Attempting to make arrangements for a homemaker-helper long distance would not be effective and the possibility of neglect could become a reality without the child's knowledge.[12] The case manager monitors the situation regularly to ensure the right person is on the job.

The responsibilities and costs associated with the geriatric case manager can be discussed as part of the advanced preparations the family makes for such situations. If there is any distance between children and parents, the subject (and how to pay for it) should be addressed.

Even though there may be cooperation from all parties in the beginning, do not assume that this harmony will continue when the actual time arrives. It is common for an older person to deny that assistance is necessary even though it seems obvious to everyone else. There may be some resistance in implementing these plans.

A third party can be of great emotional assistance here. Whether it's a case manager or a doctor or a social worker, nurse, insurance agent or friend, enlisting help should be part of the planning process.

PLANNING

It all comes down to planning. As an insurance agent and financial planner, your role in long term care planning with a family involves both emotional and financial planning. Often the emotional issues dictate the financial choices that are made.

Above all, the agent should remember that there is the likelihood of the same situation happening in one's own family. There is a need to plan your actions and those of aging parents and relatives in the event a long term care situation arises.

The emotional aspect of what to do with one's own parents will be followed by the financial situation and consequences of each action. As a plan is formed, it is important to note the financial impact of each decision. It can create its own emotional burdens on family members.

CHAPTER NOTES

1. "How Much Can I Give?", *Parade*, January 29, 1995, p. 4.
2. "Miles Away and Still Caring", A Guide for Long Distance Caregiving, AARP.
3. "Emotional, Financial Costs Can Be High", *USA Today*, Special Edition: Baby Boomers And Their Parents, July 17-20, 1995.
4. "At The Mercy of the System", *The Sandwich Generation*, Spring, 1995, p. 23.
5. "On Patience", *The Sandwich Generation*, Issue 1, 1995, p. 3.
6. "Roles Now Reversed for Mother, Daughter", *USA Today*, April 9, 1992, p. 11A.
7. "How Much Can I Give?", *Parade*, January 29, 1995, p. 4.
8. "Long Term Care Facts", CNA Insurance Co., 1991.
9. National Institute on Aging, as quoted in "LTC Facts", published by CNA, 1991.
10. "Becoming Responsible for A Parent's Care", *USA Today*, Special Edition: Baby Boomers And Their Parents, July 17-20, 1995.
11. "When You Can't Be There", *Health*, October, 1993, p. 54.
12. "After the Fall", *Modern Maturity*, November-December, 1994, p. 62.

Chapter 3

THE FINANCIAL STRAIN OF AGING

No one expects to outlive his or her money. Yet that is exactly what's happening to many Americans around the country. Take central Floridian Elsie Ryan, for example.[1]

Elsie's husband passed away in 1978 when she was 80 years old. "We weren't millionaire-wealthy" she says but she had a decent trust fund that she figured would last her the rest of her life. She's now 97 and living in a nursing home in Orlando.

The nursing home cost Elsie over $33,000 a year and after a few years in the nursing home, the trust fund was depleted. The nursing home personnel assisted Elsie in applying for Medicaid, the joint state-federal program for those living at or below poverty level.

Her mind still sharp, Elsie has endured a hip replacement and is crippled with arthritis. She no longer has the use of her right leg and is legally blind. "I've lived much too long," she says. Her trust fund was a lot of money seventeen years ago, but longevity of life and nursing home costs have created a situation that has forced her to become dependent on welfare.

THE FINANCIAL BLACK HOLE

One investment publication calls the need for long term care "the biggest threat to most Americans' wealth" topping inflation, recession, real estate or other investment-related danger.[2]

Let's say you retired at age 67 with a retirement income of $40,000 a year. You have money in the bank, no debts and nothing but a comfortable lifestyle ahead. But then...

Your spouse was diagnosed with Alzheimer's and in the early stages of the disease. Anticipation of days of relaxation are now filled with taking care of your spouse, trips to the doctor and pharmacy, general housekeeping and preparing meals. You can no longer leave your spouse alone, so every trip is a joint trip.

You realize you can't cope with it alone and you hire a home health aide. The aide is there during the day while you have night duty, but even that is getting to be too much of an emotional strain for you. Your finances are almost exhausted because the cost for the home health care is $80 per day.

The only alternative left is a nursing home and even at a reasonable rate it will run $105 a day or $38,000 a year. The $75,000 in savings will be exhausted in less than two years. Although your spouse's condition is slowly deteriorating, it is more than likely he or she will live longer than two years. The retirement you were so looking forward to has been sidelined by the financial (and emotional) realities of long term care.

What do you do when you're suddenly faced with an additional expense of $30,000 to $60,000 per year? How does this affect your retirement? What about your children or heirs?

These questions should be asked by an insurance agent and financial planner when assisting individuals with their retirement and estate planning. If they aren't addressed early on, the alternatives are limited and decisions to be made will inevitably be unsatisfactory and potentially financially devastating.

NUMBERS THAT CAN'T BE IGNORED

The amount of spending on health care costs increases dramatically with old age. Statistics show that spending by age group breaks down as follows:[3]

AGE GROUP	ANNUAL HEALTH CARE SPENDING
0 - 5	$1,389
6 - 17	730
18 - 44	1,242
45 - 64	2,402
65 +	4,840

Nursing home and other long term care costs certainly contribute to higher medical expenses among the senior population. As the body ages and begins to weaken, the recovery period is longer and results in higher costs for medical services provided.

What are some long term care costs? Looking first at nursing homes, Figure 3.1 is a 1994 survey of the daily costs of a nursing home facility stay, state by state.

Figure 3.1

NURSING HOME COSTS BY STATE			
STATE	MEDIAN	MINIMUM	MAXIMUM
Alabama	$ 85.00	$ 60.00	$235.00
Arizona	89.25	69.00	240.00
Arkansas	62.50	46.00	208.00
California	106.25	20.83	462.50
Colorado	87.25	44.00	200.00
Connecticut	175.00	125.00	248.00
Delaware	92.50	80.00	211.00
Florida	98.00	15.83	414.50
Georgia	79.75	18.33	199.50
Idaho	80.50	28.00	108.00
Illinois	80.00	15.13	265.00
Indiana	86.50	54.00	207.50
Iowa	64.00	30.00	250.00
Kansas	63.00	37.50	160.50
Kentucky	81.75	22.00	163.00
Louisiana	64.00	54.00	91.00
Maine	130.00	89.00	398.50
Maryland	101.00	20.00	185.00
Massachusetts	142.00	17.35	250.00
Michigan	96.00	34.00	231.00
Minnesota	104.00	71.00	227.50
Mississippi	65.25	51.00	122.50
Missouri	62.25	25.42	204.50
Montana	78.25	67.50	122.50
Nebraska	67.50	16.83	150.00
Nevada	113.50	94.50	169.00
New Hampshire	123.00	65.00	160.00
New Jersey	134.25	17.25	210.00
New Mexico	116.00	77.50	162.50
New York	152.00	18.48	267.50
North Carolina	89.50	44.83	138.00

Figure 3.1 (continued)

STATE	MEDIAN	MINIMUM	MAXIMUM
North Dakota	96.50	63.00	117.50
Ohio	98.00	16.67	240.00
Oklahoma	56.75	48.00	212.50
Oregon	101.25	51.00	181.50
Pennsylvania	105.00	39.00	270.00
Rhode Island	129.00	84.00	243.50
South Carolina	79.00	65.00	127.50
South Dakota	75.00	46.50	175.00
Tennessee	93.75	53.00	270.00
Texas	72.50	45.00	263.00
Utah	90.00	65.00	230.00
Vermont	111.25	71.00	343.50
Virginia	99.50	49.50	290.00
Washington	118.50	72.50	375.00
Washington, D.C.	144.00	100.08	167.50
West Virginia	91.50	35.35	240.00
Wisconsin	94.00	55.50	170.00
Wyoming	80.25	71.50	125.00

These costs, as you can see, range widely with each state. It is important to keep in mind that while the median cost gives an average daily cost of a nursing home, where your client lives will ultimately be the measurement used to determine the cost of a nursing home facility.

In Florida, for example, the daily average of $98.00 is representative of nursing home costs in Orlando or Tampa.[4] A stay in a nursing home in Tallahassee would likely be less than a nursing home confinement in South Florida.

It's easy to see how someone like Elsie Ryan can run out of money even if she was reasonably financially set when her retirement began. According to the Employee Benefit Research Institute, two-thirds of single people and one-third of married people exhaust their funds after just 13 weeks in a nursing home. Another source cited the state of Connecticut, indicating that the average time it takes for married couples to reach the Medicaid poverty level is just 52 weeks.[5]

Information on nursing home costs in your state can be found by contacting one of the state resource numbers listed in Appendix B. Working recently with an agent whose parents live in Florida, I contacted the Agency for Health Care Administration in Tallahassee and I received a listing of the nursing home facilities in two counties.

One listing in Palm Beach County was for the Abbey Delray in Delray Beach, Florida, the actual city where this agent's parents resided. In addition to the address and phone number, the information listed:

Number of licensed beds: 100
Number of beds that could be used for Medicare patients: 24
Number of beds that could be used for Medicaid patients: 100
Payment Forms Accepted: Medicare, Medicaid, private-pay
Date of last licensed inspection: 12/94
Inspection rating: Superior
Daily Semi-Private Room Rate: $123
Additional charges: Laundry (per item) no dollar figure given
Special resident services provided: Alzheimer's, quadriplegic, paraplegic, comatose, unit dosage system, I.V., tube feeding

According to the General Accounting Office, more than 12 million Americans required some type of long term care at a cost of nearly $108 billion in 1993.[6] Nearly 40 percent of those needing long term care were under the age of 65.

Typically, the elderly spend more money and require longer periods for recovery. A February, 1991 report by *The New England Journal of Medicine* cited that of the 2.2 million people turning age 65 in 1990, 43 percent of those (or 946,000 people) could expect to spend some time in a nursing home before they died. Of that group, 21 percent (approximately 200,000 people) would stay at least five years in a nursing home facility.[7]

The article further stated an estimated average cost of $25,000 to $50,000 annually for a typical nursing home stay, nationwide. That means at least 200,000 of the "Seniors Class of 1990" should plan on spending between $125,000 to $250,000 for a nursing home confinement. How many of our clients can absorb that cost during their retirement years? These are sobering numbers.

In 1993, according to a University of Missouri-Columbia study, more than 1,500,000 people live in the nation's 20,000 nursing homes. The report projected the number of nursing home residents to rise to 3,000,000 by the year 2020 when more than 55 million Americans will be over age 65.[8]

LONG TERM CARE IS MORE THAN
JUST A NURSING HOME

Nursing homes are not the only contributor to the high costs of long term care. In 1993, there were only 1.5 million residents in nursing homes. However, 12 million people overall needed long term care services in 1993.

Today, more than ever, advances in medical science have permitted medical technology to be transported right into one's own living room. Nurses and aides can provide the same type of care as one would receive in a nursing home. Since many people prefer the convenience and familiarity of their own surroundings, a large part of long term care services are provided in this fashion.

Typically, the costs are not as high as for those staying in a nursing home unless 24-hour care is needed. As Karen Parker learned in the introduction to this book, full-time home health care can run as high as $250 a day.

The average cost of a home health aide visit is $50 to $60, while an eight hour stay averages $70 to $90 a day.[9] An aide can assist the individual at home with the basic activities of daily living (ADLs). Alzheimer's patients and those with severe arthritis are usually in need of this kind of assistance. The simple tasks of bathing and dressing are particularly difficult to do if you have any type of infirmity. The home health aide can also assist in the essential household chores and even grocery shop for the homebound patient.

Adult day care centers, serving the same purpose as day care centers for children, are becoming more common today. Couples who are working and have a dependent adult staying with them use these facilities and the average cost is $15,000 or more a year.[10] (Adult day care centers are further explored in Chapter 4, Defining Long Term Care Services.)

Assisted living facilities are growing in popularity also. Assisted living facilities offer full-time adult day care with apartment-type living and aides on staff to assist with ADLs. (In addition to bathing and dressing, these can include eating, mobility or transferring positions and continence.) The cost of the average assisted living facility is $18,500 annually.[11]

COSTS, COSTS AND MORE COSTS

In addition to the expected health problems that occur with age, out-of-pocket expenses can have a severe impact on retirement. Health care costs for seniors that are paid for by public funds are substantially higher than any other age group. Skepticism about the future of Medicare and Social Security have sent the younger generations looking for other financial outlets that will be their source of future retirement income.

Today's age-50-plus population has fewer options than the youth of America. Social Security and Medicare are focal points of their retirement planning. There isn't much room for the additional expenses of long term care. The necessity of a nursing home stay can financially ruin a retired couple in a relatively short period of time.

It's no wonder that The Prudential, the provider of the AARP Medicare Supplement program, is raising its premiums. The average rate increase is expected to be about 30 percent.[12] A subscriber paying $1,200 annually for the AARP Medicare supplement policy will now pay a new premium of $1,560, or an additional $360 per year. The elderly often do not have the additional money to pay the increase in premium, much less a 30 percent increase in one year.

Today's seniors are conservative with their investments and are afraid to do anything aggressive for fear of losing their "nest egg."

WHERE DO THE ELDERLY TURN FOR HELP?

The obvious answer is their children. When financial help is necessary, what else can they do? That answer is Medicaid (See Chapter 6, Government Programs.) However, the repercussions from this underfunded government program are not widely understood by those who encourage their parents to qualify for Medicaid benefits.

Part of the Republican proposal to balance the budget was to block grant Medicaid to the states. The federal government has long contributed half the cost of this program and imposed a number of federal rules in doing so. The proposal would modify or lift the rules and each state would decide who qualifies for Medicaid and what amount of dollars would be spent. Some states have already indicated that they intend to drop the existing prohibition against using a child's assets to pay for the long term care costs of a parent.[13]

This is a shock to adult children who may see funds for their children's education and their own retirement used to pay for a parent's nursing home stay. What is the financial responsibility of an adult child for his or her parents? To what length can the state go to attach a child's assets to help pay for long term care costs for his or her parents?

It may take several years to arrive at answers. Public funds are diminishing and the reluctance to pay more taxes may result in other alternatives such as requiring an adult child to participate in paying the cost of a parent or relative's long term care.

PLANNING AHEAD

These numbers give you a familiar ground with which to approach existing and potential clients about the importance of planning ahead. The financial impact of long term care is already being felt by millions of Americans. Countless more await a similar fate unless some advanced preparation is done.

CHAPTER NOTES

1. "Her money ran out long before she has", *Orlando Sentinel*, August 6, 1995, p. A-1.
2. "Long Term Care", Special Supplement to *Adrian Day's Investment Analyst*, 1991.
3. 1993-1994 Cost of Nursing Care Survey, CNA Insurance Company.
4. Florida Agency for Health Care Administration, 1995.
5. "Asset Protection: Planning Ahead for Long Term Care", *Inside Self-Storage*, May, 1995.
6. "Health Care and Benefits", *The Bureau of National Affairs*, May 15, 1995.
7. "Nursing Home Costs", *The New England Journal of Medicine*, February, 1991, pp. 597, 599.
8. "Nursing Home Care Demand Increasing", *USA Today Monthly*, August, 1993, p. 2.
9. Health Care Financing Administration, 1994.
10. Health Care Financing Administration, 1994.
11. Health Care Financing Administration, 1994.
12. "Medigap Rates for AARP Members Rise", *The National Underwriter*, December 25, 1995, p. 3.
13. "Proposal: Children may have to help with parent's nursing home bills", *Atlanta Constitution*, December 18, 1995, p. A5.

Chapter 4

DEFINING LONG TERM CARE SERVICES

What long term care services might an individual need? It was mentioned in Chapter 3, The Financial Strain of Aging, that long term care goes well beyond the need for nursing home care. In actuality, more people access long term care services *outside* of a nursing home setting.

It is important to understand exactly what constitutes long term care. As an insurance agent, you must understand exactly what a long term care insurance policy will cover. This should include an intimate understanding of the various types of long term care services.

LEVELS OF HEALTH CARE

The type of care accessed is generally based on the severity of the health problem. The health care service administered is divided by the length of time a patient is monitored. The type of long term care whether it is maintenance, ADL assistance, or therapy can be provided in a variety of settings.

Intensive care: This is the most serious of medical situations where a patient is monitored at all times. A person may be placed in intensive care following surgery and is monitored for any negative signs usually on a 24-hour basis. A hospital-type setting is the most common facility for this type of care.

Acute care: For those individuals who are no longer on the critical list and do not need 24-hour care, there may still be a need for a patient to be monitored periodically to warrant the patient remaining in a hospital-type setting. In a 24-hour period, medical personnel may spend up to eight hours with a patient.

Skilled care: A decrease in the monitoring levels of acute care, skilled care may be needed up to half the time necessary at the acute care level.

This type of care can be administered in the home, an assisted living facility, nursing home or hospital.

Intermediate care: This type of care is similar to skilled care except it is provided on a periodic basis. The changing of a bandage every eight hours for example is considered intermittent treatment. Skilled medical personnel would deliver or monitor this type of care also.

Custodial care: This care involves assisting individuals in activities of daily living (ADLs). These ADLs include, but are not limited to, bathing, dressing, eating, and walking. This type of care is usually performed by a trained nurse's aide. As people get older, this type of care is common. Spinal cord injuries for example may also require this type of care.

Intensive care and acute care are short-term in nature and are often covered by comprehensive major medical insurance. HMOs and PPOs and other managed care programs also provide benefits for this type of care.

Skilled, intermediate and custodial care are considered long term levels of care. The objective of this type of care is to prevent a patient's health from deteriorating any further. This "maintenance" care is often not covered to any degree in a comprehensive major medical insurance policy.

The lack of coverage available for skilled, intermediate and custodial care has left the door open for the emergence of long term care insurance. As the population continues to age, the chance that more individuals will have a need for this form of medical treatment will increase dramatically.

Care for the elderly is still burdened with risk. It is easy for a long term care situation to escalate into an acute or intensive care need. For example, a 92-year-old woman with severe arthritis and bad circulation was on long term care maintenance when she developed a foot ulcer. She had two medical alternatives — amputation, a "simple" procedure with a high degree of success, but resulting in the loss of her foot; or an operation where healthy blood vessels are grafted in an attempt to save her foot.

Doctors make difficult choices for elderly patients, an oppressive situation compounded by having to deal with well-intentioned family members. Whichever alternative was selected, there was the limited chance of walking normal. Her family, of course, wanted the foot saved. The 92-year-old woman had little say in the matter.

During the operation she suffered a heart attack. She was taken to intensive care and placed on a respirator. The grafting on her foot soon became infected and was treated with antibiotics which triggered debilitating diarrhea. The long hours of anesthesia also led to a prolonged post-operation mental confusion.

The surgery only worsened the woman's already declining health and she still had the foot ulcer — the only other alternative was amputation.[1]

LONG TERM CARE SERVICES

Skilled Nursing Care

Skilled nursing care is care provided on a regular basis by licensed medical professionals such as registered nurses (RNs) or professional therapists, working under the order or direct supervision of a physician. Some people need skilled care for only a short period of time following an illness.

In Chapter 1, Today's Changing Demographics, Medicare's prospective payment system illustrated this type of skilled care. The person was not sick enough for acute care, but was still in need of skilled care and some monitoring. The recognition of skilled care became widespread as more and more Medicare patients were discharged from the hospital only to go into another type of facility, such as a nursing home to receive skilled care.

A person in need of skilled nursing care other than on an acute basis often receives a treatment plan. This program details the specifics of the treatment needed, both in description and frequency.

Today, retirement communities include independent living and personal/health care assistance. In Cartersville, Georgia, for example, Felton Place and Felton Manor represent both independent living and a personal care facility at the same location. The independent residence has 48 one-level, one or two-bedroom patio apartments with a single car garage, for $550 to $650 a month. The personal care residence has 38 private and semi-private bedroom suites. The residents receive three meals a day, medication assistance, and a nurse call system and services with a 24-hour staff. The buildings have kitchenettes, a library, fireplace, beauty/barber shop and screened porches for $1,125 to $1,800 a month.[2]

Immediate Nursing Care

Intermediate nursing care is provided for stable conditions that require daily medical assistance on a less frequent basis than skilled nursing care. The type of care to be administered is ordered by a physician and normally carried out under the supervision of a registered nurse. While intermediate nursing care is less specialized than skilled care, it is often administered over longer periods of time.

With skilled care, you are often working towards a stated goal. In a long term care scenario, that objective isn't always full recovery. More likely, it may be to bring the patient to a level where the care needed is only intermediate, allowing more independence from supervised medical scrutiny. Intermediate care could be as simple as giving medication to a group in physical therapy once a day. Intermediate nursing care is generally in the patient's home.

Custodial Care

Custodial care provides assistance with everyday activities of daily living (ADLs). While less intensive and complicated than skilled or intermediate care, the individual providing it must have some training in order to become proficient at assisting someone in necessary daily activities. Even a family member who might provide this assistance at home would be wise to seek training in ADLs for a small fee.

Custodial care may also be called personal care. It is usually defined by the actual ADLs that require help — bathing, dressing, eating, walking, getting in and out of bed, continence and taking medication are the more common ADLs defined.

ADLs originated 30 years ago from *The Index of Independence in Daily Activities*. Daily activities are defined by a person's ability to perform normal functions. This book also linked the ability to achieve the normal function with a person's behavioral level.

There is a unique correlation between childhood and the elderly stage. The lack of independence and inability to function is the same during childhood as it is in the elderly stage of life. Children generally learn and perform the following functions independently in this order:

- eating — first with hands and then with utensils;

- walking — first crawling and then culminating with baby's first steps;

- using the toilet; and

- bathing.

As people age, the inability to perform normal functions follows the adage "last learned — first lost":

- needs assistance to bathe;

- needs assistance in performing the task of going to the toilet including getting undressed;

- mobility becomes more and more difficult for an elderly person slowed by arthritis and other ailments; and

- eating — inability to hold a utensil or feed themselves.

The definition of each of these activities of daily living is more complex than one might think. The majority of long term care insurance policies measure eligibility for benefits on the basis of the ability to perform, or not perform, the usual ADLs. The following definitions are important:

Bathing — washing oneself in a bathtub or a shower, including getting in and out of the bathtub or shower, or giving oneself a sponge bath constitutes an independence from any assistance.

Bathing is the most problematic ADL for an elderly person. A lack of balance or an unsteady gait may necessitate assistance in getting in and out of a bathtub or shower. A wet surface combined with the fragility of an older person can be a hazardous combination.

Dressing — ability to get clothes from the closet or drawer and dress one's self or attaching a brace or prosthesis without any assistance. These activities require a certain dexterity of the hands and motor coordination. It's easy to take for granted the simple tasks of buttoning a shirt or tying a shoelace. And it is even more difficult to perform these tasks with decreased motor skills.

Toileting — the act of going to and from the bathroom, getting on and off the toilet and performing the necessary hygiene associated with going to the toilet without assistance. The location of the bathroom will have some impact on a person's ability to perform this daily activity. If access is difficult, assistance may be required.

Bathing and getting dressed are activities easily lost or made more difficult for an older person. It is not unusual to require assistance as one gets older and it doesn't necessarily mean the individual is severely disabled and in need of significant assistance. The need for toileting assistance, though, may well be the benchmark by which doctors measure the need for ongoing long term care services. Toileting is the critical point in the typical ADL hierarchy. Lack of independence in performing this function is the warning sign for future loss and eventual total dependence and often results in the need for around-the-clock care.

Mobility (also called transferring positions) — the process of walking without the assistance of a mechanical device (from cane to wheelchair) and moving from the bed to the chair without assistance. A considerable amount of strength in the arms and legs is necessary to adequately perform this function.

Continence — refers to one's ability to control bowel and bladder function voluntarily and to maintain a reasonable level of personal hygiene. This is independent from the physical ability to use the toilet and may involve the mental capacity of an individual to recognize the need to use the bathroom.

Eating —means the process of getting food from the plate into one's mouth without assistance. It requires the coordination of at least one of the hands. A person can use a straw or a modified utensil and still remain independent.

Administering medication is an activity of daily living and requiring assistance in taking the prescribed amount at the designated time and in the proper manner is a loss of independence.

It has taken several decades of gerontological and health research to place these ADL measurements into universal, standardized categories by which their loss can be calculated and diagnosed and medical assistance can be prescribed.[3] This medical assistance is often in the form of long term care. The loss of independence in performing these ADLs is often irrecoverable at an advanced age. Unless a person has had a specific trauma which renders him temporarily unable to perform some of these functions, the loss may be permanent. Thus, the individual may require assistance for the rest of his life.

Figure 4.1 lists ADL losses per 1,000 persons at older ages.

Figure 4.1

ADL Losses Per 1,000 Individuals At Older Ages

ADL	Age	Total (Male & Female)	Male Only	Female Only
Bathing	65-74	35.2	33.4	36.7
	75-84	80.9	68.2	88.8
	85 +	217.2	194.9	227.9
Dressing	65-74	29.3	32.5	26.8
	75-84	50.8	56.6	47.3
	85 +	132.3	126.5	135.7
Mobility	65-74	17.7	17.4	17.9
	75-84	36.7	28.8	41.8
	85 +	89.6	66.7	99.1
Toileting	65-74	12.4	13.6	11.4
	75-84	29.3	22.7	33.4
	85 +	82.8	56.4	95.3
Eating	65-74	6.3	8.5	4.7
	75-84	15.3	17.6	13.9
	85 +	27.4	23.9	29.0
Loss of 1 or more ADLs	65-74	47.4	48.1	46.7
	75-84	95.2	89.5	98.6
	85 +	238.8	218.8	247.7

Source: Supplement on Aging Survey, 1984

These statistics are used by actuaries to compute long term care morbidity rates and benefit eligibility when pricing a long term care insurance policy. Bathing and dressing are the overwhelming loss leaders in ADLs. The inability to perform these functions qualifies a person for long term care insurance reimbursement.

The table below illustrates the number of people needing assistance with these activities of daily living. The need for assistance in personal care will grow dramatically in correlation to the increasing number of people living longer lives.

Age	1980	1990	2000	2010	30 yr % change
65-74	737,139	869,412	863,487	996,042	35.1%
75-84	735,990	945,052	1,142,015	1,159,308	57.5%
85 +	535,386	779,486	1,106,664	1,462,926	173.2%
TOTAL	2,008,515	2,593,949	3,112,166	3,618,276	80.1%

Source: U.S. Census Bureau Projections multiplied by Table rates provided by the Supplement on Aging Survey

Between 1980 and 2010, the increase in the number of people needing long term care assistance is projected to be a phenomenal 30 year growth of 173.2 percent among the 85-and-older crowd. This type of care is usually associated with the assistance in performing activities of daily living.

Custodial care is the most common type of long term care assistance needed. This type of care will become more commonplace in the future and the need for funding, other than the current sources available, will certainly be needed. Long term care insurance can fill this gap.

CARE AT HOME

All of the long term care services mentioned above can be performed within the familiar confines of one's home. Physicians often recommend this care at home as it provides an important foundation to the emotional well-being of the person in need of care. Care at home, if it can be provided, is important to all ages but particularly to the elderly.

Long term care in the home is associated with the following positive factors:[4]

- control of one's lifestyle including the designated times for daily activities and social life;

- being within one's own environment;

- emotional and physical security;

- independence;

- privacy and the maintaining of one's own space;

- memories, magnified by being in the presence of personal history;

- source of financial security; and

- extension of one's self-expression.

All of these positive factors can have a profound effect on a person's health. Thus, if care can be delivered in the home, it is often preferred by the person receiving long term care.

The advances in medical science bode well for the future of home health care. Most care can be provided at home from custodial care (assistance with ADLs) to the highly skilled care performed by an RN. For example, a stroke or an accident renders a person temporarily incapacitated and in need of hospitalization. Both bed rest and assistance with household chores and common ADLs are needed. Where better to obtain the needed bed rest than in your own bed? A home health aide or family member can perform the rest of the assistance necessary.

Care in the home can be divided into two categories: home health care and home care. Home health care may include skilled nursing care, physical and speech therapy, lab services and intermediate care. Home care is a supportive service which includes assistance with ADLs and everyday activities — shopping, meal preparation and light housekeeping.[5]

These services are provided by home health care agencies which may be independent or affiliated with a nursing home or hospital. Private duty nurses operating independently can perform many skilled care functions for the individual patient at home. Chapter 5, The Growth Of Elder Care Services, takes a detailed look at the growth of this market.

OTHER LONG TERM CARE SERVICES

Adult day care centers are becoming more and more common with more than 3,000 programs nationwide in operation today.[6] An adult day care center functions much like a child day care center. With the majority of couples working, the likelihood of needing a place providing day care for a dependent adult is increasing.

A dependent adult in an day care center is supervised, fed, administered medication and in some cases, receives skilled care. Adult day care is not designed to replace the nursing home environment where a significant amount of skilled care is required, but it is a perfect place for an adult who cannot stay home alone and function on his own during the course of the day.

Some adult day care centers provide activities with speakers, music and even field trips. Many dependent adults may have diminished physical capabilities but are still sharp mentally and this type of stimulation is both healthy and helpful.

Finally, respite care is a service whereby temporary professional care is employed to give the caregiver some time off. With so many adults today providing care for a dependent parent or relative, the need for a break can be as often as once a week to run errands or perhaps to take a vacation.

Home health care agencies are a common source for providing personnel such as a nurse, home health aide or personal care attendant and who can be retained depending on the level of need for the patient for short periods of time.

The various types of long term care discussed in this chapter are the primary long term care services being provided today. Remembering the various definitions and context of these services will be important for you when analyzing a long term care insurance policy. The type of care, the eligibility requirements for benefits, and specific types of assistance are all tied into the care provided in a long term care setting.

CHAPTER NOTES

1. *Daytona Beach News-Journal*, "Assessing Medical Needs for the Elderly", by Judy Foreman, 1995.
2. *Southern Lifestyles*, A Complete Guide to Georgia Area Facilities, Special Supplement, 1995.
3. *Journal of the American Society of CLU and ChFC*, "Financial Gerontology", March, 1992, p. 23.
4. *The Sandwich Generation*, "Home: What Does It Mean?", Issue 1, 1995, p. 12.
5. AARP Home Care Handbook, "Who Benefits From Home Care?", p. 5.
6. *Parade*, "How Much Can I Give?", January 29, 1995, p. 6.

Chapter 5

THE GROWTH OF ELDER CARE SERVICES

During the 1960's, 65 percent of older parents lived with their children. Today that has dropped to 15 percent.[1] When both husband and wife work, the burden of caring for elderly parents at home is overwhelming.

When caring for an older relative or parent in one's own home is too difficult it remains for the adult children to make other arrangements for their loved ones to receive the long term care needed. These alternative choices have resulted in a rising tide in the growth of elder care services nationwide. As the population continues to age, it is clear that this upward spiral will continue or even accelerate.

The setting in which long term care services are rendered has become an important factor in determining eligibility for benefits under a long term care insurance policy. As policies become more refined, the variety of long term care settings acceptable to insurers has broadened considerably. Considering that many new types of facilities for long term care are available and are less costly than a nursing home — it makes sense to encourage individuals to elect a more inexpensive environment.

This chapter will examine the variety of the types of places where an individual can receive long term care from the original standard — the nursing home — to one's own home to assisted living facilities.

THE NURSING HOME

From the introduction in this book, it was obvious how both Mrs. Doan and her daughter, Karen Parker, felt about nursing homes. For many, the term *nursing home* has a negative connotation.

Compounding this public relations problem are the costs and reputation of these skilled facilities. The August, 1995 issue of *Consumer Reports* noted "...the quality of care at thousands of the nation's nursing homes is poor or questionable at best. Facilities allow life-threatening bed sores to develop, violate residents' dignity, fail to produce required care plans to assure a decent quality of life, improperly use physical restraints such as vests and waist belts, and fail to meet basic standards for sanitary food preparation."[2]

If you think that the certification of a nursing home by the Health Care Financing Administration (HCFA) on behalf of Medicare gives the institution a clean bill of health, think again. Approximately 40 percent of the facilities certified by HCFA have repeatedly violated federal standards over the last four inspection surveys.[3]

The question then becomes, why would anyone consider placing an individual in a nursing home? Only about 5 percent of people over age 65 live in a nursing home at any given time and for most families, like Mrs. Doan's, it is the last resort when long term care services are required.[4]

But for some, a nursing home may still be the best situation. If there is no one to care for them elsewhere, a nursing home represents a place where they will receive some attention, be close to medical services, and be able to socialize with others. In some cases, a person will receive reimbursement for the cost of care provided from Medicare, insurance, or Medicaid.

The key is to find the right nursing home for a parent or aging relative. This is not easily done. Help from state and local ombudsmen (individuals who resolve complaints on behalf of nursing home residents) rarely draw negative reviews concerning a nursing home. This leaves the research for finding the right nursing home to the individual family. And why not? If you are looking for a home, you wouldn't leave it up to someone else to make the choice for you.

As an insurance agent you will often be asked to recommend a benefit amount (usually a daily benefit) for a policy and in order to give proper counsel, it will be necessary for you to visit some of the nursing homes in your area to determine which facilities would be acceptable and average the costs among the more favorable facilities. This will give you the information and opportunity to endorse those facilities to potential clients.

Recommending a nursing home facility requires a visit. An insurance agent informally researching nursing homes in his community would be wise to ask a friend in the nursing field to accompany him for an "unofficial inspection". Nurses often spot problems well before most others and can help avoid a facility that looks good on the surface but may harbor problems internally.

A retired coal miner living in Tampa, Florida had back surgery in 1992. During the surgery, his heart stopped which resulted in his brain not receiving enough oxygen. Although doctors revived him, without special medication, he would become violent and when left alone, would wander off.

None of his children could care for him or afford home care so they consulted state officials for a recommendation of a nursing home facility that accepted Medicaid, since he would qualify due to low income and assets. In October, 1993, he was checked into a local facility and the family was advised by the nursing director to give him a few days to adjust.

When they returned four days later for a visit, they found him tied to a chair, incoherent, dirty, unshaven and wearing someone else's clothes. This was just the beginning of a nightmare. On several occasions they would find their father with cuts, bruises and other evidence of mistreatment. When his family questioned the management of the facility about the mistreatment, they were advised they had 30 days to find another residence for him as he was being discharged. Before that month was up, the man died of a lung disorder. Over a year later, the nursing home was cited for several violations and new management was ushered in.[5]

It is important to view several facilities rather than rely solely on a recommendation.

Where would a person begin researching nursing homes? In Florida, for example, the Agency for Health Care Administration can provide a list of nursing home facilities by county (See Chapter 3, The Financial Strain of Aging). The list contains useful information about nursing homes — number of beds, whether they accept Medicare or Medicaid reimbursement, the special services offered and similar data. It also offers the address and phone number of the facilities and will help you map out geographically unofficial inspections of the facilities.

Most facilities will be glad to give you a tour if someone is available, especially if you've indicated that you have a parent or relative who may be a potential resident. Upon inspection, there will be obvious signs to look for such as smell, lighting and cleanliness. If, for example, there's an undesirable smell, this is an indication that the staff does a less than acceptable job of keeping the residents and facility clean. If the building is dark with only a few windows or is poorly lit, it will likely become a gray, brooding atmosphere for the resident that can often lead to prolonged depression.[6]

A copy of the nursing home's latest inspection report should be requested. Federal law requires this report to be public record and you have the right to ask for and receive a copy. If a copy is not provided, the questions to ask are why would they not release the inspection report and what does the facility have to hide?

Another key area to explore would be the nursing home's contract. The contract typically is about 20 to 30 pages long and should be reviewed by an attorney before the elderly adult (or person with a durable power of attorney) signs it. An insurance agent can assist clients with this procedure. There are a growing number of attorneys specializing in elder law and, though a fee will certainly be charged, it is well worth the expense. Other family members do not have to sign this contract. Federal law prohibits co-signers as a requirement for admission. An adult child considering a nursing home for a parent or relative does not have to take financial responsibility at the present.[7]

In an attempt to ensure payment from someone, institutions often push for a responsible party signature from someone other than the incoming resident. This is not required to secure admission.

Despite the fact that a nursing home is considered a last resort, there are 1.6 million Americans with an average age of 83 living in nursing homes.[8] There will most likely be an increase in admissions over time. The average nursing home cost nationwide of $30,000 annually, is typically incorporated in a long term care insurance policy. The average American cannot afford this type of care for very long, if at all, and a long term care insurance policy represents an invaluable source of funds for this type of care.

Even though nursing home residency is expected to increase, nursing homes are taking on a new type of patient — those in need of *subacute care.* It is an attempt by nursing homes to mirror hospitals by providing skilled nursing care for stroke rehabilitation and cardiac care for people who recently had surgery or are recovering from a serious illness.[9]

This is a fallout from the managed care shakeup in the health care industry which has stepped up the pressure to cut medical costs and discharge people earlier, giving nursing homes another revenue source for those individuals considered too healthy to stay in the hospital but not well enough to go home. Since the nursing home can receive four or five times the dollar reimbursement to provide subacute care than what would be received for a nursing home resident, there is a flurry of activity to make way for more subacute patients.

This also has an effect on the number of beds available in a nursing home. In particular, low-profit elderly patients on Medicaid are often the first to have to give up their beds if it's a choice between a subacute patient or the Medicaid resident. Subacute care will increase the popularity of other, lower-cost elder care living choices in the future.

Nursing homes will continue to exist and the insurance agent will play a key role in helping to advise elderly clients on options available. *Consumer Reports* recently ran a ratings list of acceptable nursing homes by geographic areas and can be used as a reference for recommendation of facilities. Keep in mind though, that a written report cannot replace a personal visit to the facility, but it can help begin the process of researching facilities.

HOSPITALS

In today's health care environment, hospitals must do something to keep their beds occupied at full capacity. Managed care systems are extracting patients from the hospital at a quicker pace only to have the patient go to another facility. Hospitals are asking why not address all of the care and services needed for patients under one roof?

For this reason, some hospitals have taken the initiative and converted wings of their facilities into *extended care* beds in order to provide the same type of subacute care that nursing homes are gearing up to provide.

Caring for the elderly is more than a case of a doctor or nurse listening to symptoms and complaints from the patient. A doctor has "read" the individual who is not capable of asking for the services he or she needs. The elderly patient may often be confused or mentally incapacitated and hospital personnel must be trained specifically to deal with this type of situation. If hospitals are to provide geriatric care, they must be prepared to spend an hour or two feeding a patient, or simply providing companionship to the patient to prevent depression or loneliness.[10]

If a hospital is to be an alternative facility for care of the elderly patient, nursing personnel trained in elderly care should be provided. The idea of "switching" beds from acute care to subacute care to long term care makes sense and could be an important revenue source for hospitals in the future.

HOME IS WHERE THE CARE IS

Family members play a vital role in the health care process, especially for a patient who is not able to communicate well or has difficulty absorbing information. There are so many decisions to be made that coherent minds are needed to understand the care choices available and select the best and most appropriate of these.

In today's "continuum of care" health system, there may be a highly-detailed plan drawn up, involving several levels of care and different facilities available to provide treatment. If an individual begins the odyssey through the health care system in the hospital, there is a discharge planner usually available to assist with some of the key decisions.[11] (In the introduction, Karen Parker received help from Mrs. Becker, the hospital's discharge planner who was also a social worker.)

The discharge planner, working in conjunction with the patient's physician, can make a full assessment of health care needs and draw up a plan of care dedicated to the patient's recovery, improvement, or maintenance of the present condition. Most often, the end result is to work towards getting the patient home. Care still may be necessary, but if it can be done at home, all the better. Given the option, it is not surprising that most choose their own home for treatment.

There is usually a psychological edge to recovering at home. Maintaining some type of routine is much easier in familiar surroundings.

Remember that the retention of independence is vitally important to the elderly individual. Being at home keeps one in a familiar environment and closer to family and friends who are often in the best position to provide much needed emotional support.

No wonder the fastest growing type of health care in the 1980's was home health care. If you look at any forecast for the top jobs in the future (not limited to health care), home health personnel are high up on the list. That the medical profession can provide more and varied health care at home indicates that the health industry has a future growth potential.

Recent medical scientific advances have reduced bulky equipment to portable size for easier access in the home. Home health care services help prevent the need for hospitalization for the chronically ill patient typically in need of long term care services with the help of the new equipment.

Looking at the membership in the National Association for Home Care, an association of agencies that provide home health care services, gives an indication of the incredible growth of home health care services. From 212 members in 1982, this organization now has nearly 8,000 members nationwide, roughly half of the home health care agencies registered in the country.[12]

Receiving care in the home is a desirable situation for many Americans. The different types of care that can be provided at home, to name a few are, skilled nursing care, physical, speech or respiratory therapy, medical equipment and supplies, occupational counseling, chore services (light housekeeping, laundry and cooking), companion services, respite care, physician services, hospice care, social services, transportation services, meal delivery, nutritional counseling and everyday assistance with activities of daily living (ADLs).

Overall, the home health care industry has $27 billion in revenue, according to government statistics. It is almost always less expensive to have the care provided at home rather than a hospital or nursing facility. In Chapter 6, Government Programs, we will look at home health care and what is reimbursed under Medicare.

A 62-year-old New York woman has been in and out of city hospitals in recent years for treatment of a perforated intestine. Unable to ingest solid foods, her weight has diminished to 85 pounds. While medical personnel have predicted her demise several times, thanks in large part to home health care visits from skilled nurses and aides who assist with intravenous feeding and the changing of bandages, she has been able to survive.

She is Social Security disability-qualified so the cost of $2,411 per week is paid in full by Medicare. A prolonged hospital stay would have been four times that amount and a nursing home stay in New York could cost as much. With Medicare paying the costs, it makes it an easy decision to receive home health care.[13]

Medicare is concerned about the growing costs associated with home health care (See Chapter 6, Government Programs). In an effort to bring the same cost controls to home health care that have been adopted for hospitals and physicians, the Health Care Financing Administration has kept the payments for home health care expenses at 1995 levels. A new cost containment program is to be introduced that addresses all outpatient-type costs.

Another problem Medicare faces is home health care fraud. There have been a number of well-documented cases that have resulted in billions of dollars being paid out to scam artists. The administration of Medicare has so many loopholes in it, the fraud is not difficult to perpetrate. The head of HCFA has gone on record as saying that Medicare unquestionably pays substantially more than anyone else for the same type of home health care services. Caremark, a large home care chain, pleaded guilty to federal felony charges involving kickbacks to doctors who recommended this home care agency and paid $161 million in settlement costs.[14]

Still, the home care market is a strong one, appealing to most everyone and likely will continue to take an ever-growing percentage share of the long term care tab being paid today. If elderly parents and their adult children have their say, home care will be the primary method of delivering long term care for the future.

OTHER ASSISTED LIVING FACILITIES

Beyond nursing home and home care environments there are an assorted number of boardinghouse-type residences that cater specifically to those needing long term care. These centers are commonly known as adult congregate living facilities (ACLFs), assisted living facilities, personal care homes, extended congregate care residences, continuing care retirement communities (CCRCs), Elder Cottage Housing Opportunity (ECHO) homes and board-and-care homes.[15]

Essentially, these facilities provide room and board as well as offer additional services. They are primarily intended to provide shelter for individuals that can no longer take care of their own home or who may need assistance with the normal activities of daily living.

Long term care insurance policies are beginning to recognize these alternative living arrangements. Due to financial considerations, a nursing home (where insurance eligibility is common) may not be feasible or circumstances may prevent the use of one's own home or the use of a family member's home yet, the need for long term care assistance remains.

Caution, however, should be exercised in evaluating this type of housing. While nursing homes have set minimum standards to follow, the laws governing the licensing and regulation of assisted living facilities vary widely. In some states it's not clear whether there are laws that govern assisted living facilities.

This new type of housing can take many forms. For example:

- Marriott Corporation has started a chain of assisted living facilities. Marriott obviously recognizes the potential growth for assisted living facilities for the aging population.

- In Daytona Beach, Florida, an advertisement appearing in the local newspaper read:

ARE YOU PART OF THE SANDWICH GENERATION?

Caught between the demands of your career, your children and the demands of your own aging parents?

Bishop's Glen Retirement Community can help you help your parents.

Bishop's Glen provides four levels of quality care on one convenient campus allowing couples to remain together as their health needs change. Stop by any day between 10:00 AM and 4:00 PM for your free copy of "How To Care For Your Parents", a U.S. Dept. Of Health and Human Services booklet.

- In Brighton, Massachusetts, a newsletter published by the Friends of the Jewish Community Housing for the Elderly trumpets the opening of additional elderly apartments at the Golda Meir House.

- In Deland, Florida, a new project broke ground for an assisted living facility that will provide closely monitored apartments specifically for Alzheimer's patients.

- In Volusia County, Florida alone, 1996 construction is expected to add 113 apartments, 200 nursing home and acute care beds plus space for 50 Alzheimer's patients at a cost of nearly $24 million dollars.[16]

- In Peachtree City, Georgia, a planned community of 26,000 residents, people can navigate a road network of 70 miles without ever getting in a car. Instead, the preferred mode of transportation is a golf cart.[17]

Assisted living facilities are intended to foster independence, dignity, privacy, the ability to function at the maximum level and connections with the community.[18] Each assisted living facility differs in the degree of its success. For this reason, any recommendations you as an insurance agent might make should only be done after careful personal inspection of any facility. Treat this research as you would if you were looking for a nursing home for your relative. Many adults will opt for this type of housing in lieu of a nursing home environment, and the quality of local assisted living facilities as well as the average cost will be good information to have.

Continuing Care Retirement Communities (CCRCs): These major developments contain both independent and assisted living space. Residents contract with the community for a living unit and any other care services that are needed. A person can start out in an independent unit and as his or her health declines, move to the assisted living units that provide long term care services. Many of these communities have built a nursing home on-site for the purpose of 24-hour care. The value of this type of community is a resident can contract for additional services as his needs change without having to leave the community. This type of care is expensive and requires an admission fee which can range from $30,000 to $150,000. The monthly fee can run from $750 to $3,000 or higher. A contract is also required for the purposes of securing a long term commitment.

Adult Congregate Living Facilities (ACLFs): These facilities are designed more for the middle to lower income groups. These facilities offer communal apartment-type living with meals served in a central dining room. There are social and recreational activities organized for residents and general housekeeping is provided. Aides are available to assist with activities of daily living and in some cases skilled care is provided. There is no admission fee instead, a monthly charge ranging from $1,000 and up is assessed. Public funds might defray some of the cost if a resident qualifies for a congregate living facility. A number of the ACLFs around the country have a bad reputation, so it pays to inspect the premises before making any recommendations. Since it is communal living, talking to residents during your visit may elicit far more information than you can find elsewhere.

Extended Congregate Care Facilities: This type of care falls somewhere between an adult congregate care facility which generally provides custodial care and a nursing home which provides all types of long term care services. For those that need more than custodial care, but are not in need of long term care services, this type of housing may be a wise selection. It is similar to an ACLF in living arrangement, but has more medical services available. The fees will run slightly higher than an ACLF and some of the extended congregate care facilities accept Medicaid reimbursement.

Assisted Living Facilities: Known by a variety of names, this type of residence may be called personal care homes, sheltered homes, residential care and other names. You'll get the idea, though, from the facility's identity. Services range from furnishing three meals a day to full assistance with ADLs. Generally, the individual here will not need constant monitoring, but will be able to function alone for a few hours at a time. These facilities usually have staff members available 24 hours per day. There are social and recreational events organized. Depending on the amount of care needed, the monthly rates could range to $2-3,000. There are public subsidies often provided. The size of the residence can range from four to six people up to as many as 100 or so.

Elder Cottage Housing Opportunity(ECHO): This type of housing is made up of small, self-contained mobile units that can be placed in the yards of a single-family home. They are specifically designed for older and disabled persons and the construction allows for mobility within the unit. This type of housing allows a person to be near family and friends without actually living under the same roof. They are economical with a one-bedroom unit costing under $25,000. Two-bedroom units are also becoming available. Whether the adult child can provide this type of housing for his parents depends upon the communities' zoning laws and utility connections.

The differences in price, services offered and accommodations makes it difficult to generalize about assisted living facilities. It is an increasingly popular option for many elderly or for those in need of long term care assistance. As such, the insurance agent or financial planner working in the long term care market should be familiar with the various options in the community. Some suggestions in looking for a nursing home are applicable here: avoid unlicensed facilities, request a copy of the latest inspection report, have an attorney review the contract and obtain a list of rules and regulations.

As the population grows older, the number and variety of elder care services will increase substantially. Long term care insurance policies will adapt and generally work with most types of facilities. Since some of these facilities are lower in cost, there may eventually be incentives within the long term care insurance contract encouraging these cost effective living arrangements.

CHAPTER NOTES

1. *Cleveland Plain-Dealer*, "Planning Ahead for Long-Term Care", September 18, 1995, p. 1C.
2. *Consumer Reports*, "Nursing Homes", August, 1995, p. 518.
3. *Consumer Reports*, "Nursing Homes", August, 1995, p. 518.
4. *USA Today*, "Seeking Out a Good Nursing Home", July 19, 1995, p. 7D.
5. *Tampa Tribune*, "Nursing Homes: A State of Uncertainty", November 12, 1995, p. 1.
6. *Consumer Reports*, "Nursing Homes", August, 1995, p. 523.
7. Choosing A Nursing Home, by Seth B. Goldsmith, Prentice Hall, 1990.
8. *Consumer Reports*, "Nursing Homes", August, 1995, p. 526.
9. *Daytona Beach Sunday News-Journal*, "Nursing Homes Shuffling Patients in Profit Pursuit", March 19, 1995, p. 2C.
10. *Daytona Beach News-Journal*, "Best Place For Extended Care", July, 1995.
11. *The Sandwich Generation*, "Smoothing the Move from Hospital to Home", Issue 1, 1995, p. 18.
12. These numbers were furnished by the National Association for Home Care.
13. *The New York Times*, "An Exam For Home Health Care", September 15, 1995.
14. *The New York Times*, "An Exam For Home Health Care", September 15, 1995.
15. Staying at Home, A Guide to Long-Term Care and Housing, AARP Publications, 1992.
16. *Daytona Beach News-Journal*, "Centers for the Aged", by Jim Witters, 1995, p. 1F.
17. *Atlanta Constitution*, "As We Grow Older, Suburbia Needs To Grow Wiser", January 7, 1996.
18. *Consumer Reports*, "The Promise and Pitfalls of Assisted Living", October, 1995, p. 656.

Chapter 6

GOVERNMENT PROGRAMS

"If I had known I was going to live so long, I'd have taken better care of myself."

- Mickey Mantle

"What is this oozing behemoth, this fibrous tumor, this monster of power and expense hatched from the simple human desire for civic order?"

- P.J. O'Rourke

If you ask the average senior citizen how will he pay for his costs associated with his long term care needs, the reply most often heard is "Medicare and my Medicare supplement". Unfortunately, this illustrates how little people understand the purpose of Medicare and Medicare supplements.

Medicaid, not Medicare, is the federal government program that funds most long term care costs today. Medicaid accounts for 71.3 percent of all nursing home and home health care expenditures made by public financing according to the Employee Benefit Research Institute.[1]

Many people confuse Medicare and Medicaid. This chapter will define these programs, the coverages provided, the qualifications required for reimbursement, and discuss how a balanced national budget might affect government benefits.

Here are two important points in understanding these programs:

1. *Medicare* pays for less than 5 percent of long term care expenditures.[2] A recent survey by the American Association of Retired Persons (AARP) showed that 60 percent of its mem-

bers believe that Medicare will be the primary source of financing for their long term care needs. Medicare, on the other hand, specifically points out in its guidebook of benefits that a person should not depend on Medicare as a primary source for long term care assistance.[3]

2. *Medicaid* is a welfare program that is based on poverty-level qualifications, not age eligibility. Medicaid pays the costs of long term care only after individuals have exhausted their personal assets including their income. Because of this qualification, one of the major sources of revenue for providers of long term care is the federally funded program, Medicaid.

With this understanding, it will be easy to communicate to your client the differences in these two programs. As an agent, you must identify potential sources of available funds that an individual might draw upon for the financing of his long term care needs. Medicare and Medicaid are two such sources.

MEDICARE

In 1960, John F. Kennedy, a presidential candidate, presented a program as part of the democratic platform that would help elderly Americans pay for health care expenses without having to go into bankruptcy. Even though there were far fewer seniors in 1960 than today, a greater percentage of the elderly lived close to the poverty line. Some analysts feel that by using the approach of a federally funded program to subsidize health care costs, Kennedy used the senior vote to propel himself into the White House by a narrow margin.

President Kennedy did not live to see this idea come to fruition. That was left to his successor, Lyndon Johnson, who witnessed the birth of Medicare in 1965 as an amendment to the 1935 Social Security Act. The Medicare program design was based on an acute care oriented medical model, to reimburse people age 65 and over for hospital and physician services.[4] Also eligible, without regard to age, were qualified disabled individuals (under Social Security's definition), and those suffering permanent kidney failure. This government program is currently administered by the Health Care Financing Administration (HCFA).

There are two parts to Medicare — Part A and Part B.

Part A benefits cover institutional care including inpatient hospital care, limited skilled nursing home care, some home health care expenses and hospice care. Part A is financed almost exclusively by payroll (FICA) taxes (1.45 percent of all income earned). There is no additional premium cost to those eligible for Medicare coverage.

Part B is a supplemental and an optional program. Coverage includes physician services, outpatient hospital care, physical therapy and other miscellaneous medical expenses. Twenty-five percent of the premium is paid by the Medicare beneficiary and 75 percent from taxpayer general revenues. In 1996, the monthly premium for Part B is $42.10. This premium is usually deducted from the Social Security benefit check being paid to the Medicare-eligible individual. The individual over age 65 does not have to elect Part B coverage and has an option of enrolling in the program within the first 90 days of each year.

MEDICARE AND LONG TERM CARE

This chapter is intended to discuss Medicare only as it relates to coverage of long term care expenses. As an insurance agent and financial planner, your knowledge of the long term care aspect of the Medicare program is vital to properly designing and communicating a solution to your client or prospect's long term care needs.

Medicare is the most misunderstood government program in identifying what is actually covered for long term care services. As noted earlier, the Medicare program was primarily designed for acute medical care needs. But the health problems the elderly are faced with today are related to the inability to perform activities of daily living (ADLs). This treatment model is primarily a disability model, not acute medical care.[5] The expectation level for comprehensive long term care coverage under Medicare should not be high since Medicare was not designed to cover chronic care conditions.

Medicare Part A addresses two primary areas of long term care — nursing home and home health care.

Nursing Home Coverage

Skilled care in a nursing home environment is the only type of care that Medicare will cover. It can be either skilled nursing care or skilled rehabilitation care. Individuals needing intermediate care or custodial care (assistance with activities of daily living) are not covered and will not receive any financial assistance from Medicare.

To be eligible for reimbursement for skilled care in a nursing home facility, the patient must meet four requirements:

1. A consecutive three-day hospital stay (not including day of discharge) must precede entry into a skilled nursing home facility and the same medical cause must exist for both hospital and skilled nursing facility admission.

2. The patient generally must be admitted to the skilled nursing home facility within 30 days of hospital discharge.

3. The skilled nursing home facility must be certified by Medicare. According to the Health Care Financing Administration, only about 50 percent of skilled nursing facilities are certified.

4. A physician must certify the need for this skilled care on a daily basis.

All four of these requirements must be met in order to become eligible for coverage for skilled nursing or rehabilitative care received in a skilled facility.[6] If these requirements are not met, Medicare will not pay the claim.

It happens. In New York, a nursing home resident required eye surgery and transferred to a hospital for two days for the procedure. She returned to the nursing home where she requested and received skilled nursing care. The patient felt that with her age, overall condition and ongoing arthritis therapy, skilled care was necessary because of the potential for complications following surgery. Medicare, however, denied the claim since her hospital stay was under the three-day requirement and skilled care was not needed on a daily basis. The woman took the case to court but her request for reversal was denied. Medicare's decision to deny the claim was based on the fact that her primary care need was for custodial, not skilled care.[7]

If all four requirements have been met, up to 100 days of skilled nursing care benefits are provided. However, it is not as simple as it may seem. Here is what Medicare will pay for skilled nursing care in a certified facility:

Days	Amount
1 - 20	up to 100% of approved amount
21 - 100	all but $92.00/day (1996 rules)
100 +	nothing

Medicare's "approved amount" for the first 20 days is based on a set rate schedule for a geographical area. If a nursing home charges more than the approved amount, the patient is responsible for the difference in the rates. The nursing home facility, certified by Medicare, will be likely to accept the Medicare rate. Thus, for the majority of cases, the full rate (for a semi-private room) will be reimbursed by Medicare for the first 20 days.

The second phase of the breakdown, days 21 through 100, requires the patient to pay the first $92 per day. As you can see, Medicare's financial responsibility has diminished significantly. In Orlando, Florida, the average cost of a nursing home stay is about $92 per day. So a person staying in a nursing home facility that charged the average rate of $92 would receive no reimbursement from Medicare during this period. If, for example, the skilled facility charged $100 per day, Medicare would pay $8 per day and the cost to the patient would be $92 a day.

The sizable co-payment required for days 21 through 100 reduces the payout from Medicare. If the patient has a Medicare supplement, the patient could be reimbursed $92 a day depending upon the type of coverage offered in the Medicare supplement policy.

After 100 days, the patient is responsible for the entire cost. Medicare or a Medicare supplement will not cover skilled nursing care after this period.

A better description of Medicare's skilled nursing care coverage under Part A of Medicare might be:

Under Medicare, one might receive benefits for up to 20 days for skilled care rendered in a skilled nursing facility if you meet certain conditions. One might also receive a small amount of money during the next 80 days of skilled care provided in a skilled nursing facility.

The *Guide to Health Insurance for People with Medicare* further cautions individuals about distinguishing a *skilled nursing facility* from a *nursing home facility*. The purpose of a skilled nursing facility is to dispense skilled nursing and rehabilitation services, not custodial care as most nursing home facilities provide. A skilled nursing facility for example, could be part of a hospital. Today, more and more medical centers are branching out and offering a multitude of services.

It is important to note that many skilled nursing facilities specifically do not accept Medicare patients. This becomes an important question to ask the management of the facility that is being considered so that the resident is assured eligibility for Medicare reimbursement.

An example might clarify the extent of Medicare's skilled nursing care coverage. Assuming that a Medicare patient met all of the previous requirements to be eligible for Medicare reimbursement for a skilled nursing facility stay, how much would Medicare cover of a $110 a day 180 day stay in a skilled facility?

DAYS	MEDICARE DAILY	TOTAL	PATIENT DAILY	TOTAL
1- 20	$110.00	$2,200.00	-0-	-0-
21- 100	18.00	1,440.00	$ 92.00	$7,360
100-180	-0-	-0-	110.00	8,800
		$3,640.00 (18%)		$16,160.00 (82%)

The coverage for a skilled nursing home facility stay is limited. The gaps in this coverage are:

1. A $92 daily co-payment beyond the initial 20 days of treatment.

2. No coverage for skilled care beyond 100 days.

3. Patient is responsible for any charges above the Medicare approved amount in the first 20 days.

4. No coverage for intermediate or custodial care.

5. No coverage if the three-day hospital stay requirement is not satisfied or if the patient is not transferred to a skilled nursing facility on a timely basis (within 30 days of the hospital stay).

Home Health Care

Long term care services usually involve custodial care. If custodial care is administered, Medicare can pay the claim as long as it is in a home setting.

Medicare will pay the costs of medically necessary home health visits. There are requirements needed to be satisfied before Medicare will approve a claim:

1. Part-time or intermittent home health care is covered. Medicare will not pay for 24-hour care.

   Medicare defines intermittent care as the need for skilled nursing care at least once every 60 days or to four or fewer days per week. Individuals requiring daily skilled nursing care at home even if not on a full-time basis, may have difficulties with their claim.

2. The patient must be house-bound. This is defined as a medical condition restricting the ability to leave the house except with assistance. If leaving the house is medically inadvisable, this also qualifies.

3. The patient must be under a physician's care and the physician must certify the need for the home health care.

4. The home health care agency providing the services must be certified by Medicare. Like skilled nursing facilities, approximately 50 percent of the home health agencies in the country are certified by Medicare.[8]

Unlike skilled nursing care provided in a certified skilled nursing facility, home health care reimbursements do not have co-payments. The only exception is the need for durable medical equipment (wheelchairs, hospital beds, etc.). In this case, Medicare pays 80 percent of the cost.

Covered services include:

- part-time or intermittent skilled nursing care

- physical therapy

- speech therapy

- occupational therapy

- medical social services under the direction of a physician (for example, counseling for emotional problems)

- part-time or intermittent services of a home health aide

- durable medical equipment

Medically necessary use of durable medical equipment, which consists of wheelchairs, oxygen equipment, artificial limbs, braces, ostomy supplies and hospital beds is covered at 80 percent. The patient must pay for 20 percent of the cost.[9] A bathroom grab-bar, for example, is not covered because it is not medical in nature. Neither are elevators or lift devices since people who are not sick or injured use them.

Medicare adheres to its requirements and the slightest infraction can result in non-payment of a claim. An 82-year-old woman suffering from heart disease, weight problems and other conditions was denied home health care coverage because she was not house-bound. She was able to leave her house for a few hours a week to do errands and attend church. She had a frequent need for a walker, but not enough to warrant being house-bound. Although her physician prescribed home health care services, Medicare denied the claim based on her failure to meet the house-bound requirements, a decision that was upheld by a court of appeals.[10]

Medicare specifically states what is *not* covered under its home health care package:

    1. Full-time nursing care.

    2. Meals delivered to the home.

    3. Prescription drugs.

    4. Twenty percent of the cost of durable medical equipment or charges in excess of the Medicare-approved amount for such equipment.

    5. Homemaker services that are primarily needed to assist in meeting personal care or housekeeping needs.[11]

The home health care benefits under Medicare are intended for part-time, medically necessary care that is associated with a skilled need. Thus, while custodial care is covered, it's important to note that if it's 100 percent custodial care without any skilled care needed, the claim runs the risk of being denied.

Medicare's contribution to overall long term care costs is approximately 5 percent. The requirements needed to receive benefits from Medicare eliminate many of the standard claims that would otherwise be filed. Long term care insurance was designed to cover these types of claims.

MEDICARE SUPPLEMENTS

Do Medicare supplements help?

Some. But these policies, so familiar to seniors, only fill in the gaps of those services Medicare designates to be paid. Supplements don't add much to those gaps Medicare has left behind.

For example, for a patient receiving skilled nursing care in a skilled facility Medicare will pay the first 20 days up to its approved amount. A co-payment of $92 the next 80 days is required from the patient, with Medicare paying the difference. The Medicare supplement will pay the $92 co-payment.

However, after 100 days, neither Medicare nor a Medicare supplement will pay anything. Supplements are *not* designed to add extra benefits to what Medicare already pays, but to supplement the existing benefit.

Medicare supplement policies today are sold in ten standard, but specific, plans labeled A through J. Not every insurance company selling Medicare supplements offers ten plans. Some insurance companies do not offer the same number of plans in every state.

Neither plan A nor plan B offers coverage for the co-payment of $92 for the skilled nursing facility. Plans C through J however, do cover co-payments. If your client has the Medicare supplement plan A or plan B, the lack of co-payment coverage should be identified.

Medicare supplement plans D, G, I and J assist with home care benefits. Here, the coverage, labeled at-home recovery benefits, pays up to $1,600 per year for short-term, at-home assistance with activities of daily living for those recovering from illness, injury or surgery. The assistance must be in the form of Medicare-covered home health care services and must be ordered by a physician.

There could be limitations on the number of visits and dollar amounts. For example, some plans pay up to $40 a visit for up to seven visits a week for a period of up to eight weeks *after* Medicare-covered home health care benefits cease. A supplement will not duplicate Medicare coverage.

The majority of seniors believe that Medicare or a Medicare supplement will pay for long term care costs. As an agent it is your responsibility to explain the gaps in these coverages. There is an increasing skepticism with which the elderly view Medicare, especially since Congress is considering further cuts in benefits during its budget negotiations. Discussing Medicare and what is covered is important to your client.

MEDICARE: THE POLITICAL HOT POTATO

There has been much speculation about what Congress will and will not do to the Medicare program. Crucial to these discussions is long term care, since it is potentially the greatest financial problem the elderly will face given Medicare's current lack of comprehensive coverage for long term care services.

Discussions in Congress have not centered on how to add more benefits to Medicare. Instead, talk of requiring home health care co-payments, for example, was part of one budget proposal but eventually was dropped. Also dropped was a provision that would prevent Medicaid from paying some or all of Part B premium for the low-income elderly person.[12]

An "experimental" program called Medicare Select, allows the elderly in some states to enroll in a Health Maintenance Organization (HMO) instead of the regular Medicare program. This experimental program offers more long term coverage — both for skilled nursing and home health care coverage than the current Medicare program. Seniors, however, are not willing to give up their choice of physicians which is limited by the HMO network.[13]

Whatever the final budget resolution, long term care coverage will remain a significant gap for those 65 and over eligible for Medicare. Medicare and Medicare supplements, while a consideration in long term care planning, do not reimburse enough of the costs to be considered as reasonable financial assistance if the need for long term care arises.

MEDICARE DISCLOSURE

For those individuals that own a Medicare supplement policy and wish to buy a long term care insurance policy (or any other type of health insurance that offers coverage for long term care services), a new disclosure form is required by the Social Security Amendments of 1994. The form, adopted by the National Association of Insurance Commissioners in 1995, is as follows:

IMPORTANT NOTICE TO PERSONS ON MEDICARE. THIS INSURANCE DUPLICATES SOME MEDICARE BENEFITS.

This is not a Medicare Supplement Insurance Policy.

Federal law requires us (insurer) to inform you that this insurance duplicates Medicare benefits in some situations.

- This insurance provides benefits primarily for covered nursing home services.

- In some situations Medicare pays for short periods of skilled nursing home care and hospice care.

- This insurance does not pay your Medicare deductibles or coinsurance and is not a substitute for a Medicare Supplement insurance policy.

Neither Medicare nor Medicare Supplement insurance provides benefits for most nursing home expenses.

Before You Buy This Policy

- Check the coverage in all health insurance policies you already have.

- For more information about long term care insurance, review the *Shopper's Guide to Long Term Care Insurance*, available from the insurance company.

- For more information about Medicare and Medicare Supplement insurance, review the *Guide to Health Insurance for People with Medicare*, available from the insurance company.

- For help in understanding your health insurance, contact your state insurance department or state senior insurance counseling program.[14]

The intent of this is to avoid scandals such as the one that plagued insurers and insurance agents several years ago concerning the ownership of, by elderly individuals, several Medicare supplement policies that duplicated benefits. Many state insurance departments have been carefully regulating and monitoring the sale and marketing of long term care insurance to avoid any future problems.

THE MEDICARE CATASTROPHIC ACT OF 1989

Late in 1988, the Medicare Catastrophic Coverage Act was passed. This legislation, propelled through Congress by Democrats Dan Rostenkowski and Pete Stark, altered both Medicare and Medicaid.

The changes to Medicare primarily concentrated on long term care benefits. Skilled nursing or rehabilitative care was extended to 150 days and home health care benefits were increased. While altering the co-payment structure for these services, the new law still failed to provide custodial care coverage in a skilled facility.

To fund this benefit expansion, a tax was levied affecting senior citizens only. The amount of tax was based on their taxable income. Wealthier seniors were going to pay the bulk of these new taxes.

The backlash was tremendous. The vocal elderly let their Congressional representatives know exactly what they thought of this bill resulting in a repeal of the bill which, although not unprecedented, was certainly a rare occurrence.

The changes to Medicare were in effect for one year. On January 1, 1990, the Medicare benefits returned to the previous levels where they remain today. Changes to Medicaid (covered later in this chapter) were not repealed.

Congress received a taste of what can happen when Medicare benefits are altered and the changes are perceived to be negative. Though this political body is asserting itself more in the latest round of Medicare discussions, Americans are discovering they have an effect at the ballot box and their voices will be heard once again when the discussions are complete and legislation is passed.

MEDICAID

Medicaid is a different program entirely. Other than the fact that both are government programs financed by taxes, there is little relationship between Medicare and Medicaid. Medicare is a health care program for Social Security-eligible seniors who automatically qualify for benefits when they reach age 65. Medicaid is a joint federal-state plan that pays health care expenses for low-income individuals. There is a significant difference in eligibility requirements:

Medicare — Individuals become eligible by reaching age 65 (Part A) and paying a monthly premium (Part B (optional)); and

Medicaid — Individuals become eligible by having income and assets at or below poverty level (amounts vary by state).

Medicaid is a welfare assistance program for low-income individuals. Many low-income elderly have come to rely on Medicaid to pay for long term care costs. Funded with state and federal money, it assures health care to 35 million low-income Americans, including five million over the age of 65. For these elderly, Medicaid pays for nursing home costs, home health care and prescription drugs. Two-thirds of all nursing home residents rely on Medicaid, making this program an important source of financial assistance for those needing long term care.[15]

Established in the 1960's, Medicaid is funded by state and federal funds, with approximately 50 percent of the costs indemnified by each. Much attention by Congress has been paid to Medicaid in recent years. The reasoning is that Congress must account for half of the funding of any new program involving Medicaid. This has led to complaints from the individual states about unfunded mandates. Unfunded mandates require local governments to find the dollars to support Congressional-passed legislation. Legislation passed in 1995 at the Congressional level is intended to prevent this from happening in the future.

While there are some federal guidelines concerning Medicaid, every state designs its own program. This creates a diversity of eligibility and plan benefits from state to state. Services covered under the Medicaid program include:

- inpatient hospital care;

- inpatient skilled nursing facility care;

- home health care;

- physician services;

- outpatient hospital services;

- transportation costs to medical facilities;

- laboratory services;

- x-ray services; and

- Medicare deductibles, co-payments, coinsurance and premiums.

Steps in qualifying and applying for Medicaid are:

1. The individual needs long term care and receives it from a nursing home, at someone's home or in an assisted living facility.

2. The patient files for Medicare benefits in the event Medicare will reimburse some of the cost.

3. If private insurance coverage exists, the patient must file a claim with the insurance company. In 1991, a study by the Health Insurance Association of America showed that only 5.9 percent of Americans over age 65 owned private long term care insurance.

4. The patient begins spending and then exhausts all of his money.

5. The patient files a claim for Medicaid benefits.

How common is this scenario? Today, almost 90 percent of the costs for long term care services are paid for by either the individual in need of care or by Medicaid.

Medicaid is available to any American who can satisfy the eligibility requirement of low-income and little or no assets. This eligibility requirement differs for single persons and married persons thanks to the Medicare Catastrophic Coverage Repeal Act of 1989. Each state has its own income and asset eligibility guidelines.

Generally, a person's assets must be at or near poverty level to qualify. Many states set the poverty level at $2,000-$3,000 of assets. The Medicare Catastrophic Coverage Repeal Act of 1989 also affected Medicaid by installing safeguards for the spouse of the person requiring long term care services. Prior to this legislation, the at-home spouse was included in the eligibility requirement of low-come in order for the person requiring assistance to qualify for Medicaid. This often left the healthier individual in a near-bankruptcy situation. The legislation established the minimum monthly income and shelter allowance for the at-home spouse to prevent bankruptcy.

While Medicaid requires individuals to exhaust their income and assets, a few items are exempt from this financial free-fall:

1. The house (while spouse is living) does not need to be sold to pay for Medicaid, regardless of value.

2. One automobile.

3. Household and personal belongings.

4. Wedding and engagement rings.

5. Life insurance.

6. Burial plots and funeral expenses up to $2,500.

For the at-home spouse the monthly income and shelter allowance can go as high as $2,000 per month. The community spouse is also allowed to retain one-half of the couple's assets up to $72,000, varying by state and indexed by inflation.

For the single individual, the need for long term care services precludes the necessity of retaining assets above $2-3,000. The nursing home resident is also permitted a personal needs allowance that is extremely low and also varies by state. Figure 6.1 illustrates the asset and personal monthly allowance by state.[16]

These numbers magnify the importance of planning ahead. To lose the bulk of one's assets and income due to the need for long term care services can be devastating.

To determine eligibility, Medicaid reviews the income and assets of the applicant and his or her spouse. The type of assets that Medicaid looks at and which must be disposed of if a person applies for Medicaid assistance are a second car, vacation home, investment properties, savings and certificates of deposit, bonds, IRAs and other retirement vehicles.

Figure 6.1

PERSONAL NEEDS ALLOWANCE	
$30 per month:	Alabama, Arkansas, Colorado, Georgia, Hawaii, Idaho, Illinois, Indiana, Iowa, Kansas, Missouri, Nebraska, New Mexico, North Carolina, Ohio, Oklahoma, Oregon, Pennsylvania, Rhode Island, South Carolina, South Dakota, Tennessee, Texas, Utah, Virginia, West Virginia, Wyoming
$31 per month:	Delaware
$32 per month:	Michigan
$33 per month:	Louisiana
$35 per month:	California, Florida, Maine, Nevada, New Hampshire, New Jersey
$36 per month:	Washington
$40 per month:	Connecticut, Kentucky, Maryland, Minnesota, Montana, Vermont, Wisconsin
$44 per month:	Mississippi
$45 per month:	North Dakota
$50 per month:	New York
$60 per month:	District of Columbia
$65 per month:	Massachusetts
$70 per month:	Hawaii

ASSETS	

All states allow $2,000 except:

Connecticut: $1,600	New Hampshire: $2,500
District of Columbia: $2,600	New York: $3,350
Indiana: $1,500	North Carolina: $1,500
Maryland: $2,500	North Dakota: $3,000
Minnesota: $3,750	Ohio: $1,500

It is possible to transfer some of these assets to another person. Transferred properties are not considered assets when qualifying for Medicaid. Although Medicaid was not designed to aid the wealthy, a growing number of Americans are making arrangements to transfer their assets to avoid spending their own money.

THE TRANSFER GAME

Attorneys specializing in elder law are consulted by many people and often an elaborate plan called reconfiguration takes place. This involves transferring assets to someone else, typically a child. The object of the transfer game is to see how many assets can be legally moved and how fast Medicaid eligibility can be achieved once the senior client becomes ill. In so doing, they are stepping up their eligibility for Medicaid assistance by avoiding spending those assets. Legally, they no longer have assets.

However, Medicaid has a catch. The 1989 Medicare legislation required that these assets be transferred 30 months before filing for Medicaid. This necessitated planning ahead. A Harvard University study found that nearly two-thirds of the inhabitants of one of Boston's wealthiest suburbs became eligible for Medicaid immediately.

As a result, Medicaid expenditures soared. States began having difficulties balancing their budgets. Long term care expenses were identified as the area largely responsible for the substantial increase in Medicaid costs. When it became clear that many middle-class and wealthier Americans were using the Medicaid program to pay for long term care expenses, the federal government acted.

The passage of the Omnibus Budget Reconciliation Act of 1993 (OBRA), in effect, eliminated most of the transfer game pieces by imposing more stringent requirements on qualifying for Medicaid assistance.[17] The purpose of Medicaid is to aid the truly impoverished.

With the passage of OBRA, regular transfers of assets must occur 36 months prior to applying for Medicaid and transfers out of a trust must occur 60 months prior. In addition, the law states that individual states must enact, by 1995, legislation concerning estate recovery. As a result, Estate Recovery or Lien Recovery Acts have been enacted in many states over the last several months.[18]

The estate recovery programs direct the recovery of transferred assets of a Medicaid beneficiary in an amount equal to that spent under Medicaid to provide long term care services. For example, let's say Mrs. Barnes qualified for Medicaid after transferring her assets and the cost to the state and federal government to take care of her until her death was $35,000. The Estate Recovery Act allows the government to recover the $35,000 (as long as her spouse is no longer living) from wherever the assets were transferred.

For example, Florida's estate recovery law states, "the estate recovery program was designed to enhance the state's rights and ability to reimburse the state treasury whenever possible without creating a new population of Medicaid recipients".[19] The individuals to whom the assets have been transferred are fair game since they are unlikely to be Medicaid-eligible.

Medicaid was intended to be a true welfare program, not an artificial one. People who do not wish to spend their own assets have legally avoided doing so and are now siphoning dollars away from the legitimate poor who need care. The Medicaid program is simply running out of money. An attempt by the government to reduce costs by cutting back reimbursements to medical providers, for example, hasn't helped either. Unfortunately by reducing medical reimbursement, it has forced many providers to not accept Medicaid patients.

The "pay me now" (spend down) or "pay me later" (estate recovery) approach has made an impact on those who would otherwise transfer assets in order to qualify for Medicaid. Although the estate recovery law is not an attractive one, it has helped to a degree in restoring benefits for those individuals who truly qualify for Medicaid.

It is worth noting that the transfer game did have some unexpected outcomes for those who played it. Many people who transferred their assets found themselves in the unwanted position of having to ask their children or relatives for money. Many nursing facilities and home health care agencies do not accept Medicaid assignment so individuals who otherwise would have had the choice of a nursing home facility or home health care agency were limited to facilities that accepted Medicaid. The nursing home facilities that did accept Medicaid patients often crowded them three to four in a room. In short, the final results from the transfer were financially acceptable but emotionally difficult.

For those desiring to transfer assets, this must be done 36 or 60 months prior to applying for Medicaid. OBRA '93 also penalizes those who transfer assets during this period. The ineligibility period will be extended based on both the amount transferred and the cost of the average daily nursing home rate in one's geographical area.

For example, let's say our Mrs. Barnes transferred assets of $250,000 and then applied for Medicaid within the 36 month eligibility period. Since the local average daily nursing home rate is $2,500, this transfer and subsequent application will disqualify the individual for 100 months ($250,000 divided by $2,500), over eight years instead of 36 months.[20] If transferring assets is desired, it's a good idea to consult with an elder law attorney.

THE BUDGET DEBATE

Congress has proposed block granting the Medicaid program to the state governments rather than have the federal government impose regulation that is not sensitive to individual states. States would have the ability to design their own eligibility requirements thus making Medicaid qualification exceedingly difficult. The transfer period in order to become eligible for Medicare has already been determined by the federal government but what is to prevent a state government from changing to a longer period in an effort to completely discourage transfer of assets? The Estate Recovery Act is a first step, a warning to let people know that Medicaid should not be an alternative for people who have assets and would not ordinarily qualify for Medicaid. Such individual should make other arrangements for their long term care needs.[21]

The proposed changes to Medicaid would almost certainly end Medicaid entitlement for the middle class and wealthy.[22] Elder care attorneys warn people about states who may even place a lien on the family home so that when the house is sold, the state can recover its Medicaid expenditures.[23] Still, many intend to play the transfer game because of loopholes found in the Medicaid system.[24]

The importance of long term care insurance, however, has been elevated to a much higher level.

VETERAN'S BENEFITS

Veterans of foreign wars may be eligible for nursing home and home health care benefits. Veterans with service-connected disabilities and low-income veterans are considered top priority applicants. Higher-income veterans not disabled in the service may also be eligible although eligibility will be based on a means test if Veteran Administration resources and facilities are available.

After determining the eligibility class of a client, contact the local Veteran Administration office for specific information on qualification.[25]

SUMMARY

Medicare and Medicaid are two separate and distinct programs that can provide payment for long term care services. But there are drawbacks to each program. In general:

Medicare — This program covers some skilled nursing care in a nursing home or at home if specific qualifications are met. Home health care is available but is subject to stringent eligibility rules. There is no coverage for true custodial care, the most common of the long term care services needed.

Medicaid — This program pays the costs for many long term care services for individuals at or below the poverty level. Medicaid benefits are usually not available until the individual's savings have been depleted.

CHAPTER NOTES

1. The *BNA Pension and Benefit Reporter*, "Long Term Care Education Urged", August 7, 1995.
2. *The New York Times*, "Planning for Nursing-Home Bills", by Laura Pederson, 1995.
3. *AARP Bulletin*, "Medicare Showdown Near", November, 1995, p. 1.
4. *Health Care Innovations*, "Managed Care, Elder Care and Medicare", July/August, 1995, p. 19.
5. *Health Care Innovations*, "Managed Care, Elder Care and Medicare", July/August, 1995, p. 20.
6. *1995 Guide to Health Insurance for People with Medicare*, National Association of Insurance Commissioners and Health Care Financiing Administration, January, 1995.
7. *The ElderLaw Report*, "SNF Medicare Coverage Denied", November, 1992.
8. *Public Policy Institute Fact Sheet*, distributed by AARP.

9. "Medicare and Home Medical Equipment", consumer pamphlet distributed by the U.S. Department of Health and Human Services.
10. *The ElderLaw Report*, "Medicare Benefits Denied Because Patient Not Confined To Home", January, 1992.
11. *1996 Guide to Health Insurance for People with Medicare.* National Association of Insurance Commissioners and Health Care Financiing Administration, January, 1995.
12. *AARP Bulletin*, "AARP's Deets Warns Against Big Medicare-Medicaid Cuts", November, 1995, p. 1.
13. *National Underwriter*, "Medicare, Medicaid Are Budget Bill's Sticking Points", December 11, 1995, p. 20.
14. This form was released for use by the Principal Financial Group in 1995.
15. *AARP Special Report*, "Scene Shifts to the States Amid Alarms", Fall, 1995, p. 1.
16. Published by the National Governor's Association, 1994.
17. *The Sandwich Generation*, "New Medicaid Laws", Issue 1, 1995, p. 10.
18. *Financial Planning*, "Federal Budget Toughens Medicaid Requirements", September, 1993, p. 14.
19. Agency for Health Care Administration, Florida, "Medicaid Third Party Recovery", March, 1995.
20. *Life Association News*, "Long Term Care After OBRA '93", June, 1994, p. 83.
21. *Business Week*, "How Medicaid Reform Could Burn the Middle Class", November 6, 1995, p. 53.
22. *The Atlanta Constitution*, "Medicaid Battle Pits Poor Against the Middle Class", Jane Bryant Quinn column, December 18, 1995.
23. *The Sandwich Generation*, "House May Be Claimed", Fall, 1995, p. 13.
24. *LTC News and Comment*, "Undaunted Divestors Dig Deeper", February, 1994, p. 5.
25. For further information and assistance, write or call: Veterans Benefits Department, Paralyzed Veterans of America, 801 18th Street, NW, Washington, D.C. 20006, 1-800-424-8200.

Chapter 7

THE NEED FOR FINANCIAL PLANNING

"Money is better than poverty, if only for financial reasons."

— Woody Allen

"You can send a message around the world in one-seventh of a second, yet it may take years to move a simple idea through a quarter-inch of human skull."

— Charles F. Kettering

Long term care services are costly. People receiving medical care at an older age are finding it difficult to pay related medical costs because they are outliving their resources. Government assistance programs are not enough (Medicare) or require too much (Medicaid). Studies have shown that 93 percent of the people who will reach age 65 in the near future will be dependent on the combination of Social Security, charity and relatives. Only seven percent will have sufficient assets for retirement and financial security.[1]

Most women spend nearly a third of their lives financially independent. They live an average of five to seven years longer than men and are more likely to need long term care services for an extended period than their male counterparts.[2]

Most people realize financial planning is important but many procrastinate thinking that there will be enough time later on to plan for the future. Yet, like Karen Parker mentioned in the introduction, the worse scenario is having to confront a long term care situation without proper financial planning.

Adult children should sit down and talk with their parents about their family's financial situation and decide on a plan of action for the future.

If their parents haven't saved enough or planned for the possibility of requiring long term care whether in a nursing home, an assisted living facility, or some other type of long term care, some of the cost or the caregiving itself will fall to them.[3]

Likewise, parents should willingly discuss financial matters with their children. This is especially difficult if it is something that has not been shared in the past. Many parents still feel their finances are not their children's business and may resist their advice on financial matters even if those children are now in their 30's, 40's and 50's.

The key to understanding the importance of long term care financial planning is that death itself is often preceded by a lengthy disability that could cost thousands of dollars. An estate could be erased within a short period of time if proper planning has not been done.

This is where an insurance agent can play a vital role. Bridging the gap between parents and children is part of long term care planning. The agent should be prepared to deal with a number of emotional issues as information is gathered. Some parents may not even want their children present. Others may not give the agent all of the information. There are people who still remember the "Great Depression" vividly and may not disclose the money hidden under the mattress, or the money that is stashed away in a safety deposit box. Talking to both parents and children is the ideal situation because it often reveals most of the information that the agent needs in order to make a recommendation.

DATA GATHERING

There are two components to the data gathering process — words and numbers. Data gathering is critical to long term care planning because the words and numbers dictate a plan of action. If the client has an attorney and/or an accountant, it is best to involve them from the beginning since they may play a role in carrying out part of the agent's recommendations. There are some legal and financial issues that should be carried out by most everyone.

Words

As the agent, it is important to construct a profile of your client. Asking specific questions can gauge the person's ability to comprehend and follow through on the proposals the agent makes. This will also help the agent assess whether or not this client is a candidate for long term care insurance.

This data gathering process will help the agent identify a person's recent health history and estate planning, if any. It will also provide important contacts in the event the agent may have to call them on behalf of the client in case of an emergency and, gives the agent an essential profile of the client. Figure 7.1 shows the questions that should be asked.

Figure 7.1

DATA GATHERING QUESTIONS TO ASK IN LONG TERM CARE PLANNING

Questions to ask:

Name: _____ Date-of-Birth _____ Age _____

Social Security Number: _____ Telephone: _____

Address: _____

City _____ State _____ Zip Code _____

Occupation _____

Employer (Current or Retired From): _____

Health Benefits Provided by employer: _____

Smoker? _____ Height & Weight _____

Current Physician _____

Have you been hospitalized in the last 5 years? _____

If so, give more details, including date and current prognosis: _____

_____

_____

Are you currently taking medication? _____

Figure 7.1 (continued)

If so, please list: _____

_____

On Medicare? _____

On Medicaid? _____

Important names and phone numbers:

Attorney _____

Accountant _____

Stockbroker _____

Clergy _____

Closest relative _____

Closest friend _____

Other agent or financial planner _____

Account number and location of key documents:

Safety deposit box: _____

Bank : _____

Home: _____

Office: _____

Other: _____

Do you have:

Will? _____

Powers of Attorney   Financial: _____   Medical: _____

Special bequests: _____

Burial instructions : _____

Before proceeding in obtaining financial information, it is important to focus on several of the key data elements.

Will: This is an important issue. There are many elderly people that do not have a will. The purpose of a will is to determine how the estate is to be distributed. Financial planning may be almost worthless without this document. If a person's net worth is more than $600,000 or a couple's net worth exceeds $1,200,000, certain trusts can help avoid probate and estate taxes.

Financial Durable Power of Attorney: This document allows the person appointed to sign an individual's name and to legally conduct affairs on behalf of the individual. If one or both parents are incapacitated, this document is crucial. Without it, bank accounts may not be accessed, bills may not be paid, checks may not be signed, and the entire family may be tossed into a frenzy.[4]

While this frenzy can be avoided with a financial durable power of attorney form, it is easier said than done. Asking a parent to give someone else (especially a child) access to their hard-earned assets and a license to handle all of the financial affairs is a scary proposition to many. It's not so much a matter of trust (although it can be) as it is a matter of giving up control and the ability to make decisions for themselves.

As long as the person who is assigning the financial durable power of attorney is capable of making decisions, he or she will continue to do so. The purpose of the financial durable power of attorney is to have a contingency plan in the event of an unexpected inability to communicate. Without someone to take over the financial affairs, control is then truly lost.

Anyone age 18 or older of sound mind can be designated as the holder of the power of attorney. The selection of the proper individual will be dictated by trust, capability, and convenience.[5] The individual chosen should be willingly to respect and honor the individual's wishes. The oldest child may not be the best choice if he lives 3,000 miles away or is not trustworthy or does not have the parent's best interests at heart. Careful consideration should be given to this issue.

Medical Durable Power of Attorney: While the financial aspect of this legal preparation allows someone to conduct financial affairs for your client, the holder of the financial durable power of attorney cannot make medical decisions unless a medical durable power of attorney form has also been signed. This form, also called a Health Care Surrogate form, puts the appointed individual in a position one hopes never to be in — to make crucial medical decisions on behalf of another who is incapable of making the decisions. Decisions such as withdrawing life support systems or authorizing the donation of vital organs can be made by the holder of a medical durable power of attorney.

Many hospitals are requiring this form today.[6] It carries legal authority that living wills do not have even though both documents may contain the same requests. There are many individuals who do not wish to be kept alive in certain circumstances for example and their wishes would have been discussed in advance with the medical durable power of attorney.

The living will is not legally binding on a physician so in this respect it is not the same as the medical durable power of attorney. With concerns over malpractice, a doctor is not likely to carry out the patient's wishes specified in a living will. A physician could however carry out the directives voiced by the medical durable power of attorney holder.[7]

If a person has specific medical requests, they should be discussed with the person given the authority to make medical decisions. Many people do not want to stay technically "alive" at enormous costs, especially if there is little hope of recovery. This can be avoided with the medical durable power of attorney form.

Longer life spans increasingly mean that people are likely to die of extended illnesses. Modern medicine enables a person to stay alive for extended periods of time, perhaps longer than a person would want to be kept alive.[8] While it is a difficult subject to discuss, there are many who have strong convictions about these matters and will be receptive to signing a medical durable power of attorney form.

These documents are vital to the success of a long term care financial planning program. Without them, a complete and proper job cannot be done for the client who relies on the agent's advice. Scenarios like the following may develop.

The daughter has been caring for her comatose mother for nearly ten years. She has been signing her mother's Social Security checks and using the money (plus some of her own) to pay for full-time home health care (not covered by Medicare). No durable power of attorney forms, financial or medical were signed. For some unknown reason, Social Security records indicated that her mother was deceased which would prevent any further Social Security payments. The daughter proved to the Social Security administration that her mother was technically "alive".

Because the daughter signed the checks, Social Security had the right to ask for an accounting of the money spent. Since the cost of the home health care exceeded her mother's Social Security check anyway, this wasn't hard to prove. However, she has to continually provide this information to Social Security in order for the checks to keep coming in. If a financial durable power of attorney form had been signed, the checks would have been automatically deposited into her mother's bank account and she would have had the authority to write checks on her mother's account. With a medical durable power of attorney, she could have also stopped her mother's life support system some time ago.

But she didn't have these options and the documentation required by Social Security would have been substantial if the cost of care hadn't exceeded her mother's check. While there were many other expenses she could have claimed on her mother to justify the check, the monthly documentation alone would have been a considerable inconvenience.[9]

Working closely with the client and his attorney will enable the agent to recommend and follow through in getting a will drawn up and the necessary durable power of attorney forms signed. From there, the next step is the numbers.

Numbers

Figure 7.2 gives a synopsis of the financial information needed to create a financial planning analysis.

An asset and liability review will yield a net worth number. Individuals with a net worth below $100,000 are often considered not strong candidates for long term care insurance. They may qualify for Medicaid in a relatively short period of time and the money spent on long term care insurance would not be worth it if there are few assets to protect.

Figure 7.2

DATA GATHERING FORM FOR LONG TERM PLANNING

Find Your Net Worth		Check Your Cash Flow	
Assets	**Amount**	**Income**	**Monthly Amount**
Checking Accounts	_____	Take Home Pay	_____
Savings Accounts	_____	Overtime	_____
Home or other Real Estate	_____	Bonuses	_____
Life Insurance Cash Value	_____	Social Security	_____
Annuities	_____	Interest Dividends	_____
Retirement Equity		Other Income	_____
(pension, 401(k))	_____	**Total Cash Income**	
Stocks (market value)	_____		
Bonds (market value)	_____	**Expenses**	
Mutual Funds			
(market value)	_____	Mortgage or Rent	_____
Other Investments		Credit Card Payments	_____
(collectibles)	_____	Alimony, Child Support	_____
Automobile	_____	Insurance (auto, home	
Household Appliances		health, medical	
and Furnishings	_____	and so on)	_____
Loans Owed to You	_____	Food	_____
Other Assets	_____	Utilities (heat, phone,	
Total Assets		electricity and so on)	_____
		Child Care	_____
Liabilities		Personal Care (clothing,	
		hair cosmetics	
Current Bills	_____	and so on)	_____
Auto Loans	_____	Medical Bills Not	
Credit Card Balances	_____	Paid by Insurance	_____
Mortgage Balance	_____	Education Expenses	_____
Student Loans	_____	Recreation	_____
Other Debts	_____	Donations	_____
Total Liabilities		Savings	_____
		Gifts	_____
Your Net Worth		Miscellaneous	_____
(Assets Minus Liabilities)	_____	**Total Expenses**	
		Income Surplus or Deficit	
		(Income Minus Expenses)	_____

The $100,000 figure is merely a guideline. There may be individuals with a net worth of $100,000 or less that desire long term care insurance and can afford it. There may be people with a $150,000 net worth who do not want the coverage or cannot afford it. Ultimately, the agent will have to use his own judgment when recommending long term care insurance.

Income and expenses are equally important. Getting an idea of an individual's cash flow will give the agent information on two key factors:

1. *Income surplus.* This indicates the ability to be able to afford the premium for long term care insurance. Long term care insurance is not for everyone. A large amount of discretionary income indicates both an ability to pay and the likelihood of a sizable income and asset base to protect.

2. *Liquidity.* The amount of cash can be important later in determining the length of time the client can self-insure before needing long term care insurance benefits. This will help in deciding on the elimination period (the deductible — the number of days before policy benefits are payable) too. For more information on this topic, see Chapter 8, A Long Term Care Sales Presentation.

The financial analysis is critical in setting up guidelines in order to establish a financial plan. The plan should be updated annually based on current circumstances.

The client will ask many questions during this process. Be prepared to answer as many as possible and elicit the assistance of the other key players (accountant, attorney) and family members.

REVERSE MORTGAGES

A reverse mortgage allows people to borrow on the equity in their home, creating a stream of monthly payments or a line of credit. For those who rely only on Social Security, this could be a critical flow of income. You must be age 62 or older to receive income payments. The "loan" is paid when the property is sold after the owner's death. It is a financial alternative for some individuals strapped for cash.[10]

SUMMARY

If an agent has done a thorough job of gathering data, he will be prepared for the variety of questions and emotional issues that will surface. It will also be easier to prepare a financial plan and, if appropriate, a long term care insurance solution.

CHAPTER NOTES

1. *The Sandwich Generation*, "Who Will Pay?", Issue 1, 1995, p. 11.
2. *Bull and Bear News*, "Women and Investing: An Untapped Resource", a publication of Princor Financial Services Corporation, Summer, 1995, p. 1.
3. *USA Today*, "How to Get Financial Affairs in Order", special edition, July 17-20, 1995, p. 3.
4. *The Sandwich Generation*, "Control Your Own Life", Spring, 1995, p. 27.
5. *The Living Trust Solution*, by Richard W. Morris, p. 42.
6. *USA Today*, "Essential Documents", special edition, July 17-20, 1995, p. 3.
7. *The Living Trust Solution*, by Richard W. Morris, p. 43.
8. *The Sandwich Generation*, "Protect Your Last Days", Spring, 1995, p. 14.
9. *The Sandwich Generation*, "Letters to the Experts column", Issue 1, 1995, p. 2.
10. *The Kiplinger Washington Letter*, August 11, 1995, p. 2. For more information on the banks that offer reverse mortgages, Kiplinger suggests sending $1 and a stamped, self-addressed business-size envelope to the National Center for Home Equity Conversion, Suite 115, 7373 147th Street West, Apple Valley, Minnesota, 55124.

Chapter 8

A LONG TERM CARE SALES PRESENTATION

My first long term care client was my mother. Approaching your own parents and relatives for the purpose of selling long term care insurance is an excellent way to enter this market. What more natural market is there than your own family?

To successfully present a product, you must firmly believe in the product yourself. With insurance, that usually means purchasing coverage on yourself. This also applies to long term care insurance. Depending on your age, selling long term care insurance to a family member is just as effective.

Selling to family members however may not be that easy. Long term care is a very emotional subject and like your clients, family members might be "guarded" on the issues involving long term care insurance too. Many parents are not enthusiastic about sharing financial information with their children, nor do they want to discuss nursing homes, moving into their children's home, or anything related to long term care.

Still, approaching parents on this subject is good practice to perfect your sales presentation and will help you prepare for any objections that might arise from recommending long term care insurance as an alternative financial solution to a potentially devastating situation. Parents can also be excellent centers of influence.

NETWORKING

A considerable amount of publicity in the last few years concerning long term care insurance has heightened consumer interest in this product. From *Consumer Reports* to *USA Today* to *Money* magazine, people of all ages have read something, somewhere about long term care insurance.

With this public awareness, it is a place to start building a base of potential prospects for presenting long term care insurance. It's easier to approach individuals about a subject that's in the news on a daily basis.

There are three types of prospects: (1) parents, relatives and their referrals; (2) professionals and organizations that are involved in long term care situations; and (3) employees.

1.   *Parents*: This is the beginning of a long list of prospects. In addition to parents, aunts, uncles, grandparents, in-laws and other family members are a great source of prospects for long term care insurance. Referrals from family members will provide daily activity and an opportunity for making long term care presentations and recommendations for a long time to come.

2.   *Professionals and Organizations*: These prospects easily recognize the need for long term care insurance and may be receptive to the idea themselves. With continual association with the elderly in some aspect or another, this type of prospect would be able to provide a long list of potential prospects. This group includes:

Health care providers. What better group to talk to about long term care insurance than home health care workers, nursing home employees, private duty nurses, durable equipment salespersons, hospital workers, and physicians? As the population continues to age, the need for long term care will increase. The medical field — providers and health care services organizations — delivering long term care services is rapidly expanding each year. The fastest growing occupations in the job market are in the long term care field. This prospect list alone can be extensive.

Attorneys. Specializing in elder care law, these attorneys deal with clients who are concerned with protecting themselves and their wealth. Making these attorneys aware of your services in the long term care insurance area could result in qualified prospects for you. When contacting these professionals, prepare a long term care sales presentation as you would for a client. This will help the attorney in understanding the need for long term care insurance and how it can benefit his clients. It will also make it easier for the attorney to refer clients to you for long term care insurance.

CPAs. The same approach used for attorneys would also apply to CPAs. Knowledge of long term care insurance will assist CPAs in their financial discussions with clients. Clarification by Congress of the tax consequences of the long term care product would also help. This issue is expected to be resolved this year.

Bankers. These individuals do a considerable amount of trust work with older people and can be an excellent source for prospects. For example, a person who has established a living trust indicates a willingness to do some financial planning and may be agreeable to a presentation on long term care insurance.

Churches and Synagogues. Your own religious affiliation can provide you with another source of prospective clients. While a minister, priest or rabbi deals with family long term care issues, these organizations also focus on older, senior members of the congregation and provide activities designed exclusively for them. Contacts here can further add to your list of prospects.

3. *Employees*: Without question, a number of people in their 40s and early 50s are discovering through firsthand experience the emotional and economic impact of a parent or relative requiring long term care services. As a result, individuals are expressing an interest in securing long term care coverage for themselves.[1] They want to preserve their independence and protect their assets — two solid reasons to consider long term care coverage. With these "younger" prospects showing an interest, insurers have begun to develop and market employer-based long term care coverage. Employers, especially those with 50 to 75 employees or more, are sensitive to employee benefit programs. With respect to how an employee would seek medical assistance and the restrictions put on health insurance, employers are softening the blow by offering additional coverage options. One of these options is long term care. If you have employer-clients already, you should contact them about this valuable employee benefit. For more on employer-sponsored long term care, see Chapter 14, Employer-Provided Theme: Taking Care Of Your Own Finances.

THE APPROACH

Now that you have a list of contacts, the question is what is the best way to approach them on the concept of long term care insurance? The best approach will vary with your own strengths and experience.

Telephone Calls

For individuals with whom you have some relationship, either personally or professionally, the phone is often the best way to try and secure an appointment. At this point, you should not attempt to sell a concept or product over the phone, but to secure an appointment to discuss a few estate planning ideas that can save money. It may be that your contact has no need for your services but this is not easily discerned over the phone.

Letters

Mass mailings are a numbers game. The more mailings you send, the more responses you're likely to get. There are lists available that can be purchased and, depending on your criteria, they can identify for example, ages, income, or net worth of people in your community. Your letter should be brief and to the point. Depending on what your approach in soliciting business is, there are several options available. A letter can indicate that you will be calling them to set up an appointment or inviting the reader to attend a free seminar on long term care. Letters #1 and #2 in Figures 8.1 and 8.2 are samples for such approaches. In Figure 8.3 Letter #3 is a sample letter for the professional or an organization. This letter suggests working as a team to meet the long term care needs of their members/clients. A letter should also state the intent to follow-up whether it is with a phone call or a postage-paid return envelope. It is up to you which action you will take. The most common is a phone call as a follow-up to a letter.

Sending a letter is one way to secure an appointment but it can be an expensive process depending on the number and frequency of your mailings. Generally, a letter should always be followed up by a phone call. This will help to increase the number of appointments you will have to schedule. A general rule to follow when mailing several letters at the same time is to mail only the amount that you are able to follow-up on a timely basis by telephone. For example, mailing 25 letters a week is usually sufficient when following up by telephone the following week to schedule appointments.

Addressing different audiences — seniors, 40-50 year olds, the professional — requires a variation in the letters sent. This will help you convey enthusiasm on the phone, an energy vital in obtaining an appointment.

Figure 8.1

LETTER #1

June 1, 1996

Mr. and Mrs. Alfred Bridge
1050 Tara Boulevard
Atlanta, GA. 30328

Dear Mr. And Mrs. Bridge:

It's a tragedy!

Perhaps you've read about it happening to someone in your town; a person whose lifetime savings is spent on health care that's not fully covered by Medicare. The costs associated with health care and aging are increasing and the alternatives to financing these necessary services are few.

If your desires are to:

1. Maintain your independence;

2. Retain your dignity;

3. Avoid depending on your children;

4. Eliminate the financial concerns of a long life span; and

5. Provide an inheritance for children and grandchildren,

you will be interested in hearing a few ideas that can let you accomplish these important wishes and goals.

I will be in your area the week of _____ and plan on calling you in advance to see if we can schedule some time to discuss these important ideas to help you avoid future financial concerns.

I look forward to meeting you.

Sincerely,

Figure 8.2

LETTER #2

June 1, 1996

Mr. and Mrs. Alfred Bridge
1050 Tara Boulevard
Atlanta, GA. 30328

Dear Mr. and Mrs. Bridge:

    Lately, you may have noticed an increasing number of news stories on the subject of long term care. Perhaps you, like many people are both confused and concerned about this important issue.

    The need for long term care is unpredictable, but the risk is higher than you think. According to the *New England Journal of Medicine*, 43% of people turning age 65 will enter a nursing home at some point during their lifetime.

    I am personally sponsoring a free seminar on the facts concerning the issue of long term care. In this 45 minute session, I will provide you with data and information that can help you sort out your own concerns about this subject.

    The seminar, entitled *Everything You Need To Know About Long Term Care* will be held at the Embassy Suites in Dunwoody at the following times: 10:00 A.M., 2:00 P.M. and 7:00 P.M. Light refreshments will be provided. There is no charge to attend.

    Please return the postage-paid card indicating your time preference as soon as possible. Or, if you'd like, call (404) 332-5671 to reserve a space for this important session.

    I look forward to seeing you there.

                      Sincerely,

___   YES, I'd like to attend your seminar at: ___ 10:00 AM
       ___ 2:00 PM ___ 7:00 PM

___   NO, I cannot attend, but please send me more information
       about long term care.

Figure 8.3

LETTER #3

June 1, 1996

Ms. Michelle Truman
205 State Street Suite 214
Springfield, MA 01106

Dear Ms. Truman:

A loved one in need of long term care services is an emotional event that we all would like to avoid. Yet, in increasing numbers, many of us are facing the necessity of arranging for care for loved ones suffering from a chronic health condition.

As a professional servicing the mature individual, you hold a unique position. You will often be sought for advice and direction on this issue of long term care. As such, my firm may be able to assist you.

The improvement in long term care policies over the last few years has made this product a viable option for many mature individuals with assets to protect. This product is becoming the program of choice for those planning ahead for their financial future. Long term care insurance can let individuals maintain independence, avoid depending on their children, retain their dignity and provide an inheritance for their loved ones.

From one professional to another, I am enclosing my card. I would like to schedule a convenient time to stop by and discuss how we can work jointly on behalf of your clients.

I will call you next week to identify an appropriate date and time to get together. I look forward to meeting you.

Sincerely,

Seminars

Seminars are a very effective tool in communicating the need for long term care insurance. A number of insurance professionals using this mass marketing approach have been very effective. Many seniors have plenty of time to attend seminars and many come just for something to do. The larger the audience, the greater the likelihood of finding a few good candidates for long term care insurance.

When sponsoring a seminar, light refreshments such as coffee, tea, soft drinks, and water accompanied with a couple of snacks should be made available. Mid-morning and mid-afternoon seminars are usually the best time for seniors. Boomers and professionals are more likely to attend evening sessions. It is a good idea to follow up with a phone call to those who did not respond to your invitation. The ideal size of an audience is 25 to 30 people. No more than 50 people should be in any one seminar. If the seminar is popular, schedule another date for the overflow.[2] Location should be convenient with plenty of parking available. Check the senior centers since they may have space available at no charge.

Keep your session on an informative and educational level. The purpose of holding a seminar is to advise how long term care insurance can be a solution to a potential financial problem, not to sell your product. Long term care can be a very complicated subject and using visuals such as cartoons will keep the presentation reasonably light. The entire seminar should not be more than an hour and audience participation by way of questions should be encouraged. You can do an effective job within that time frame. If the seminar runs more than an hour, you run the risk of people walking out. It's important to keep the audience's attention by telling them everything they want to know about long term care and not everything you know about long term care. Keep it light and simple.

In concluding a seminar, an evaluation form as shown in Figure 8.4 can be given to the attendees. This form will provide you with feedback on your presentation and will also provide important information on a prospect that could possibly result in a sale.

When the seminar evaluation form has been returned, distribute the prepared packet of information that should include the *Shoppers Guide to Long Term Care Insurance* (available from the National Association of Insurance Commissioners (NAIC), your state insurance department or

Figure 8.4

SAMPLE EVALUATION FORM

Please indicate your rating of this seminar:

	Excellent	Good	Fair	Poor
Subject Matter				
Presentation				
Material				
Location				
Time				

Additional comments and suggestions:_____
_____
_____

Your name: _____ Spouse's name_____
Date-of-birth: _____ Date of birth:_____

Address:_____
City _____ State_____ Zip Code_____

Home Phone: _____

Please check one:

____ I would like to review my long term care insurance options. Please contact me for an appointment.

____ I already have a policy with _____. Please contact me to receive a free analysis of this program to ensure that it is up to date with my needs.

____ Please send me more information about your long term care insurance program.

---

many insurance companies), one or two articles about long term care insurance and a copy of the outline of your presentation with key topics highlighted.

The seminar approach is an excellent tool for making a sales presentation to many people at the same time. Specific details can be addressed during a follow-up appointment. This is one way to enter the long term care insurance market.

WORKING WITH SENIORS

Seniors view the insurance industry and related services in a negative light including long term care, insurance agents, Medicare, doctors, nursing homes and other topics related to long term care insurance. This negative perception stems from the Medicare supplement scandal when seniors carried several extra (and worthless) Medicare supplement policies. Although the insurance industry is trying to rebuild its reputation in a positive way, there is still a mistrust among seniors.

To be successful in working with mature individuals, a bond of trust must be established. This can be accomplished by building credibility with the potential client. A seminar on long term care for example, may firmly establish you as an expert in the area of long term care insurance. A referral from a family member, relative or friend can also assist in building their trust in you as an agent.

Once you have gained that trust, you can maintain your credibility by asking questions and listening to their answers. You'll find their answers will tell you a lot about their situation, both emotionally and financially. Completing the financial analysis covered in Chapter 7, The Need For Financial Planning, assures the senior client that you are working to find a solution for them and not just to make a sale. Tell them at the outset what you hope to accomplish and then review these key points reinforcing your recommendation.

As an agent, you will need to educate your client on Medicare, Medicaid, and other statistical data with respect to long term care services and cost. This background information is of great interest to the client because it directly affects them. During your presentation frequently ask your client whether they agree or disagree with what you're saying. This approach allows you to keep the client involved in the process and at the same time allows you to continue with your sales presentation.

THE BASIC SALES PRESENTATION

Establishing the need and providing a solution by identifying the alternatives are basic steps used in a long term care sales presentation. It does not matter whether it is a one-on-one interview or in a seminar environment.

Establishing The Need

This initial phase of the presentation can be handled in two parts. First, a fact finder must be completed to gather important financial details that will assist you in making a sound recommendation. Much of this phase is accomplished by the financial data that is gathered as discussed in Chapter 7, The Need For Financial Planning. By identifying your client's assets, including his or her spouse's, and their cash flow situation, the need for long term care insurance is established.

Prospects should already have priorities set for their retirement years. To further establish the need for long term care insurance, certain questions need to be asked. Do they plan to see their families as often as they can? Do they want to travel? Do they have the finances to accomplish these goals? Reinforce the fact that they have worked hard to build up their assets to make their retirement a pleasurable one and then ask what they think the need for long term care will mean to them financially.

At this point, you are into the second part of establishing the need — indicating the likelihood of needing long term care insurance. In a 1991 study, as referenced in the *New England Journal of Medicine*, it was predicted that 43 percent of the 2.2 million people turning age 65 in 1990, (946,000) would enter a nursing home at some point during their lifetimes. Of that 946,000, 21 percent (198,660) would stay five years or longer.

Since the likelihood of a nursing home stay has already been factored into your client's financial analysis, now you must identify the potential cost to your client. It is this cost factor that can now be brought to the forefront and discussed in relationship to your client's financial situation.

To illustrate the costs involved, you must be aware of the average cost of a quality nursing home in your area. The national average cost for a nursing home today is $36,000 a year.

Using the national average cost of $36,000 a year, for a five-year nursing home stay (should your client be one of the 21 percent staying in a nursing home five years or longer), the cost would be $180,000. Now, ask your client if he has this much money "tucked away for a rainy day" when the need for long term care arises.

Most people do not have an extra $180,000 nor do they realize the potential devastating impact that long term care can have on their finances. Using local nursing home rates and the *New England Journal of Medicine* statistics, you can "bring home" these calculations to relevant status for your client. And, while the likelihood of a long term care need is greater for someone age 65 or older, there are many younger people that need and receive long term care services. A 1988 Congressional study published by the United States Health Cooperative predicted that 40 percent of functionally dependent adults would be under the age of 65 in the year 2000. This can make the long term care story relevant to everyone.

Younger people are not immune to requiring long term care either. An auto accident, a boating mishap, a skiing incident, can leave anyone with a long term care need. A spinal cord injury for example, necessitates physical dependency on someone else for the rest of one's life. It can and does happen and, as such, you can make long term care relevant for a younger audience as well.

A lengthy nursing home stay is not uncommon. Nursing home data compiled at the end of 1991 in Florida indicated that:

Current Length of Nursing Home Stay	Number of Residents (Percentage)
0 - 90 days	17.8%
91 - 180 days	9.5%
181 - 365 days	15.1%
366 - 730 days	19.9%
731+ days	37.7%

On average, a nursing home stay for two years costs $72,000. Many people do not have $72,000 available to pay for long term care. In a 1991 report by the House Select Committee on Aging, two-thirds of single people and one-third of married people exhaust their finances after just 13 weeks in a nursing home.[3]

Identifying The Alternatives

How is long term care paid for today? An exploration of who pays the cost today can set the stage for dispelling the myths surrounding Medicare and Medicare supplements paying for long term care.

The majority of funds come from either an individual's own finances or from Medicaid. According to a 1993 AARP Congressional briefing, the following is a breakdown of the responsible parties that pay long term care costs:

> Individual: pays 45% of the overall long term care costs.
> Medicaid: pays 45% of the overall long term care costs.
> Medicare: pays 5% of the overall long term care costs.
> Private insurance: pays 1% of the overall long term care costs.
> Other sources, including veteran's benefits pay 4%.

Ninety percent of all long term care costs are paid by the individual needing care or by Medicaid because the individual has little or no income or assets left. This is easily the largest unfunded liability in the country.

In Chapter 6, Government Programs, a detailed study breaks down what Medicare will cover — the result is a five percent contribution to the overall costs of long term care. This certainly dismisses the notion that Medicare pays much of the long term care costs.

Reviewing various financial options to paying for long term care:

1. *Medicare.* Medicare is clearly designed to cover acute medical expenses such as doctor's visits, hospital stays and surgery. This government program does not reimburse personal care or custodial services which are the primary reasons long term care is administered.

2. *Medicare Supplement.* This policy is important to seniors because it covers many of the acute medical expenses that Medicare does not pay including deductibles and coinsurance. There is virtually no coverage for custodial or personal care

and additional benefits are not substituted in the ten mandated Medicare supplement plans available.

3. *Savings*. How much will be enough? A financial analysis of your client's liquid assets compounded with nursing home costs, will indicate how long his savings will last. People do not want their entire life savings spent on health care. What if they eventually recover? What happens then if their savings are nearly gone? This alternative can help determine the elimination period (the number of days before benefits are paid). As statistics indicate, savings can help fund a short-term stay or the need for long term care in any setting, but would not likely last for a long period of time in the event long term care is needed on a continual basis.

According to a 1992 Merrill Lynch survey, 50 percent of all retirees in the latter part of the 1980s went into retirement with less than $10,000 in savings. This study also showed that today's average 50-year-old has only $2,300 in savings. Thirty-five percent of pre-retirees and 54 percent of baby boomers had no IRAs, no annuities and no savings accounts.

Our general savings rate as a nation has been plummeting since the early 1970s. This does not bode well for general retirement living let alone paying for long term care services.

4. *Family Members*. Children and other members of the family are often placed in the position of caregiver for lack of any other alternative. Today, this option has become more difficult with two income earners, single parents, long distances between parents and children, and delayed parenting which places potential caregivers already in the position of raising young children.

This option can be an emotional burden for all parties involved. Many parents do not want to move in with their children and, should that be the only option, resentment between the caregiver and caretaker and of the entire situation will affect all concerned.

This option may not be financially feasible for the children either. If a parent has very little money and the only choice is to try and care for this person, the added expense of another dependent may be overwhelming to the family budget.

While this alternative is often utilized instead of Medicaid qualification, it is one which both parent and child would like to avoid.

5. *Borrow/Charity*. Borrowing money unless it's from a relative or friend is unlikely because an elderly person or disabled individual is not considered a good risk to loan money. However, some banks will consider reverse mortgages (see Chapter 7, The Need For Financial Planning).

With the many volunteers assisting senior-based groups, charity would be a possibility. Charity can also be from an individual's religious affiliation. Many churches and synagogues have programs for those in need of long term care. If nursing assistance is necessary, however, it is unlikely these charitable groups can be of assistance.

6. *Medicaid*. This is often the last resort. When personal funds are exhausted and family members are not able to provide care, application for Medicaid is the only other option. (For a full discussion of Medicaid, see Chapter 6, Government Programs.) If residence state guidelines are met, Medicaid will pay for nursing home and home health care. The drawback of this program is the person needing care will have to go to a facility or home health care agency that accepts Medicaid payments. Because Medicaid reimburses at a low rate, many facilities and agencies do not accept this form of payment.

Nursing homes accepting Medicaid patients are generally packed three or four to a room because of the low reimbursement. Some of these facilities would not be selected if the individual had a choice. With Medicaid, for the expenses to be covered, you take what you can get.

For those individuals who transferred assets in order to qualify for Medicaid, this money was simply a loan from the government. State governments have legally promised to look for the money spent on long term care services after the patient (and spouse) have passed away. Forty-five percent of all long term care services are paid by Medicaid because of the transfer of assets "loophole".

Transferring The Risk

The alternatives described above are less than perfect and it would make sense to look into private long term care insurance. The sole purpose of insurance is to pay for significant financial events that otherwise can't be easily handled. Long term care fits this definition nicely. The nature of long term care from the onset will likely require medical services on a long term basis. High cost for long term care medical assistance will eventually deplete one's personal finances.

With long term care insurance, the insured pays an allotted premium today for the insurer's promise to take care of the larger, ongoing bills later. The younger the individual, the lower the premium cost. People in their late 40's and 50's should seriously consider this product because the price is very low. Waiting until one is 65 or 70 will have a significant impact on the premium rate for a long term care policy.

Long term care insurance is the best solution for those that can afford the premium comfortably. People with few assets to protect and very little income after expenses are not usually good candidates for this type of coverage. These individuals will probably qualify for Medicaid in a short period of time after the need for long term care begins.

For people of middle to upper class in assets and income, long term care insurance presents a wonderful opportunity to plan in advance. By not planning for future long term care expenses, the entire family will be at a disadvantage when the need for long term care arises such as the case with the Doan family described in the introduction.

Long term care insurance policies today can cover both nursing home and home health care in the same plan. In addition, most policies now cover care provided in a variety of assisted living facilities. Depending upon how accurate the daily benefit selection was, out-of-pocket expenses will often be small once the claim commences.

Long term care insurance provides an excellent alternative to financing the long term care need.

That's it! You've just been through a basic sales presentation. The concept of long term care insurance is simple; the financial analysis portion is more complex. Once the financial details are filled in — liquidity, income, and assets, the remainder of the presentation should proceed smoothly.

OBJECTIONS

Naturally, there will be some objections. This is a normal reaction when buying most items. Most of the objections come down to cost — a buyer's remorse. Here's how to answer some of the objections.

"I'd like to think it over."

This is a delay tactic that you might be tempted to allow, following up later. However, before adopting the waiting position, ask the client why he wants to think it over. At this point, the real objection should surface — most often the concern is the cost of coverage.

The cost issue comes down to two scenarios. Outline each one (as shown below) and ask the client which one would he feel more comfortable with.

Scenario #1: The client pays $150.00 per month for $100 a day of long term care coverage in any type of facility or at home.

Scenario #2: The client pays $3,000.00 per month for long term care services when needed.

If the insured pays a premium of $150 a month for 25 years before using the policy, total premiums paid (without any rate increases) would be $45,000. If the cost for long term care services remains at $3,000 per month (which is unlikely in today's economy), it would take 15 months to recoup the total premiums paid of $45,000. Twenty-five years of premium repaid in 15 months!

Then ask the client which expense is more likely to alter his retirement lifestyle, $150 a month or $3,000 a month. The $150 a month is a known expense, while the $3,000 a month could be needed next week, next month or next year.

Ask your client again if there is a reason to wait since the $150 per month premium will increase based on an age change.

"I'd like to talk with my children first."

This response can come up often and can be avoided by involving the children in the presentation and discussion. There may be a considerable distance between the parent's and children's residences so this is not always practical.

Ask your clients what their children would think about long term care insurance. Would they rather take care of their parent(s) if the need for long term care arises or would they rather they purchase long term care insurance that promises to pay the bills for future long term care services.

When interviewing prospective clients, I ask them if they would like their children to receive copies of all the material being presented. If so, I mail proposal information along with a letter of explanation. Children rarely balk at their parents' attempt to protect their assets which will eventually be passed along to them. In some cases, the children have offered to pay the premium if the parents object to the coverage, understanding the consequences even better than their parents.

Involving as much of your client's family in the solicitation and presentation of long term care insurance usually strengthens your overall position. You have nothing to hide — long term care insurance is an alternative to financing future long term care services. The more up-front you are in demonstrating a willingness to work with family members, the greater the likelihood of making a sale.

"I'd like to talk with my attorney (or physician or CPA)."

As with family members, you should ask the client early on who he would like involved in the discussions. If not included originally, ask your client why, at this time, does he feel he needs a professional's advice. Would an attorney or CPA or doctor sign a statement advising a client *not* to purchase long term care insurance?

Advise that the physician's input will be important later on when the need for long term care arises. Otherwise, this objection is another smoke screen for the concern about the cost of the plan. If this is the case, you can respond with the same explanation concerning costs used earlier (see the objection entitled "I'd like to think it over."), or refer to the section, "To Buy or Not To Buy - That Is The Question!" presented later in this chapter.

"I would like to shop around a little more."

This objection can be avoided by doing the shopping yourself. To satisfy your client, you should have at least three quotes from companies offering long term care. For a complete listing of long term care companies, please refer to Appendix A — *Companies Selling Long Term Care Insurance.* In addition, several industry publications including *Life Insurance Selling* and *Life Association News* have issues devoted each year to reviewing long term care insurance companies and their products.

In the financial analysis phase, ask your client if there are any insurance companies or policies he is interested in. If possible, obtain quotes from the companies he has identified. This gives you the opportunity to shop for your client. If only one quote is presented, this does not offer him the opportunity to compare quotes thus, the objection is valid.

"I'm not going to a nursing home under any circumstances."

This objection occurs if you dwell only on the nursing home aspect of long term care. However, since the majority of claims are home health care oriented, it makes more sense to place a greater emphasis on this aspect of long term care services. The product you are recommending should have benefits payable in a number of settings. It's vital that this be stressed when reviewing the policy benefits as part of the proposal process.

Very few people voluntarily enter a nursing home. A nursing home confinement is generally the alternative if no other means of providing long term care services is feasible. The client needs to know that if a nursing home is the only alternative for treatment, the insurance policy will provide reimbursement.

"I'd like to wait since I'm in good health now and don't need the coverage."

This is another tactic used to delay having to make a buying decision. Delaying the purchase of a long term care policy will not only drive the cost higher, but ultimately will not save money. It also runs the risk of your client incurring a health problem which may hinder his chances in the future of purchasing long term care insurance.

Although your client isn't planning on getting sick, he is probably paying for some type of medical insurance. He isn't planning on getting in a car accident, yet he is paying for automobile insurance. He doesn't think his house will catch on fire, but he is paying for homeowner's insurance.

Insurance is always a gamble. The client shouldn't take the chance and wait because the need for long term care services is unpredictable and could cost them the opportunity to transfer a significant potential liability to a third party. If the premium is affordable now, there is no reason to wait.

"The government is going to take care of long term care."

This objection came up during the months of debate over President Clinton's national health care plan. Even that program, as wide in scope as it was, failed to do much in the way of long term care. Nursing home coverage was not covered. Home health care was covered for a short time, but the qualification to receive it was more stringent than most private insurer's policies. Even the Clinton administration realized that the cost of long term care was too high to be rolled into his health care program.

Considering the heated debates over the budget, it is unlikely that the Medicare and Medicaid programs are going to enjoy any expansion — Medicare to include more long term care benefits or Medicaid to lower the qualification requirements.

TO BUY OR NOT TO BUY — THAT IS THE QUESTION!

As a final means of closing the sale, you can illustrate the difference between one who buys long term care and one who chooses to self-insure the risk.

At age 70 the premium for long term care is significantly higher and the key to understanding the coverage for some is to see how the numbers work.

Both candidates, age 70, own their own homes, a car, a comfortable retirement income of $2,250 per month and $120,000 in other liquid assets. The $120,000, invested in various vehicles, earns an average of six percent per year. They would like to pass along as much of that $120,000 to their heirs as they can. Both are interested in buying the following coverage:

$100 per day in long term care coverage

20 day elimination period (number of days before policy benefits begin)

unlimited benefit period (policy pays for as long as LTC services are needed)

inflation option (which increases the daily benefit of $100 by 5 percent each year)

The premium cost for this plan is $3,800.00 annually. One individual pays the premium despite the high cost, using money from his money market account. The other individual decides against purchasing the coverage, citing high costs. He assumes the $120,000 will be more than sufficient to cover the costs of long term care.

Both individuals live another ten years before the need for long term care arises. When the need does arise, both individual's medical conditions require skilled nursing care and personal care assistance. The individual with long term care insurance chooses home health care which averages about $140 a day. The inflation option benefit in his policy increased to $145 a day, ensuring him there will be enough in the policy to pay the increase. The person who elected to self-insure chooses to enter a nursing home for $125 a day since it is less expensive than home health care. See Figure 8.5.

Demonstrating how a third party (insurance company) can assume the financial risk of long term care better than an individual is a powerful argument. The costs of long term care can quickly erode even a presumably safe nest egg. Most people are not in a financial position to pay for long term care on their own for a long period of time and would be eligible for Medicaid sooner than the fifth year in this example.

Figure 8.5

INSURED VS. SELF-INSURED

INSURED	SELF-INSURED
$120,000 in various investments earning 6 percent	$120,000 in various investments earning 6 percent
Needs long term care at age 80	Needs long term care at age 80
Spent $41,534 in total premium payments	Elected not to buy long term care insurance
Age 80, liquid assets have accumulated to $157,589	By age 80, liquid assets have accumulated to $214,901
Care at home: $140/day	Nursing home costs: $125/day
Costs:	Costs:
1st year: 20 day elimination period insured pays $2,800 ($140 x 20)	1st year: Nursing is $45,625
2nd yr +: insured pays -0- as policy (daily benefit is sufficient to pay full costs. Unlimited benefit period and inflation rider should continue to assume full costs.	2nd year: Nursing home costs $49,275 (assume 8 percent nursing home inflation) 3rd year: Nursing home costs $53,217 4th year: Nursing home costs $57, 474
Liquid asset balance left after 4 years of long term care: $195,796 and growing, earmarked for children's inheritance.	Liquid asset balance left after 4 years in a nursing home: $34,302. This individual will qualify for Medicaid in the 5th year. $120,000 original nest egg for children's inheritance is gone.

Moreover, the insured *elected* to receive the care at home since his long term care policy covered it. The individual who was self-insured had little choice but to enter a nursing home in order to stretch his dollars as far as possible.

This financial scenario should help in closing cases where a high premium is objected to. The premium must be affordable. In the example above, both individuals had the means to pay for the coverage. When working with clients with different financial situations, you can alter benefits such as the daily benefit, elimination period, benefit period, or inflation feature to fit within a person's budget.

THE WAIVER STATEMENT

For any number of reasons, people will turn down long term care insurance as a financing alternative. If this is the case, it is important to have the prospect sign a waiver form, a copy of which you and the prospect will keep.

The waiver form itself is not legally binding, but it can be a powerful closing tool or used to discourage a potential lawsuit later down the road. As a closing tool, this form will give the prospect a second chance to reconsider purchasing the coverage. Once he has read the form, he may question the reason why the form needs to be signed.

You can point out that it is necessary to clarify the result of the sales interview for both parties and, since the insurance wasn't purchased, a signature attesting to this fact will go in the prospect's file. Offer to follow-up at a later date (usually three to six months) to further discuss long term care insurance as a financing alternative. The individual may sign the form or may reconsider and ask for an explanation one more time. Sales have been made when this form has been presented. A sample form appears in Figure 8.6.

In any event, secure a signature! Insurance agents have been sued over the lack of a certain coverage within a person's portfolio. Don't take that chance!

Figure 8.6

ACKNOWLEDGMENT OF RESPONSIBILITY

I understand the risk of needing long term care as explained to me by _____. I understand that neither Medicare or Medicare Supplement policies will satisfy that need.

I choose to decline the insurance protection shown to me at this time and, in so doing, acknowledge that I am assuming responsibility for arranging funding of any long term care services that I may need in the future.

_____	_____
Name	Date
_____	_____
Signature	Agent's Signature

The agent might also consider having a form signed stating that coverage accepted is less than the amount recommended. This waiver of liability form would indicate that the individual had the opportunity to purchase one amount and elected another. Claims have occurred where the reimbursement received was less than what the insured expected. The insured's memory may not be as good as the agent's file records. This form will help to clarify the position taken by the insured at time of application. A sample form appears in Figure 8.7.

Both your client and you should sign this form and keep a copy. This can clear up any confusion in the future.

OTHER CONSIDERATIONS

Impaired Risks: Initially, underwriters of long term care coverage adopted an "accept or decline" approach and people that had health problems were automatically declined because of high risk.

Today, several insurers have classified health risks and created rate classifications that would allow insurance companies to insure people

Figure 8.7

WAIVER OF LIABILITY

By my signature below I acknowledge that I have elected to obtain long term care insurance that provides less coverage than that recommended by _____ who has offered this coverage as protection for my assets.

The plan recommended would have paid a daily benefit of _____ with an elimination period of _____ and a maximum benefit period of _____.

Instead, I have selected a daily benefit of _____ with an elimination period of _____ and a maximum benefit period of _____.

---

with health conditions by charging additional premium for the coverage. The extra increase can run from 20 percent to 100 percent. While the cost for the health-impaired individual is higher, insuring the extra risk means that there are no restrictions on the coverage when a claim occurs. The benefits, elimination period and benefit period are unaffected.

Some companies may choose to insure a risk by increasing the elimination period or reducing the benefit period. The more serious the condition, the greater the likelihood that this approach may be taken. The alternative would be no coverage offered but many people with health conditions who are trying to obtain insurance will gladly settle for the modified coverage and/or the extra premium.[4]

This openness to writing impaired risks has resulted in long term care coverage being issued for people who have osteoporosis, arthritic conditions, pulmonary problems, history of heart problems, diabetes or current high blood pressure controlled by medication. One company even has a lengthy book of underwriting guidelines and classes, listing a number of conditions and their respective rate classes. There may even be an offer to review the modified coverage at a later date or the extra premium may be only a temporary charge removed after a specified time if there are no changes in the insured's health.

Substandard cases are sometimes easier to close because the applicant is perfectly aware of his medical condition necessitating the modifications in the coverage. Impaired risks have a higher probability of needing long term care in the future than healthier individuals and, as such, usually desire the coverage more than the healthy person.

Internet: Some insurance agents, agencies and companies have taken to advertising their services on the Internet. One such marketing firm placed a page about a new long term care product on the information super highway and received an overwhelming response. In a three week period, the inquiries about the plan on the World Wide Web site averaged between 480 and 620 per day. Electronic mail responses were also high, with 18 messages waiting the day after the page appeared on the Internet.[5] These requests were for more information with name, address (often the E-mail address) and telephone number included. It's another marketing alternative for those who want to prospect in the long term care market, especially for younger clients.

The basic long term care sales presentation works because it is simple and uses the prospect's own numbers. You can't do a proper financial analysis and recommendation without the individual's financial picture. Your presentation is based on selling a program that is a financing alternative for long term care costs. The presence of insurance coverage gives people more of a choice about their long term care when it is needed. It's a control issue, one that is very important to stress as many fear losing independence more than going to a nursing home. Remember this, and your sales presentations will be very successful.

CHAPTER NOTES

1. *Best's Review*, "LTC Insurance Market is Growing Younger", July, 1995, p. 76.
2. *The Agent's Sales Kit Magazine*, "Long Term Care Seminar Selling", June/July, 1995, p. 32.
3. *Spotlight*, "Why People Need Long Term Care Insurance", Principal Financial Group newsletter, July, 1994.
4. *The National Underwriter*, "Some Impaired Risks Can Be Insurable", November 13, 1995, p. 11.
5. *The National Underwriter*, "LTC Marketer Surprised At Response to Web Site", November 13, 1995, p. 35.

Chapter 9

BAD PRESS: EARLY LONG TERM CARE PRODUCT ATTEMPTS

A person seeking automobile or homeowners insurance, which is generally required by a third party, looks toward an insurance company for these coverages. Products such as long term care insurance however, are sales driven. The need for products like long term care is not always apparent despite the avalanche of publicity that has been accorded long term care.

The need for long term care must be identified and alternative solutions presented using the basic sales presentation described in Chapter 8, A Long Term Care Sales Presentation.

If a product is viewed by the media in a negative way, as has been the case with long term care insurance, this often will surface during a sales presentation. Bad press represents yet another obstacle in establishing long term care insurance as a viable financial alternative.

This chapter will trace the history of long term care as a product, from its modest early beginnings and questionable policy forms to today's current liberal approach of underwriting and payment of benefits.

THE BIRTH OF LONG TERM CARE

There are two key points to remember:

1. Long term care coverage was created virtually without data.

2. Long term care coverage is one of a handful of products developed during the information age.

When a product is introduced, there is an expectation of profit by the insurance company. Affordability and profitability are two considerations with product development. Insurance company actuaries rely on data and experience for the predictability of usage. Without the data and experience, claims frequency is a guessing game that most insurers don't want to play.

In the beginning, actuaries had very little information available — only a few tables showing the admissions and duration of stays in nursing homes — to rely on for the development of a long term care insurance product. The first long term care policy introduced over 30 years ago (by the CNA Companies) covered nursing home care only. Home health care was a fledgling industry, with only a few agencies and arrangements with private duty nurses to provide care. Home health care was not incorporated as a benefit in a long term care policy for several decades after the first policy was written.

Pricing a policy without historical data and experience in order to predict future usage is an actuarial nightmare. Assumptions, generally made with a high degree of certainty, gave way to a pure stab in the dark. Moreover, there was no way to predict the average buyer of long term care since the product was not in existence. Insurers pioneering long term care were placed in the difficult position of developing and pricing a policy based on pure assumptions. To avoid high claims experience, the companies implemented "gatekeepers". These safety nets were:

- a requirement of a three-day hospital stay prior to becoming eligible for benefits

- requiring skilled nursing care be administered prior to becoming eligible for policy reimbursement for intermediate or custodial care

- high premium

Most long term care services are custodial in nature and quite often a three-day hospital stay is not necessary prior to long term care being administered. The purpose of this requirement was to eliminate all but the most severe claims from being paid under the earlier long term care policies.

When long term care insurance was introduced in the late 1960s and early 1970s, the only other program available to pay anything for long term care services was Medicare. As a result, much of the language used in policies by the insurance companies was identical to Medicare. For the last three decades coverage under Medicare, except for a few improvements, has remained the same.

Insurers have handled their products differently. Long term care insurance was developed during the information age, a time in our history where data availability had become greater and more easily accessible. As more reliable data became available, insurance companies were able to fine tune their long term care products. As a result, six or seven generations of the long term care product have evolved. Many insurance products developed 100 years ago have not seen nearly that many changes.

The three-day hospitalization requirement mirrors Medicare's language. The skilled care requirement reduced claims from individuals who needed assistance with activities of daily living. The conservative premiums were priced high based on the data available at the time and assuming the worst in terms of claims experience. It was reasoned that it would be easier to lower premiums later, rather than underestimate the potential for high claims experience and run the risk of financial jeopardy for the entire company.

The goal was to effectively reduce the number of potential claims. With the three-day hospital stay and skilled care requirements under private policies, the insured could count on assistance from Medicare for the first few days of nursing home treatment. The high premiums diminished the product's attractiveness even further. Long term care products early on were clearly not as helpful nor as affordable as insurance is intended to be.

It is difficult to place the entire blame on the insurance companies. The development of long term care policies was an answer to a growing need — certainly a prediction that has come true. Without substantial and reliable data however, it is nearly impossible to feel comfortable with either price or policy language. The earlier long term care policies as first introduced were available for an extended period of time because it takes several years for this type of insurance to accumulate reliable claims experience and allow contract adjustments to be made.

Nursing home costs varied widely geographically, making it difficult to predict the benefit amount that would consistently be elected. As mentioned earlier, home care costs were virtually unknown as the current medical technological advances permitting most health care to be administered in the home were still several years away.

For decades mortality (death) and morbidity (disability) rate tables have been around and patterns used in developing a life or disability product could easily be discerned. So, one can feel some empathy for the long term care trailblazers — it wasn't an easy job.

The media backlash for long term care products took some time to emerge. Earlier, the nursing home plans enjoyed relative obscurity for twenty years until Medicare's diagnostic-related groups (DRGs) brought the skilled nursing facility to national prominence (see Chapter 1, Today's Changing Demographics). By then, up-to-date nursing home data was available, home health care was beginning to emerge as a major growth industry and, there was a rapidly increasing community focus on the need for long term care. Product sales began to accelerate, often by selling a Medicare supplement and pointing out the scarcity of nursing home coverage under both Medicare and Medicare supplements. The country's population was beginning to age and the time for this product had come.

BATTERED

Early policies didn't change as quickly as the demand for them did. During the early 1980s a number of claim denials and the obvious similarity in safety nets between private insurance and Medicare became more apparent and attracted a hailstorm of criticism. These opinions were echoed in the following headlines:

Chicago Tribune, Section One, September 21, 1988:

   "Study finds big holes in home care coverage"

Greensboro North Carolina News and Record, page A-15, September 23, 1988:

   "This insurance doesn't pay"

U.S. News and World Report, page 62, August 13, 1990:

   "Many long term care policies are too restrictive
      to offer much genuine protection"

Harsh criticism or an accurate appraisal? These headlines did not surprise many buyers of earlier generations of long term care coverage.

These buyers had experienced the safety nets when filing claims against their policies. They were naturally upset when measuring the dollars paid for the product versus the lack of dollars the plan paid for long term care services.

There were two more factors to consider that made the media (and insurance regulators) suspicious of long term care coverage. First, the age range of the individuals eligible for the earlier policies was generally limited to those 60 years and older. This meant that the policies were being sold to the age group with the highest probability of utilizing policy benefits. Marketing an insurance product to its primary users makes it impossible to properly distribute the risk. The principle of insurance is based on the *law of large numbers*. Many people pay for a product and only a few actually use the benefits. Healthy people subsidize the unhealthy, but because everyone is at some risk, there are many buyers who gladly purchase the plan and hope never to use it.

With long term care insurance, the odds that most seniors will use the policy benefits are good, making the pricing of the plan even more difficult. When in doubt, insurance companies price high.

Secondly, abuses in the Medicare supplement market were beginning to emerge and the public was genuinely outraged. Senior citizens who had paid a lot of money bought seven or eight Medicare supplement policies when one policy would have been sufficient. Seniors demonstrated a lack of understanding about the coverage and insurance agents apparently were hesitant in filling in the gaps necessary for their clients to make an informed buying decision. The complexity of the Medicare supplements made it difficult for both the insured and the agent to sort through the different policy benefits. The federal mandate of ten specific Medicare supplement policies has lessened this lack of understanding and has made selling supplement policies more manageable.

At the time these problems were identified, it was easy to compare the abuses in the Medicare supplement market with another product aimed directly at the senior market — long term care insurance. When the gatekeepers reared their heads on these contracts, the media was ready to pounce. It was a period where apparently the policies weren't worth the paper they were printed on.[1]

CORRECTION

Long term care products and their sales presentation to the public are still evolving. While today's products in no way resemble the early products, several factors (aside from negative media) have contributed to the positive product changes in the past decade.

NAIC

The National Association of Insurance Commissioners (NAIC) is composed of state insurance commissioners across the country. Insurance is not federally regulated due to the McCarran-Ferguson Act passed in the 1940s by the House and Senate. Instead, each state regulates the insurance industry in its own state. State insurance commissioners attempt to bring consistency to this jurisdiction by meeting regularly and adopting model laws for each state to add to its own specific statutory law. Despite this apparent semblance of order, not every state sees fit to adopt the model laws as is; still other states don't adopt any of these laws.

The problems with Medicare supplements that eventually had to be sorted out by a federal law mandating standard plans had to be embarrassing to the NAIC and further gave impetus to those in Washington who would love to see the McCarran-Ferguson Act repealed and the federal government regulating the insurance industry. The NAIC was determined not to lose control of this new product line for seniors.

The late 1980s saw the creation of standardized language for long term care insurance. One of the first corrections to the existing policy language was the removal of the three-day hospital stay requirement and the necessity of skilled care administered before any benefits for intermediate or custodial care were allowed. This eliminated two gatekeepers that stood in the way of benefit eligibility.

The purpose of the model policy is to give the states statutory language for long term care policies. Once the states adopt policy language, insurers filing policies with that state must use contract language that conforms to the state's statutory language. Companies that do not comply are rejected by the state.

A model policy is intended to cover essential aspects of a policy. This gives the states and insurers leverage to add other provisions to expand coverage. This type of flexibility, along with the reluctance of some states to use the model policy language, results in a number of policy variations for insurers that market a product nationwide.

The NAIC has continued to work with and update its original long term care model policy. For example, a requirement that home health care benefits be offered as part of, or as an optional benefit to a long term care plan has given these policies a wider scope of coverage beyond the early nursing home only plans. Age banding to determine rates was eliminated — rates can only be increased on a class basis not on a predetermined basis. The inflation option must be offered on both a simple or compound increasing basis. Currently, the NAIC's Long Term Care Task Force is looking at a nonforfeiture benefit provision that would preserve some policy benefits even after the insured ceases paying premiums.[2]

The model policy immediately improved policy benefits under a long term care policy and steered insurers towards offering plans with more flexibility.

Increased Competition

With an interest in long term care insurance and the emergence of qualified and thorough data on the usage of long term care services, more and more insurance companies have introduced new products. Insurance companies offering long term care coverage went from a total of 75 companies in 1987 to a high of 143 companies in 1990, currently settling around 118 companies in 1993.[3] For a complete listing of long term care companies, please refer to Appendix A.

As more companies entered the long term care market, competition forced insurers to stay abreast of market and product changes, resulting in even better products available today. Still, while insurers have been tempted to follow the same liberalization steps taken by disability insurers during the 1980s (which resulted in a claims disaster), some caution has prevailed due primarily to the "newness" of the benefits and claims experience. It was clear that some insurers entering the market had no idea how to design, price, market, and underwrite this product. Some of those carriers have since withdrawn their contracts, preferring to focus instead on programs they are familiar with and understand. This may explain the drop in the number of insurers in the long term care marketplace from the 1990 high.

Another reason for the diminishing number of insurers in the long term care market is the regulation of the product by state insurance departments. Certainly, this has to be the most regulated product the industry has ever introduced. Much of that is due to the Medicare supplement debacle that the NAIC does not want to see repeated.

Still, the high number of carriers today marketing long term care insurance bodes well for accumulating thorough and valid experience, leading to better predictability of claims and assurance of the accuracy in the pricing of long term care policies.

Expanding the Age Range

Insurers have branched out by offering long term care insurance to younger people. While consideration of this product may not be a priority for younger people, those ages 40-45 and older should give serious consideration to this coverage. It's important in the overall design of a pre-retirement plan which people should consider well before they reach retirement age.

The initial success in the sale of long term care insurance is due to the efforts of those agents specializing in Medicare supplement sales. Long term care insurance is a different type of sale and involves detailed financial planning. A long term care sale often requires 2-3 interviews, while Medicare supplements are usually sold on the first appointment. The agents working in the long term care insurance market today are more traditional and focused on financial planning working with all age groups. With long term care insurance expanded to younger age groups, it is a product many agents propose routinely now as part of an overall financial plan.

The younger buyer likely will not use the policy for several years, but it's easier to qualify for the coverage and the premium is much lower if purchased early on. Since the NAIC banned automatic age band increases (where premiums typically increased every five years), any rate increases filed by an insurer for a class of policies will be exercised on lower premiums if the policy is purchased at an early age.

The younger buyers help spread the risk from the older age buyers who are more likely to use the benefits. The effectiveness of spreading the risk steers long term care insurance into a "comfort zone" for insurers and allows insurers to continue offering better policy benefits.

The long term care insurance market is unprecedented in insurance history. While it usually takes years for a product to reach a second generation of language revision, long term care has seen seven or eight revisions over a period of three decades. These rapid changes make it difficult for insurance agents, let alone consumers, to absorb these alterations to the product and to explain them to the insured or prospect.

While these changes have been generally positive for the consumer, it is more complicated for the insurance agent as a full examination of both product and price is necessary to properly compare and evaluate long term care insurance policies. While some policies are in their seventh generation, there are others that have not seen current changes. Chapter 11, Today's Basic Long Term Care Policy, reviews the basics of current plans, giving the agent a basis upon which to compare other programs.

GOTCHA!

Although long term care products improved, initial media reaction did not. The June, 1991 issue of *Consumer Reports* placed long term care insurance on the front page with the tag line "Gotcha!" While the assessment of long term care policies was considered unfair given the improvements already made, the assessment of a lack of knowledge on the part of the agent concerning long term care was more likely accurate. Change had come so fast that few agents could comprehend it well enough to explain it to a prospective buyer.

Insurers and states moved quickly to rectify this "gap" in education. Educational programs for agents were implemented by insurance companies, while states began introducing continuing education requirements for an agent in order to retain his or her license. Some states had pre-licensing requirements specifically for long term care.

As agents' knowledge progressed and coverages improved, even *Consumer Reports* begrudgingly acknowledged long term care insurance as a viable financing alternative — for some. The September, 1995 issue of *Consumer Reports* stated "...another way to pay for a nursing home stay is with a long term care policy - a relatively new form of insurance coverage."[4] Even though the article was cautionary in its praise, this was a long way from "Gotcha!".

However, not all consumer magazines are endorsing long term care insurance. In the December, 1995 issue of *Smart Money* (a Wall Street Journal publication), an article stated "The numbers certainly suggest you can do without this insurance... If you are among the unlucky seniors who do need a nursing home, chances are that it will cost you no more than $57,600."[5] The implication here is that most people have $57,600 in liquid assets that can be spent on long term care services. This is a consumer financial publication? Maybe the unlucky senior who takes this advice can send his bill to the magazine.

The articles cited are now in the minority as the long term care insurance market has changed dramatically. And more changes are expected. This is a remarkable rebound from a rocky start. Sales are increasing but on a less than expected basis. More than 1,351,043 policies have been sold nationally by 1994, up from 666,665 in 1991.[6] Given the improvement in benefits, the increase in age range availability, the media publicity about the subject and the aging of the population, one would expect those numbers to be higher.

Some feel that the NAIC has done too fine a job in including benefits in its model policy, causing the price to rise beyond affordability for the consumer. The average age of the buyer of long term care insurance is 65, a time when rates are starting to accelerate rapidly. A focus on the younger buyer would increase sales. Currently, the policies that are owned demonstrate very low lapse rates, which means consumers are keeping what they buy. Clarification of tax issues may also help the sale of this product. Endorsements from accountants and attorneys might help the long term care market reach new heights over the next several years.

CHAPTER NOTES

1.   *Kiplinger's Personal Finance Magazine*, "Long Term Care Insurance - It's Better Now", October, 1993, p. 97.
2.   *The Washington Post*, "State Regulators Target Long Term Care Insurance", 1995.
3.   *The National Underwriter*, "Fewer Companies in Market, But LTC Sales Grow", May 8, 1995, p. 3.
4.   *Consumer Reports*, "Who Pays for Nursing Homes?", September, 1995, p. 591.
5.   *Smart Money*, "Shelter From The Storm?", December, 1995, p. 130.
6.   *The National Underwriter*, "Why Aren't Consumers Buying More LTC Policies?", July 31, 1995, p. 2.

Chapter 10

LONG TERM CARE vs. DISABILITY
INCOME PRODUCT DESIGN

Earlier long term care policies were narrow in scope and easy to explain. If an insured entered a nursing home, the policy paid a specified daily benefit, usually in cash, directly to the individual. When home health care policies became available, the arrangement was the same — the daily cash benefit was paid directly to the insured.

The earlier policies were popular with agents who specialized in the Medicare supplement market. The products were targeted at seniors and could usually be handled in one sales interview. Insureds could easily see what they were buying.

Today's long term care products take a more comprehensive approach towards the reimbursement of long term care expenses. There are several reasons for this approach:

1. The NAIC's model program prompted a more comprehensive policy form. The program has allowed the NAIC to refine contract language while expanding the range of benefit options.

2. Insurance companies, while struggling to get a handle on the proper design of the policy form, turned to the actual providers of long term care services for input. Feedback resulted in expansion of benefit choices and a variety of settings in which long term care services could be administered and be reimbursed.

The feedback from the providers was also helpful to companies when modifying contract language in the areas of qualification for benefits and types of covered services. For the first time, insurance companies in the marketplace began developing a comfort level when an actual claim occurred — how services were rendered and who was administering the care. In effect, policies today are far more practical and accurate in providing benefits for most long term care situations. This evolution might never have happened had the industry not tapped into the growing medical field for its knowledge of long term care.

GOOD NEWS FOR THE DISABILITY INCOME SPECIALIST

Agents that are apprehensive about the long term care market and lack an understanding of its products can take solace in the knowledge that today's long term care product is very similar to a disability income product. While product development has moved long term care policies beyond the scope of traditional Medicare supplement policies, the long term care policy of today closely resembles a disability income policy.

When I first explored the long term care market in the late 1980s, I did so in search of a program for my mother. She read an article about long term care insurance and called me to find out if it was in her insurance portfolio. Upon hearing that it was not, she instructed me to find her long term care insurance.

I contacted several companies I knew that were marketing long term care insurance and requested quotations. The questions asked by the marketing representative concerned elimination periods and benefit periods. It wasn't until the question, "Did I understand that if my mother was disabled, there were several ways to qualify for benefits?" that I realized: 1) I obviously knew very little about this coverage and; 2) it was going to be easier to learn than I thought.

I read all the information including the specimen policies sent. The long term care product was indeed a disability-based product with a design similar to the disability income policies I'd been marketing. Now, I was on familiar ground.

More importantly, it was a product I could market to my existing clients. My disability income clientele was aging and starting to focus on retirement. For many of them, it was only 10 or 15 years away and preparing financially for retirement had taken on an immediacy previously missing from our discussions. A long term care policy would be central to their retirement planning because a disability could severely hamper one's lifestyle at retirement just as easily as it could threaten income flow during their working years.

The more I thought about it, the traditional definition of "own occupation" in a disability income contract was similar to the disability definition in a long term care contract. The last line of the "own occupation" definition of disability read:

> If you are not working, your duties will be considered to be that of a retired person.

What did this mean? The first part of the definition addressed eligibility for benefits if a person was unable to work at his own occupation — the job held at time of claim. What did not working have to do with it?

I then called a claims administrator for the answer. Because the disability policy was a guaranteed renewable and non-cancelable policy, the company could not cancel the policy for any reason other than for non-payment of premium. It was anticipated that there would be individuals who might retire from work, but continue to pay the premiums for their coverage. Even though no occupation was involved, the insured was still eligible for benefits because of the injury or illness suffered.

This meant there had to be another measurement established to determine the insured's inability to perform duties — the essential key to qualifying for benefits. If not working, the insured was assumed to have retired, hence the policy language stating that supposition.

What are the duties of a retired person? The claims department uses an activities of daily living measurement — bathing, dressing, eating, mobility — the ordinary activities being performed every day. If these were modified in any way, the insurance company at least had a way to measure the disability and any subsequent recovery. Activities of daily living, as you will see, is the primary disability definition in a long term care product.

Understand that this was all conjecture on the part of the claims administrator. This particular insurance company had no claims that were filed utilizing this language but it was a perfect transition to understanding a long term care policy.

Two basic concepts resulted from this research:

> *Disability income* policies protect the insured during his working years.

> *Long term care* policies protect the insured during his retirement years.

To explain it simply, disability income benefits could be paid to retired people. Certainly, long term care services are reimbursed to a number of people under the age of 65.

Both disability and long term care policies should be purchased early on — disability income for people in their 20's and 30's and long term care for people in their 40's and 50's. Disability income is protection in the event of a disability while working and long term care is protection against a disability after retirement (when the need for long term care is the greatest).

If an agent sells disability income coverage, he can easily move into the long term care market. I made some minor alterations in my basic disability income sales presentation and created a basic long term care story to share with existing clients and prospects.

OTHER PARALLELS

The basics of my disability (and now long term care) sales presentation are:

1. Explanation of the need.

2. Introduce statistics.

3. Identify financing alternatives.

4. Present the product as a better financial alternative.

In reviewing each of these key areas, you will see how a minor change in wording or emphasis placed on a particular benefit can transform a discussion on disability income into one about long term care.

Explanation of The Need

During a sales presentation for disability income, prospects are asked what is their greatest asset. Their reply will vary (spouse, car, home, children — not necessarily in that order) and eventually they are steered towards understanding that income is their central asset. Loss of income would be a serious financial setback for them and their family.

Disability insurance is intended to protect the insured's ability to work and earn an income. There are tables available that indicate the potential earnings a worker will make over the course of a career. It is the potential income and assets derived from income, that disability insurance is designed to protect.

Long term care is intended to protect income and assets, too, except it is designed to protect retirement income and assets already built up. For the person who is retired, his lifestyle is dependent upon money accumulated during his working years and any investment income. This can be reduced drastically should the need for long term care arise. Recovery is not certain at this point in life. If anything, a return to normal health will take longer.

Introduce Statistics

For disability income, the statistics on the chances of a disability occurring are currently based on the 1985 update of the Commissioner's Disability Table (CDT). A measurement of the chances of being disabled for 90 days or longer, noted at benchmark ages (25,30,35,40,45,50,55,60) is introduced during the sales presentation to give the client some idea of the frequency and chances of becoming disabled. Other statistics include the rate of recovery based on the length of the disability and the chances of a disability versus premature death for any given age. In addition to a discussion about the risk to income and assets should a disability occur, the chances of a disability occurring can be clarified by using these statistics.

Long term care does not have access to historical data and statistics like disability income has. However, the *New England Journal of Medicine* has provided the most telling statistics to date. In a 1991 study of 2.2 million people turning age 65 in 1990, it was estimated that 43 percent of those could expect to spend some time in a nursing home before they died. Of that group, 21 percent would spend at least five years in a nursing home facility.[1]

More and more studies and statistics will emerge in the future, but, importantly, these numbers give the prospect some idea of the need for long term care insurance. There are no reliable numbers to date on home health care.

Introduce The Financing Alternatives

Prospects are aware of the impact a disability will have on their income, especially during their working years. They know how much they make and how much they spend. They understand that a disability can completely eliminate that income.

With long term care, the agent must quantify the income need. It is important to know the average daily nursing home rate for your state and surrounding counties where you work. On average, the annual cost for a nursing home stay is $36,000 nationwide. A five year nursing home stay would cost $180,000 — a major financial setback. Using local data is important and it is up to you to provide this information. In Miami, Florida, for example, the average cost for a nursing home stay is approximately $60,000 per year. A nursing home in a rural setting would average a lower rate. See Appendix B for a complete listing of the state agencies on aging for more information.

For disability there are several financing alternatives — savings, borrowing, relatives and friends, unearned income, Social Security, other disability income coverage, a working spouse's income or selling one's assets. The financing alternatives for long term care are the same except Medicare replaces Social Security and selling one's assets is replaced by Medicaid. Other long term care coverages available are Medicare supplements.

Some of these financing alternatives may provide sources for financing income during a disability. In all likelihood, the gap between what is needed and the money coming in will be substantial.

Present The Product As The Best Financial Alternative

Generally, setting aside an allotted premium for a disability income or long term care policy is better than any of the alternatives to fund the income need should a disability occur. A disability can occur any time, any place, anywhere. It is often unexpected and there are few ways to properly prepare for the financial need occurring during the recuperation period. Transferring the risk of funding the income need during disability makes sense for many people.

With a few modifications, your disability income sales presentation has become a long term care story. The audience may have changed somewhat, but the story is still essentially the same. But, the parallels between disability income and long term care don't end there.

PRODUCT SIMILARITIES

The plan design of a long term care policy utilizes language comparable to a disability income policy. The key plan parameters are:

Disability Income	Long Term Care
Monthly Income	Daily Benefit
Elimination Period	Elimination Period
Benefit Period	Benefit Period

Monthly Income vs. Daily Benefit

Monthly income versus a daily benefit is the primary difference between plan designs. For long term care you will have to do a little more homework so that you can make a daily benefit recommendation. The information is available and should be updated on an annual basis. Look for newspaper articles about the costs of nursing home and home health care in your area and state. Long term care is a popular subject and this information is an excellent source for making daily benefit recommendations.

Elimination Period

The disability income salesperson will recognize this plan parameter. This, in effect, is the policy deductible — the number of days that the policyowner must self-insure before benefits are payable.

With individual disability policies, we have witnessed the demise of the shorter elimination periods. The plans with 14 day and 30 day elimination periods have been shelved and the 60 day elimination period is probably near extinction for the professional and executive disability risk. Gray and blue collar applicants will likely find 30 day and 60 day elimination periods still available. For the rest of the working world, the starting point of elimination period discussions is a 90 day elimination period.

For long term care, first day eligibility with a zero day elimination period is available. This means as soon as the insured qualifies for benefits, reimbursements begin, providing immediate coverage. So far, the premium for a zero day elimination period is not any higher than other elimination periods available in a long term care policy. For example, when presented with a choice of several elimination periods, my mother selected the zero day option since the premium difference between a zero day elimination period and, in her case, a 30 day elimination period was minimal. However, I did caution her that claims experience could subject her to future rate increases, but that didn't deter her. Since she purchased the policy she has had seven rate renewals and is still paying the original premium quoted.

In addition to the zero day elimination period, long term care elimination periods are also available for 15, 20, 30, 60, 90, 100, 120, 150, 180 and 365 day periods. Some states place limitations on the longest elimination periods. A twenty day elimination period is a common choice because Medicare's skilled nursing coverage ceases 100 percent beginning on the twenty-first day. The primary selection however, has been the zero day elimination period. Whether these short options will expire over time in the face of deteriorating claims experience as with disability income, will not be known for some time.

The longer one can wait before benefits begin, the lower the premium cost. How long one can wait depends on the retirement cash flow and the availability of liquid assets to pay the premium. In Chapter 7, The Need

For Financial Planning, there is a detailed discussion on how to arrive at these numbers. Until premiums increase significantly for the zero day elimination period, most prospects will continue to elect the zero day option.

Some policies have dual elimination periods available — nursing home confinement and home health care. Selecting a shorter elimination period for home health care (a more common and popular long term care need) and a longer elimination period for a nursing home stay results in a lower premium and is helpful when trying to keep within a strict budget.

Benefit Periods

Benefit periods are familiar ground for the disability income agent. A benefit period determines the maximum length of time that benefits will be payable. For disability income, the choices generally range from 12 months to lifetime, although the lifetime benefit is currently being modified. Just as insurers are ushering the front end of a claim outward by eliminating the shorter elimination periods, they are moving the maximum length of time benefits are payable inward. Lifetime benefit periods are substituted with "to age 70" plans, a finite exposure period. Benefit periods for two and five years, and "to age 65" are also available.

For long term care, the lifetime benefit period (often called "unlimited") is available. Combining a zero day elimination period with an unlimited benefit period offers a more complete financing alternative to fund the income need during long term care than any other alternative.

Also available are two, three, four, five, six, and ten year benefit periods and there may be more options to come. The longer the benefit period, the greater the premium. With the different benefit periods available, the agent will be able to reduce the premium and stay within a prospect's budget. As mentioned earlier, *The New England Journal of Medicine* predicted that of the 2.2 million people turning age 65 in 1990, 198,660 or approximately nine percent could expect to spend at least five years in a nursing home facility before they died. Also, Medicaid requires a five year grace period when transferring assets irrevocably from a trust before becoming eligible to apply for reimbursement under this federal/state government program.

Thus, a five or six year benefit period could save premium dollars and provide ample coverage for the nine percent who will need benefits longer than five years and those who need long term care after the transfer of assets has been completed. There can be a significant premium difference between an unlimited benefit period and a five or six year benefit period. Of course, qualifying for Medicaid under these circumstances will eventually leave assets vulnerable but many people elect to construct their long term care plans with the transfer of assets in mind.

Like the dual elimination periods (for nursing home and home health care), it may be possible to elect separate benefit periods for these services in a long term care insurance plan.

Because of the similarities of long term care and disability income, the disability agent is familiar with the terminology and the underwriting process. This will easily help the agent with marketing long term care insurance.

PRODUCT DEFINITIONS

Renewability

For years, the disability income industry touted its non-cancelable renewal provision as a benchmark of quality coverage. Non-cancelability meant that not only could the insurer not cancel the contract (except for non-payment of premium), but rates could not be increased until age 65. This was a strong unilateral policy provision with the insured holding most of the cards.

Recently, poor claims experience has caused most disability income carriers to steer away from this type of renewable provision. It's not the cancelable aspect of the renewal that has been the headache, but the inability to adjust the rates on a particular block of business. Because of this, the non-cancelable feature has become expendable.

Instead, insurers are substituting a guaranteed renewable provision which retains the non-cancelability feature, and allows the insurer to raise rates in the future on a class basis. The class basis is often a specific policy form (insurers cannot isolate individual bad risks) that incurs the rate increase. These increases are not an automatic adjustment. Due to the extensive requirements in obtaining approval of premium changes from the state insurance departments, rate increases are made only when absolutely necessary.

The NAIC established the guaranteed renewable provision as the minimum standard for long term care policies, meaning that virtually all long term care plans have conformed to this requirement even in states that have not adopted the NAIC model. Insurers have yet to emerge with a non-cancellable provision for this coverage. Given the recent poor claims experience of disability insurers and the lack of credible experience for the long term care product to date, there is little chance the renewal provision will advance beyond the reasonable guaranteed renewable language.

Definition of Disability

The definition of disability is considered the core of disability income and long term care contracts. It determines how an insured qualifies for benefits, certainly an important matter to discuss with a prospect. There are distinct parallels between the two products in this area.

"Own Occupation" vs. Activities of Daily Living. Earlier in this chapter, it was mentioned that the "own occupation" definition of disability was to base qualification on the ability of the insured to perform the duties of a retired person — the ability to perform activities of daily living.

The disability income definition is considered met if the insured cannot perform the typical duties of his own occupation. Each occupation may have a different set of key tasks upon which eligibility for benefits will be considered. The long term care definition is based on the inability of the insured to perform such activities as bathing, dressing, eating, toileting and transferring positions. While Chapter 11, Today's Basic Long Term Care Policy, will look at these activities of daily living in more detail, know that the primary method under both policies of qualifying an individual for benefits is based on the ability to perform tasks — work duties for disability income and essential activities for long term care.

Presumptive Total Disability vs. Cognitive Impairment. In a disability income policy, another way of qualifying for benefits is a catastrophic-type event that automatically makes the insured eligible to receive benefits. These catastrophes are the irrecoverable loss of sight, speech, or hearing, or the use of two limbs. Should one of these types of disabilities befall the insured, no other qualifications need to be met and benefits are often paid from date of loss thus, the elimination period no longer needs to be satisfied.

The long term care equivalent is called cognitive impairment. Part of the NAIC model policy's objective was to ensure that benefits would not be denied for organic mental disorders like Alzheimer's disease. A diagnosed cognitive impairment — any kind of organic brain disorder — is another way to qualify for benefits under the long term care policy. No other qualifications need to be met with a cognitive impairment diagnosis.

Under A Doctor's Care vs. Medical Necessity. Most disability income policies require the insured to be under a doctor's care to be eligible to receive benefits. A condition could be waived if future treatment would have no impact on an individual's recovery.

For a long term care policy, a "medical necessity" (under a doctor's care) resulting from an illness or injury is another possibility for benefit eligibility. The insured can qualify for benefits if a physician directs that long term care services are needed to help further an individual's recovery.

The definitions for disability income and long term care are very similar and the experienced disability income salesperson can easily transfer the disability income concept to long term care insurance.

RESIDUAL DISABILITY

It took disability income carriers several decades to add the residual disability benefit to disability income policies. Under a total disability definition (as described above), there was little provision for benefits should the insured actually return to his own profession. In the early 1970s, claims experience indicated that the majority of claimants did go back to their own jobs — without much in the way of benefits.

The development of the residual benefit established an intermediate definition of disability for the insured. If the insured's time, duties and income were partially reduced as a result of an attempt to return to work, a portion of the total monthly disability benefit based on the actual earnings loss incurred was payable. This allowed the insured to return to work without being penalized. Studies have shown that the earlier the insured returned to work, the shorter the duration of the claim.

Currently, for benefits to be paid in a long term care policy, the insured must require full assistance in an activity such as dressing or toileting to qualify under this definition. Partial or intermediate assistance, while increasingly common, is not yet a staple in long term care products.

Some long term care insurance companies have added the "residual" definition to their measurement of activities of daily living. The insurer will pay nothing to the insured who can perform activities independently. Full daily benefits are paid when full assistance is needed and 50 percent of the daily benefit when partial assistance is needed.

Partial assistance still requires a visit from a medical technician, most likely a home health aide and there is a cost the insured incurs for partial assistance. As the policies continue to be fine tuned, look for the inclusion of this "residual" feature, making it even closer in appearance to a disability income policy.

Still uncertain about your command of knowledge in the long term care market? If you're currently selling disability income insurance, this chapter should have increased your level of understanding while preparing you for Chapter 11, Today's Basic Long Term Care Policy, which will detail the essential policy provisions under a long term care insurance policy.

CHAPTER NOTE

1.   "Nursing Home Costs", *The New England Journal of Medicine*, February, 1991, pp. 597, 599.

Chapter 11

TODAY'S BASIC LONG TERM CARE POLICY

Long term care products today are going through the same evaluation process that disability income policies underwent fifteen years ago. In the early 1980s, companies selling disability income policies were rewriting policy provisions, adding new provisions and evaluating the contract language. This created a wide disparity in the products offered. Insurance agents and consumers found that a comparison of various policy forms required a review of a dozen or more provisions to ensure a thorough and accurate analysis. Premiums fluctuated depending on the benefits and definitions included in any given policy.

Long term care products are experiencing the same evaluation process today. There are a wide variety of definitions and various policy provisions that have a significant effect on the premium being charged. How disability is defined, what long term care services are reimbursable and where these services can be rendered make for a diversity of products. Sorting through the policy language is important for an in-depth understanding of the product being offered. It will also ensure a reliable explanation of the information when recommending long term care insurance to a prospect.

The involvement of the National Association of Insurance Commissioners (NAIC) has accelerated product changes as well as impacted the rate at which a number of individual states have imposed specific requirements on policy design. Mandated policy provisions, varying by state, add another layer of complexity to the analysis of a product. While no where near the number of mandates health insurance faces, these requirements still present a challenge to long term care insurers. The result is a "confusing panorama of permutations" in the long term care market, keeping agents and consumers off-balance when trying to make an informed buying decision.[1]

For those selling (and buying) long term care insurance, it is imperative to take the time to carefully review the coverage that is offered in a
policy — specific limitations, policy exclusions, definitions of disability,
and premiums.[2] There are many insurers that are established in the long
term care market but there are a number of insurers that are not experienced in the long term care market. The inexperienced insurers offer broad
policy benefits without regard to a potentially high claims experience.
Like disability income coverage, a block of written business will take
several years before results of any profit or loss are realized. There have
already been products withdrawn by inexperienced insurers due to substantial rate increases.

A knowledge of the key policy provisions (and their variations) will
help the insurance agent and financial planner understand the benefits and
potential claims liability. While it is important to avoid the truly restrictive
products, it is equally critical to stay away from the very liberal plans
where poor claims experience can translate into substantial rate increases.

THE POLICY DESIGN BASICS

The key design parameters of a long term care insurance policy are
daily benefits, elimination periods, and benefit periods. Recommendation
of these policy elements is based on the agent's own research combined
with the financial analysis completed on each prospect.

Daily Benefits

The cost of care in a nursing home is generally the criterion used to
initially choose the benefit amount. Information should be available in
written form on the average cost and specific costs of nursing homes in a
given area. A visit to several nursing home facilities is also important in
eliminating those that fall below standards.

In some policies, the daily benefit amount selected is used to determine the coverage payable for other long term care services such as home
health care. Often a percentage of the daily benefit amount can be chosen
to dictate the amount paid for home health care and adult day care, two
reimbursements that are usually less than the cost of staying in a nursing
home.

For example, if your client has chosen a $100 a day benefit based on local nursing home costs, the policy may pay 50 percent of this amount (or $50 a day) for any home health care services and 25 percent ($25 a day) for adult day care that is needed. These percentages can vary, allowing flexibility in selection. Home health care can be 50, 75 or even 100 percent of the daily benefit amount selected for nursing home confinement. In some cases, a higher benefit level can be elected for home health care instead of a skilled nursing facility.

Many policies today offer level daily benefit amounts without regard to the service needed. For example, if an individual chooses a daily benefit of $100, the coverage, whether it is for a nursing home stay, home health care, adult day care, or other covered services, would be $100 a day. Other plans allow a selection of individual daily benefit levels for primary services.

The daily benefit amount can be paid two different ways:

1. Pay the full daily benefit (or appropriate percentage) selected regardless of the actual charges for long term care services provided, or

2. Pay the actual charge incurred for long term care services provided up to the daily benefit amount selected.

There is a difference and the policy language should be reviewed to determine how the daily benefit is paid. The first option pays the insured the specified amount elected under the policy for the long term care services provided regardless of the actual cost (higher or lower) of the services rendered. For example, if an insured receives home health care at a cost of $60 a day the selected daily benefit amount of $75 is paid to the insured regardless of the actual cost.

The second option will pay either the daily benefit amount elected or actual cost if it is lower than the daily benefit. Using the same example, if the selected daily benefit amount is $75 and the actual cost for home health care is $59, the policy will pay $59 since the actual cost is lower than $75. If the actual cost was higher than the daily benefit amount, the policy will pay $75, the maximum daily benefit amount selected.

Daily amounts should also be indexed annually to offset the effects of inflation. This is usually an optional benefit for the policy and will be discussed in Chapter 12, The Essential Optional Benefits.

Zero Day Elimination Periods

The zero day elimination period (see Chapter 10, Long Term Care vs. Disability Product Design) remains one of the best deals in the long term care insurance market. When balanced against a policy that offers reasonable benefits, the zero day elimination period has so far withstood the test of time. A zero day elimination period allows benefit payments to begin immediately and many insurers have not yet experienced the anticipated adverse claims.

A word of caution to anyone considering the zero day elimination period — a few insurers have experienced adverse claims. If it is sold in combination with a remarkably easy qualification for benefits provision, the results will undoubtedly be high claims and equally high rate increases. The downside is for those policyholders who are now in their late 60's or early 70's (when the likelihood of long term care increases). If they have had the policy for some time but not yet made a claim, they will soon be facing a rate increase which may render the policy unaffordable. What kind of service does the agent and the industry provide when a policyholder has to drop the plan or significantly modify the coverage at a time when the product is most needed?

If you will recall, this happened with health insurance and it almost brought us a national health insurance program run by the government. So, use caution when recommending the zero day elimination period.

Benefit Periods

There are two types of benefit periods available today. The first type is the traditional benefit period where policy benefits can be paid within a specified number of months, or years. Typically, 12 months, 2, 3, 4, 5 and 6 years are examples of benefit periods. Policies can be sold with an unlimited benefit period — as long as the insured needs covered long term care services, benefits will be paid. This is a popular benefit period despite its higher cost in comparison to the potential payout with shorter benefit periods.

Historically, the choices in benefit periods began with a six month maximum introduced in CNA's first long term care policy in 1965. Today, many states require a minimum of 12 to 24 months for payout of benefits.

The second type of benefit period available is not measured in days, months or years, but rather in dollars. This is called a "pool of money concept" and is becoming popular among insurers, agents and consumers. Rather than specify a period of time, benefits for long term care services are paid from a single lifetime maximum number of dollars[3]. Benefits are payable for as long as the maximum amount lasts, regardless of the time period.

The lifetime maximum amount is calculated using the daily benefit selected multiplied by a specific number of days elected by the person buying the coverage. The specified days may be 1,000, 2,000, 3,000 or 365, 730, 1,095, 1,460, etc. The following are examples of the lifetime maximum:

$$\$100/\text{day} \times 2,000 \text{ days} = \$200,000$$

$$\$100/\text{day} \times 1,460 \text{ days} = \$146,000$$

It can be compared to purchasing a lump sum amount except the benefits will be disbursed over an unspecified period of time instead of all at once.

Pool of money plans pay expenses as they are incurred in an amount up to the daily benefit level (see #2 in the daily benefit explanation above). Thus, expenses that are consistently below the daily benefit amount would likely mean a longer payout period than the number of days used to calculate the lifetime maximum.

The pool of money concept integrates the benefits so the prospect does not have to choose a benefit percentage for home health care or other long term care services. When the need for long term care arises and it is a covered service, the payout will come out of the lifetime maximum pool. This flexible approach allows consumers to generally receive the type of long term care they wish in the setting they prefer.[4]

Benefit Coordination

Some insurers coordinate their policy benefits with Medicare. This is typical in the pool of money concept where dollar for dollar offsets can be achieved. If a service, for example, costs $88 and Medicare reimburses $75 of the cost, the policy would pay the additional $13.

The administrator of Medicare benefits, the Health Care Financing Administration (HCFA), is as excited about this prospect as it was about health insurance being secondary to Medicare. In the early 1980s, HCFA influenced the passage of legislation ensuring that in the event of duplicate benefits, Medicare would *always* be secondary to health insurance coverage. In August of 1995, HCFA issued a ruling prohibiting any long term care policy, regardless of when it was issued, from coordinating benefits with Medicare.[5] In other words, in the event of duplicate coverage, Medicare will *always* be secondary to long term care policies — policy benefits must be paid first before deciding on what financial responsibility, if any, Medicare would have.

This could create a problem for insurers who priced their policies with the consideration that benefits may not be payable at times since Medicare would cover the majority of costs. This is more likely for home health care than nursing home care, but it will certainly impact insurers' claims results. As such, there may be a need for an increase in premiums in anticipation of a higher than expected claims experience.

Of course, Congress could reverse this ruling with specific long term care legislation, which is still pending at the time of this writing.

RENEWABILITY

Once the agent has recommended to the insured the basic policy selections careful review of the various policy provisions is necessary. The first discussion should be about renewability.

This policy provision is usually found on the face page of the policy itself. As noted previously, the minimum renewal provision called for by the NAIC is guaranteed renewability. This means that the policy cannot be arbitrarily canceled (except for non-payment of premiums) nor can any policy provisions be altered in any way except for the betterment of provisions. However, insurers do possess the right to impose a rate increase on a specific class of long term care business.

The term "class" consists of a specific policy or policy series. State insurance departments will allow reasonable and justifiable rate increases on a policy form since it affects all purchasers of this product.

Nearly all comprehensive long term care policies have this type of renewal provision. This makes it easy to compare this product feature. To my knowledge, there are no non-cancelable renewable (the premium is guaranteed for a specified period of time) policies for long term care. Given the recent troubles of the non-cancelable renewable provision in disability income policies, it is not likely to be a policy feature offered in the near future.

Be wary of policies that are not written on a guaranteed renewable basis. Policies that pay for a specified service rather than taking a more comprehensive approach may offer renewability on a conditional basis. This type of renewal, while keeping premium costs low, also gives the insurance companies the opportunity to refuse to renew the policy form based on poor claims experience. Policies that provide benefits for nursing home coverage only or for home health care could contain this type of provision.

DEFINITIONS OF DISABILITY

This product feature dictates how a prospect qualifies for benefits. The definitions of disability, as in a disability income policy, are the key measurements of a long term care policy.

Most long term care policies today are utilizing a "triple-trigger" means of qualification for policy benefits. This approach gives the insured three possible ways of qualifying for benefits.

The insured's ability to function independently is the framework for benefit eligibility. The three definitions for benefit eligibility are:

1. Inability to perform a certain number of activities of daily living (ADLs).

2. Suffering from a cognitive impairment, such as Alzheimer's or Parkinson's disease.

3. A medical necessity, as prescribed by a physician, for long term care services.

This triple-trigger feature allows the insured to qualify for benefits by meeting the requirements under any one of these definitions. The primary definition is the inability to perform a certain number of routine activities of daily living (ADLs).

The most common activities of daily living are bathing, dressing, eating, toileting, transferring (mobility or transporting), continence, or taking medicine.

Insurers generally list and define these qualifying activities of daily living in their policies. The total number of required activities can range from four activities to all seven activities. Some insurers combine bathing and dressing into one ADL called personal care.

To qualify under the primary definition, the inability to perform a certain number of these ADLs, usually a minimum of two, must be evident. Thus, this definition is usually written as "the inability of the insured to perform two or more activities of daily living". Some insurers require three, while there are a few insurers that require the loss of only one ADL to activate a claim.

The requirement that an insured lose three or more ADLs seems too strict while the loss of one activity makes it too easy to qualify for benefits. Insurers marketing the latter and, in effect, competing by policy liberalization, are probably making a mistake which will eventually fall back on policyholders. The ease of qualification could lead to higher than expected claims experience and will necessitate the application for an increase in policy rates. In my opinion, this is a risky definition and given the experience of the disability insurance industry, should be avoided. This is a great definition to use during a sales interview, but it could be subjected to a heavy rate increase later on leaving the client in a vulnerable position if premium affordability becomes an issue.

The loss of two ADLs may be liberal enough if bathing and dressing are among those activities listed. According to UNUM, a long term care insurer, in over 85 percent of long term care cases, bathing and dressing are the first ADLs requiring assistance. Think about it. Getting in and out of the bathtub can be dangerous because of a slippery surface. A fall can immobilize an already frail person or compound problems for someone who already has health problems. Likewise, dressing requires being somewhat limber when bending down to tie shoelaces or simply buttoning a shirt. Arthritis could significantly hamper one's ability to get dressed.

The insurers that combine bathing and dressing into one ADL (personal care) are trying to avoid the easier qualification of a separate listing. Many insurers do keep them apart and, as such, the loss of these two ADLs first triggers benefit payments quicker than the other activities.

One of the quirks of aging is that the ability to perform activities of daily living are lost in the reverse order in which they were learned. The last activity a parent lets a child do independently is bathing. The chances of an accident are too numerous to mention. Dressing, such as buttoning a shirt or tying shoelaces, also requires a parent's help for some time. Yet these same two activities, last learned, are the first activities lost for the elderly.

The importance of how the inability to perform activities of daily living is defined has prompted much speculation. Most companies prefer to take a "black and white approach" to claims adjudication. An insured is either independent, needing no assistance, or dependent, requiring assistance. The problem lies with a number of people who are receiving long term care assistance with an activity which they can occasionally perform themselves. Assistance with dressing may be to help tie shoelaces while the rest of the activity of getting dressed is performed by the person needing assistance. This isn't independence — this person can't leave the house without shoes (although one could buy shoes without laces). But is it truly dependence since other articles of clothing can be negotiated?

There is an interim level of care between dependence and independence which most insurers have yet to recognize. It is partial assistance with certain activities and, as such, should generate a partial claim payment. It took disability income insurers many years to acknowledge the importance of residual disability. Residual disability pays a portion of the total monthly disability benefit upon the insured's return to work and is based on the percentage of loss of earnings incurred as a result.

Assistance, the middle ground between independence and dependence, will eventually have a defined benefit level that a number of insurers will incorporate into their policies. Otherwise, claims handling can be harsher than intended or, at least, difficult to administer. This definition is the most common way to become eligible for benefits.

The second definition is usually an alternative to the primary definition. One of the most severe disabilities affecting the elderly is Alzheimer's disease, an organic brain disorder. As millions of Americans battle this difficult disease, the condition poses a difficulty for insurers using the "ability to perform ADLs" test. Under the primary definition of disability, it is necessary for the insured to suffer a continuing inability to perform two or more ADLs. Alzheimer's patients may enjoy days they function normally, and are thus disqualified from satisfying the continued loss of an ADL requirement.

In addition, as part of the NAIC Model Act, it was mandated that insurers cover Alzheimer's disease, Parkinson's and other organic brain disorders that occur after the policy has been purchased. To do this, a second definition of disability, cognitive impairment, was developed where the insured automatically becomes eligible for benefits. Policy language for this definition may read:

> Cognitive impairment means the deterioration in or loss of the insured's intellectual capacity and may include exhibition of: (1) abusive or assaultive behavior; or (2) poor judgment; or (3) bizarre hygiene or habits, which requires continual supervision to protect the insured or others. Cognitive impairment is measured by clinical evidence and standardized tests and is based on the insured's impairment as indicated by loss in the following areas: (1) his/her short or long term memory; or (2) his/her recognition of who or where he/she is, or time of day, month or year; or (3) his/her deductive or abstract reasoning.

There is no universal definition of cognitive impairment recognized by insurers to date so the terminology will differ from policy to policy. Recent breakthroughs in the research of brain disorders will help future victims. A gene believed to cause 40 percent of all Alzheimer's cases has been identified as "apo E4".[6] A genetic test is available that will help solidify the diagnosis of Alzheimer's in people that are starting to show signs of dementia. This will help to qualify an individual who will need long term care assistance for benefits.

While virtually all plans use the first two definitions to qualify an insured for benefits, a growing number are adding a third definition as an eligibility requirement. If the insured needs long term care services according to his or her doctor, but does not meet the requirements of the first two definitions, what happens? For those policies with the triple-trigger definitions, the policy has a back-up — medical necessity. This definition allows eligibility for benefits to be established if the need for long term care services is substantiated by a physician, usually the insured's own physician.

If an illness or injury occurs and it necessitates the use of long term care services, verified by a physician, benefits will be payable. Some insurers require the medical condition that precipitated the need for long term care must be the same as the original injury or illness. Other insurers require that the physician certify the need for the care. Continuous verification of a long term care need from the physician is necessary for benefits to continue under the medical necessity definition.

These definitions are a fair and flexible approach in qualifying for benefits and seem to satisfy most insurers and insureds. The language for these policies is still being fine tuned and the need for the addition of an "assisted" definition of ADLs is widespread and will likely be the next phase of product refinement. Today's policies are far more generous in qualifying for benefits than earlier policies. Look for the most comprehensive language for activities of daily living, cognitive impairment and medical necessity. If you can read it and interpret it easily, it will be easy to explain to a client or prospect.

LONG TERM CARE BENEFITS

Chapter 4, Defining Long Term Care Services, identified the types of long term care services offered today. Now let's see how the following benefits are treated in long term care policies:

skilled nursing care	intermediate care
custodial care	home health care
home care	adult day care
respite care	hospice care

Most comprehensive policies cover these services in some fashion. Look for reference to them and their definitions in every policy.

Skilled Care: Requires the service of trained medical personnel with the authorization of a physician. Skilled care can be administered in a skilled or intermediate nursing facility, a hospital, at home, or in an assisted living facility. These various settings may not be in every policy and actual reimbursement can vary based on where the services are rendered.

Intermediate Care: Requires the skill of trained medical personnel on a less frequent basis than skilled care, and with the authorization of a physician. Intermediate care is generally administered to patients who need medical care or therapy to resume their ADLs. In a skilled or intermediate care nursing facility, the nursing home daily rate would likely be paid. Home health care, adult day care centers, and assisted living facilities would also receive reimbursement at a different level.

Custodial Care: Primarily assists with ADLs, this level of care does not have to be authorized by a physician or require trained medical personnel. Most often custodial care is received at home, delivered by qualified home health aides. If care is received in a custodial care facility, the nursing home rate would likely apply. Reimbursement at a different level for care received in an assisted living facility is also likely.

Home Health Care: Medically necessary skilled or intermediate care with the authorization of a physician and performed by trained medical personnel. Benefits could be paid as a percentage of the nursing home daily benefit, at the same level, or a larger reimbursement depending on the complexity of the product.

Home Care: This is custodial care — assistance with ADLs and household chores. Benefits could be paid as a percentage of the nursing home daily benefit amount, at the same level or a greater amount. This care is usually delivered by a home health care aide or possibly a licensed practical nurse.

Adult Day Care: This long term care service is considered custodial care or intermediate care provided in a licensed adult day care facility. The caregivers who work during the day will find this a convenient alternative.

The policy may have a specific rate for adult day care reimbursement or could pay from the pool of money at rates up to the daily benefit level.

Respite Care: This benefit provides temporary relief for those in a caregiving role by hiring temporary help to care for a dependent adult. Depending on the policy language, more than one temporary helper can be hired at the same time. This help is reimbursed up to the limits of the policy. Typically, the policy pays for up to 21 days for temporary help. The substitute can most often be obtained from a local home health care agency.

Hospice Care: Many long term care policies provide some benefit for hospice care, a program primarily designed for pain and symptom control for terminally ill patients. Benefits could be paid as a percentage of the nursing home daily benefit, at the same level, or a larger reimbursement depending on the complexity of the product. In addition, an amount may be paid for bereavement counseling for other family members. Medicare also provides some assistance for bereavement, but in view of HCFA's ruling concerning long term care policies as the primary insurance, the long term care plans that include this benefit may find reimbursements being made in more cases than originally intended. Whether this will ultimately affect inclusion of this benefit in the policy is not yet known.

These are the most common services and reimbursement structures in long term care today. It is vitally important to be as accurate as possible in choosing the daily benefit since virtually all benefit services and reimbursements are based on this selection. It is important to do your homework in the areas of long term care you plan to market so that the proper recommendations are made.

Alternate Plans of Care

Many long term care policies today contain a provision which allows claim payments for long term care services delivered outside the scope of the usual policy definitions. Most insurers recognize that most of these "non-covered" services are less expensive to cover than the services defined in the policy, making it easier for them to provide a means for the insured to receive this care without penalty (withholding of benefit payments). Several examples are described below:[7]

1. A person confined in a skilled nursing area of a nursing home was transferred to a "home for the aged" type facility. This type of facility was not defined in the long term care policy as a setting for policy benefit reimbursement. Medical documentation received from the physician substantiated the need for consistent intermediate care and some skilled care. The "home for the aged" staff verified that the services rendered were similar to those received in a skilled nursing facility. Benefits were paid under the policy.

2. A 71-year-old man has a medical condition where the pressure of fluid builds up inside his head, causing violent hallucinations and behavior management problems. He is also legally blind. His wife could not effectively care for him on a daily basis. While a nursing home confinement was recommended, his wife argued for an alternative that would allow her husband to receive care at home, feeling it would be better for him. She would do as much of the caregiving as possible but would need some help. Working together with family members, the physician, and a home health care agency developed a schedule for where he would have adult day care twice a week, respite care for his wife, and home care as needed.

   The result was a lower reimbursement — $38 per day for adult day care rather than the $105 a day for a nursing home, care in a familiar environment, no pressure on the spouse for full-time care. The spouse requested very little respite care or home care assistance — two days of adult day care per week seemed to be enough.

Those familiar with disability income claims know that every case is different even if two people suffer a similar ailment. People adjust differently to adverse medical circumstances and what works for one may not necessarily work for another. Long term care insurers have been contracting case managers to assist in fully evaluating each claim, making recommendations based on the most effective treatment at the most reasonable cost, taking into account the wishes of the family, and the circumstances which would either speed recovery or make one more comfortable. Not all of this can be defined in the policy language, so carriers include "alternate plans of care" to cover other, non-contract options.

Under this option, a number of assisted living facilities like adult congregate living facilities (ACLFs) are recognized by the insurer as a setting for receiving long term care services. Whether it's a "home for the aged" or the most expensive nursing home in the area, alternate plans of care can encompass the entire range of services. Growing at a phenomenal rate, the variety of long term care services and facilities is expanding far beyond the capacity of an insurance policy to include the latest service or type of facility. The terminology for the policy option, alternate plans of care, alleviates the burden to keep up with the trends on paper. Insurers are always looking for ways to improve coverage, and careful monitoring of long term care trends is constant.

Another extension of this alternate care is to recognize that many people receive care from a family member or friend. Some insurers are paying for caregiver training for family members or friends to help them learn to effectively care for their loved ones.[8] No benefits are paid beyond the training allowance, which usually has a maximum limit listed in the policy.

There are policies that pay benefits when a non-licensed individual is providing the caregiving. This is often in the form of household chores, but may involve duties such as administering medication. The non-licensed individual cannot be a family member nor can he already be living in the household. A neighbor or friend, for example, would qualify and benefits would be paid.

Other Policy Provisions[9]

Waiver of Premium: This policy feature is designed to eliminate the burden of premium payments by the insured during the time of claim. Depending on the insurance company, waiver of premium can begin on the first day the claim commences, (which may be immediately under a zero day elimination period), or for example, after 90 days. Some insurance companies will waive the premium after a stipulated period of time in a nursing home.

The best waiver of premium provision is the premium that is waived after the elimination period (even zero day). If care is essential, why add further to difficulties by requiring premium payments? Read this policy feature carefully, however, as many insurers will only waive premiums during a nursing home confinement. This means receiving home health care does not qualify for the waiver of premium benefit.

Restoration of Benefits: When an insured selects a benefit period other than "unlimited" or "lifetime" periods, this policy provision will restore claim days already used. If the insured has a claim, then recovers, and is claim-free for a set period (6 to 12 months), the claim period can be fully restored. For example, an individual with a three year benefit period uses the entire period for a claim, eventually recovers and goes treatment-free for a year. The three year benefit period may be restored in whole or in part for the individual.

This concept is popular with *true* benefit period policies. There is generally no corresponding provision for the "pool of money" benefit.

Bed Reservation Benefit: A person in a nursing home, assisted living facility, or a hospice facility may need to be hospitalized for several days due to a medical condition. If the facility he lives in charges to hold the bed until his return, the policy can reimburse the insured up to a specific number of days, usually with a maximum limit of 21 to 31 days. This allows for continuous care and ensures that an insured will have a bed at the same facility, providing a consistency of treatment that is important.

Cognitive Reinstatement: Traditionally, insurance policies, by law, have a 31 day grace period beyond the premium due date. This allows the insured to make a late payment without any interruption or change in the coverage. Long term care policies have extended grace periods. If it is satisfactorily demonstrated that the missed payment was due to forgetful-ness or even a cognitive impairment, reinstatement of the lapsed policy can be made as long as nine months after policy lapse. The payment of back premiums is required to reinstate the policy. This allows individuals a maximum range of flexibility under which to continue the policy in good faith.

This provision may also be written in conjunction with a third party notification provision under which an individual, often a family member, receives lapse notices. This ensures that another individual can inquire about the missed payment and keep the policy in force.

Pre-Existing Conditions: There are situations that are specifically excluded from claims consideration under a long term care policy. Most states require that a complete list of policy exclusions, including pre-existing conditions, be displayed on any sales material that is published. A pre-existing condition is one that is not disclosed on the policy application and for which the person received treatment or medical advice within a specified period of time (usually six months) before the policy went into effect. This means that if the individual was aware of a medical condition and treatment or advice was sought in the months prior to obtaining the long term care insurance, and did not disclose this condition on the application, it is considered pre-existing and there is no coverage. If the pre-existing condition is disclosed on the application, and the policy is approved with or without restriction, it is no longer considered a pre-existing condition.

Other more common exclusions from coverage are:

1. War, or act of war, declared or not declared.

2. Intentionally self-inflicted injury or attempted suicide.

3. Injuries sustained while attempting to commit or committing a felony.

4. Services rendered for treatment of drug, alcohol or chemical dependence.

5. Non-organic brain disorders. (Alzheimer's is an organic brain disorder.)

6. Care covered by any state or federal workers' compensation, employer's liability or occupational disease law.

7. Care provided by a member of the insured's family.

8. Care received for which a charge would not have been assessed except for the presence of insurance such as a free service provided by a church organization for which no obligation to pay would be the normal course of affairs.

Each policy may have other exclusions and should be evaluated on its own merit to see if it is legitimate.

Spouse Discounts: Many companies offer a ten percent discount if both spouses apply for long term care insurance. The reasoning behind this offer is a clear relationship between the amount of time spent in a nursing home and marital status. One study found that seven percent of those married at time of death spent five years or more in a nursing home, compared to 16 percent of those who were widowed, 17 percent of those who were separated or divorced, and 29 percent of those who had never married.[10] Most companies who offer this provision will let one spouse keep the discount even if the other is turned down for coverage because of health reasons.

Policy Upgrades: Although most companies don't state it in the policy, these carriers offer improvements in coverage than can be added retroactively to the policyholder's current coverages. In most cases, there is no charge to do this. Other states require a premium although evidence of medical insurability is not required. This helps the insurer to keep the policy from being replaced by newer plans and better benefits. For policyholders, it is a simple way to keep the policy up to date without changing carriers.

Non-forfeiture Benefits: This is a recent addition to many companies' policies. The NAIC added a mandated non-forfeiture provision to their policies in 1993. This feature requires insurers to preserve some of the policy benefits even if the insured stops paying premiums. The policy should be held for a certain number of years before eligibility for these non-forfeiture benefits is allowed.[11]

In life insurance, after a certain number of years, the premiums paid have achieved some ownership or vesting in the policy. In long term care, the insured can elect to take a paid-up policy where the money paid in has been calculated to refigure the benefit level to allow coverage to continue for the same length of time with the same elimination period at a reduced daily benefit amount. Or, the insured may elect extended term coverage whereby the policy stays in force for a number of days, months and even years, and the policy benefits stay the same without paying any further premiums.

This provision ensures that premiums paid have some significance if the insured should decide to stop paying the premium. Otherwise, although the money was paid and the protection was present, the insured has little to show for that investment when premium payments cease.

This feature will increase the cost of the policy and it is unclear just how much it will affect the premium because insurers are still struggling to develop and price this feature. While non-forfeiture benefits are included in the NAIC Model Policy, not every state adopts the changes and many states are slow to react to the changes.

Premiums

The cost for a long term care policy fluctuates between insurers, issue ages, and benefit levels. This makes it difficult to compare premium cost between two plans.

For example, two quotes are ordered from two different insurance companies with the premiums ranging from $1,000 annually for one plan to $1,350 annually for the other plan. The differences in the coverages must be reviewed before recommending the lower premium plan. It may be that the $1,000 plan does not include inflation protection, for example. Or, the $1,350 plan allows the insured to receive care in virtually any setting while the $1,000 plan limits coverage to a nursing facility or in the home.

There are some basic assumptions regarding premiums in general. Individuals in their 40s and 50s can expect to pay relatively low premiums for long term care coverage. Typically, this age group won't file a claim for some time. The premiums begin to accelerate each year around age 65. Rates increase dramatically for those buying the coverage in their 70s and 80s.

A nationwide study by the Health Insurance Association of America (HIAA) released March, 1995, on coverage and premiums in 1993 revealed:[12]

- a person buying a basic long term care policy at age 50 pays $405 annually for a $100 nursing home daily benefit and a $50 daily benefit for home health care;

- a person buying the same policy at age 65 would pay $1,086 annually; and

- a person buying the same policy at age 79 would pay $4,372 annually.

The relationship between premium and age in this study underscores the need to plan ahead and consider the coverage in pre-retirement years. Since premiums can be increased by the insurer in the years after purchase, a premium starting out low will be less affected by any change.

For example, if a prospect was paying $405 for a policy and the insurance company raised the rates by ten percent, the increase would be $40.50 annually for a new annual premium of $445.50. If a prospect was paying $1,086, the increase would be $108.60 for a new annual premium of $1,194.60. For a $4,372 annual premium, the rate increase would be $437.20 for a new annual premium of $4,809.20. The chart below illustrates the rate increase relationship.

Premium	Rate Increase	Dollar Increase	New Premium
$ 405.00	10%	$ 40.50	$ 445.50
$1086.00	10%	$108.60	$1194.60
$4372.00	10%	$437.20	$4809.20

In addition to age, other factors can increase the amount of premium:

Elimination Period—the shorter the elimination period (0, 15, 20 days), the higher the premium.

Benefit Period — the longer the period of time benefits are paid, or the higher the lifetime maximum benefit in a pool of money plan, the higher the premium.

Daily Benefit — the higher the daily benefit, the higher the premium.

Gender—insurers generally charge the same rate for male and females (some states require this), so this isn't usually a factor.

Health Risks — some insurers have tiers of risk classification and those applicants with health conditions may pay a higher rate than those who are relatively healthy.

Optional Benefits — if additional coverages such as inflation protection and return of premium are selected, the cost of the policy will be higher.

Earlier policies often had rate bands for certain ages and the premiums automatically went up when one moved from one rate band to another. The grouping of ages were typically 40-49, 50-54, 55-59, 60-64, 65-69 and so on.

For example, if a policy was purchased at age 47, the premium would automatically change at age 50, again at age 55, at age 60, and so on. This increase was in addition to any other rate increases the insurer levied based on overall claims experience.

The NAIC (and many states) outlawed this rate banding practice for comprehensive long term care policies several years ago. Now, when a policy is purchased, the only rate increases filed by the insurer will be based on claims experience. These increases may happen periodically or they may not happen at all.

A new premium feature available is the limited pay program. The insured can pay the premium in several large premium installments which will pay for the policy for life in a few short years. This gives individuals in their 50s an opportunity to purchase a paid-up long term care policy before retirement when their income and assets are higher.[13] Future rate increases would be a moot point since there would be no effect on this paid-up plan. More and more insurers may offer this option in the future.

Policy Review

Here is a checklist of questions for reviewing the basic policy design when evaluating a long term care insurance program:[14]

1. What levels of care are covered? Does the policy cover skilled, intermediate care, home health care and adult day care?

2. How long will the policy pay benefits? How great is the pool of money?

3. Will the policy pay for care in all settings? Nursing homes, one's own home, assisted living facilities, adult day care centers?

4. What is the minimum and maximum daily benefit that can be purchased?

5. How long is the elimination period? What is the premium relationship between various waiting periods?

6. How are pre-existing conditions defined? What are the specific policy exclusions?

7. Is there a triple-trigger definition of disability (ADLs, cognitive impairment, medical necessity)?

8. Is the policy guaranteed renewable?

This brief checklist can help you identify the key features of the policy for your clients and ensure that you are keeping up to date with the latest policy trends in the long term care marketplace.

CHAPTER NOTES

1. *Estate Planning*, "Long Term Care Insurance Helps Preserve An Estate", March/April, 1993.
2. *The Bradenton Herald*, "Long Term Care Insurance Can Bring Peace of Mind", October 27, 1995.
3. *Life Insurance Selling*, "The Leading Edge in Long Term Care Product Design", December, 1995, p. 150.
4. *The National Underwriter*, "Fortis Uses Pool of Money Approach For LTC Payouts", January 1, 1996, p. 19.
5. *Life Insurance Selling*, "The Leading Edge in Long Term Care Product Design", December, 1995, p. 150.
6. *The New York Times*, "Alzheimer's Group Finds Many Members Want Test For Risk", December 13, 1995.
7. These cases were published by the CNA Insurance Companies.
8. *The National Underwriter*, "Plan Pays Friends To Be Caregivers", June 5, 1995, p. 45.
9. For a review of the latest in long term care policy design, *Life Association News* publishes an annual survey of long term care products, usually in July.
10. *The New England Journal of Medicine*, "Long Term Care Study", February 28, 1991, p. 597.
11. *The Washington Post*, "State Regulators Target Long Term Care Insurance", 1995.
12. *The Bradenton Herald*, " Long Term Care Insurance Can Bring Peace of Mind", October 27, 1995.
13. *Life Insurance Selling*, "The Leading Edge in Long Term Care Product Design", December, 1995, p. 150.
14. *The National Underwriter*, "Expert Tells How To Evaluate Long Term Care Insurance", November 6, 1995, p. 14.

Chapter 12

THE ESSENTIAL OPTIONAL BENEFITS

The basic long term care policy does a reasonable job in providing comprehensive coverage. There are additional benefits, however, that can enhance the basic program and tailor a long term care program to an individual's specific needs. The optional benefits available in a long term care policy are few but are considered extremely important.

INFLATION PROTECTION

A study conducted by CNA Insurance Companies in December, 1991 addressed nursing home inflation. The study tracked 1,069 nursing homes over a one year period (May 1990 to May 1991). The average rate increase was seven percent. This study was similar to another study released through the Agency for Health Care Administration on nursing home rates in Florida a year later.[1]

Based on the average cost of nursing homes in a given area, a $100 a day cost today may be closer to $200 a day in ten years. If the basic policy benefit is not changed, the insured will have a $100 a day benefit to pay a $200 a day cost.

Insurance policies of every type have alternatives in keeping benefit levels from eroding due to inflation. Long term care insurance is no different. The best time to buy a long term care policy, from a premium and an insurability standpoint, is when a person is in his 50's, even though it may be many years before benefits are actually needed. It is very important to consider inflation protection as an optional feature for long term care coverage.

One alternative for providing inflation protection is to buy a much larger daily benefit amount than the average local cost of a nursing home at the time application is made. For example, if the current average nursing home rate in the area is $100 a day, the purchase of a $200 a day benefit would provide some protection against rising long term care costs for a few years. Of course, the premium would be double with this example, but if the policy is purchased early on, the cost should be affordable.

A better approach is to add an inflation rider that will automatically increase the benefit amount by a specific percentage each year. This percentage, for most companies, is fixed at five percent. The NAIC has required that this option be offered two ways: (1) increases made on a simple basis and (2) increases made on a compounded basis. This has an effect on both the daily benefit and the premium for this option. Figure 12.1 illustrates the effect of the inflation rider for a $100 a day benefit.

Figure 12.1

Policy Year	Daily Benefit (no inflation)	Simple 5% Inflation Rider	Compounded 5% Inflation Rider
1	$100	$100	$100.00
2	100	105	105.00
3	100	110	110.25
4	100	115	115.76
5	100	120	121.55
6	100	125	127.62
7	100	130	134.01
8	100	135	140.71
9	100	140	147.75
10	100	145	155.13
11	100	150	162.89
12	100	155	171.03
13	100	160	179.59
14	100	165	188.56
15	100	170	197.99
16	100	175	207.89
17	100	180	218.29
18	100	185	229.20
19	100	190	240.66
20	100	195	252.69

While differences in the daily benefit increases are more obvious in the later years, a couple of dollars difference in the early years can make a substantial difference in the daily benefit. Figure 12.2 illustrates the differences in an annual payout based on 365 days.

Figure 12.2

Year	5% Simple	5% Compounded	Annual Difference	Cumulative Difference
1	$100	$100.00	-0-	-0-
2	105	105.00	-0-	-0-
3	110	110.25	$ 91.25	$ 91.25
4	115	115.76	277.40	368.65
5	120	121.55	565.75	934.40
6	125	127.62	956.30	1,890.70
7	130	134.01	1,463.65	3,354.35
8	135	140.71	2,084.15	5,438.50
9	140	147.75	2,828.75	8,267.25
10	145	155.13	3,697.45	11,964.70
11	150	162.89	4,704.85	16,669.55
12	155	171.03	5,850.95	22,520.50
13	160	179.59	7,150.35	29,670.85
14	165	188.56	8,599.40	38,270.25
15	170	197.99	10,216.35	48,486.60
16	175	207.89	12,004.85	60,491.45
17	180	218.29	13,975.85	74,467.30
18	185	229.20	16,133.00	90,600.30
19	190	240.66	18,490.90	109,091.20

These numbers show the difference between the simple and compounding effects on increasing the daily benefit. Though the simple inflation rider provides adequate protection, the compounded inflation rider provides better coverage. However, the premium cost for the rider may influence the option selected.

A simple inflation rider will increase the premium by 25 to 30 percent or more. The compounded inflation rider option will double the simple inflation rider premium.

While the compounded inflation rider is the ultimate protection, every client should seriously consider adding the simple inflation rider. It will increase the cost somewhat, but the resulting increase in protection will be vital when the policy benefits are needed. While the cost of the compounding inflation rider is prohibitive for most, the simple inflation rider (as illustrated in Figure 12.1) is still considerably better than leaving the daily benefit on a level basis.

There may be a few inflation riders available that increase daily benefits based on the Consumer Price Index (CPI). With the CPI consistently under five percent in the last few years, and generally under the medical inflation measurements, the CPI increases will not keep pace effectively with long term care inflation. It is still better, however, than buying a level daily benefit without an option to increase the daily benefit amount.

Unlike the cost of living options available under disability income insurance policies, the inflation rider for long term care insurance increases the daily benefit each year the policy is in force. For disability insurance, the insured has to be on a claim first before any increases are made. A 50-year-old who purchases a long term care policy with an inflation benefit rider and who doesn't use the benefits for 20 years, will have 19 increases in the daily benefit amount before a claim is filed.

Generally, increases to the daily benefit under this policy are not available past the age of 85. At that point, the daily benefit stays at the attained level.

GUARANTEE OF INSURABILITY

The guarantee of insurability option increases the daily benefit at specified option dates. Also called the guaranteed purchase option, the increases can be significantly larger than the increases under the inflation option.

For example, the insured may have the option to increase a $100 daily benefit level by $25 a day or $50 a day every two or three years. This increase can be taken in one step, bringing the daily benefit to $125 a day or $150 a day. A five percent simple inflation rider would increase the daily benefit to $110 a day by the third year. The guarantee of insurability option has a notable effect on the daily benefit increase.

In addition to larger daily benefit increases, this option requires no evidence of insurability. Once the original policy is issued, there are no health questions involved when an increase in the daily benefit occurs. As the insured grows older, this option becomes more and more important.

The cost for the increases, when exercised, is based on company rates and the attained age of the insured. The additional benefit amount is subjected to new rates and the original benefit remains as issued and rated.

The insured can waive the option to increase the daily benefit only once. If, for example, an increase is scheduled every three years, the insured can exercise the option at that time or waive the option — once. In addition, these increases are not available past a certain age, usually age 80 or age 85.

The guarantee of insurability option can be an alternative to the inflation protection rider or the purchase of a higher daily benefit than needed at time of application.

RETURN OF PREMIUM

Prior to the inclusion of non-forfeiture benefits in NAIC's model policy, a few insurers offered a return of premium benefit to give individuals something in exchange for the premiums paid — especially policy benefits that were never utilized. The drawback to this option was that the policy had to be surrendered or the insured had to die before the premium was returned.

The amount of premium returned may vary depending on the language of the rider. Some insurers return all of the premiums paid beyond a certain date less any policy benefits utilized. Others may pay a stipulated percentage (30 percent, 50 percent, 80 percent) depending upon the year the insured surrenders the policy or upon the insured's death, less any claims benefits paid.

Examples of each type are:

#1:   Annual premium: $1,125.00
       Policy kept for 11 years before surrender
       No claims
       Calculation: $1,125 x 11 = $12,375 - benefits (-0-) =$12,375

#2:   Annual premium: $1,125.00
       Policy kept for 11 years before surrender
       No claims
       Percentage returned in year 11: 80%
       Calculation: $1,125 x 11 = $12,375 x 80% = $9,900 - benefits (-0-) = $9,900

The additional premium for this option is exceptionally high (50 - 100 percent more than the base policy cost) and may not be worth the money, especially if the option of selecting non-forfeiture benefits is available (see Chapter 11, Today's Basic Long Term Care Policy). An insured may be better off to take the extra money that would have been used to purchase this option and invest it in another vehicle that earns interest rather than let the insurer hold it for future payout.

The insured would collect the money if the policy is surrendered which would also leave him without coverage at an age when benefits may be needed. If the insured is changing insurers for some reason, there could be some return of premium from the original policy that can be applied to the new plan. However, any substantial return of premium would accumulate only after a number of years of the policy in force. Changing policies and paying a significantly higher premium due to the age change makes little sense despite a return of premium. The insured may be better off buying additional coverage than investing in this option.

MANAGED CARE

Although this benefit is not an option, it is worth mentioning because there are only a few insurers using this concept. A long term care claim can be a fairly complex matter. This is partly due to a variety of services and treatments provided by a number of different health care personnel.

A treatment plan may consist of a skilled nursing facility stay, follow-up treatments at home, or adult day care. To coordinate these types of care and effectively manage the claim to maximize recovery at the most efficient cost, insurers are turning to claims managers (often third party) who can meet with the insured's physician to map out a plan of care.

Flexibility is the buzz word in long term care today and the inclusion of coverage for alternate plans of care in the basic long term care policy makes the managed care approach more sensible.

Managed care eliminates the multitude of claim forms that the insured (or a family member) would have to provide the insurer. It is also clear from the beginning what the treatments consist of, when they are scheduled, and the cost. The treatment plan can be modified as necessary depending on the course taken for recovery.

Some companies attempt to establish a claims file long before any benefits are needed. For example, my mother's long term care insurer, CNA, contacted her in the second year of the policy to obtain some basic information about her that would be forwarded on to a claims manager if and when a claim occurred. Her past medical history, any current medications, her personal physician and other health preferences are already noted within her claim file to make it easier to discuss treatment plans with her doctor. Also, it does not require my mother's input which she may or may not be able to give at time of claim.

Some insurers have set up relationships with nationwide nursing home and home health care agency chains to obtain preferred rates for their long term care charges. Use of these facilities (an option) may have an advantage for the claimant if the daily benefit level normally wouldn't be high enough to cover the normal costs of care.

Managed care is an integral part of health insurance today and inevitably will be an important part of long term care insurance.

As you can see, only a few optional benefits are available with a long term care insurance policy. Some insurers may offer home health care as an optional benefit, rather than include it in the basic policy, so check to be sure that this important coverage is included.

CHAPTER NOTES

1.   *The National Underwriter*, "Nursing Home Inflation Rates", December 2, 1991, p. 25.

Chapter 13

ALTERNATE FINANCING OPTIONS USING INSURANCE

While most of the product discussion to date has centered on individual long term care policies sold on a stand-alone basis, it's important to note that there are other ways to finance the long term care risk. These additional methods utilize other forms of insurance and give consumers other choices in meeting their long term care needs.

In this chapter, the focus will be on the various hybrids of long term care coverage being marketed today. An outline of the most common benefit provisions for an individual long term care policy appears in Chapter 11, Today's Basic Long Term Care Policy. Group coverage marketed through employers, a growing long term care market, is covered in Chapter 14, The Employer-Provided Theme: Taking Care of Your Own Finances.

LIVING BENEFITS

For years insurance companies focused on death benefits and how important it was to protect against premature death, estate tax, debt settlement as well as to provide income for the surviving family members. While most people know that life insurance is an important financial tool, many dreaded reviewing these plans since the central issue was about death. There also was an emphasis on cash values which were receiving only four percent interest while the market rate was closer to 20 percent. In the late 1970s the life insurance industry was hit hard with huge losses and competitive products on the market. The shift to pure death benefit protection in the form of term insurance began in earnest. This shift significantly altered the premium flow of the life insurance industry.

Ironically, at the same time, a growing realization concerning the impact of substantial advances in medical science started to take hold. Life spans were increasing with regularity. Many were living into their 80's, especially women. The financial services industry not only had to deal with premature death but all of a sudden it was confronted with people living longer.

The new era of living benefits was ushered in. This aspect of life insurance was appealing to the insurers — what life insurance can do during one's lifetime added a positive spin to the subject. It had the same positive aspect that disability income offered — providing income during the lifetime of the policyowner. With mixed reviews on universal life insurance to ponder, the industry set about adding features to the life insurance policy that highlighted living benefits as a new approach in sales.

The first idea to be launched successfully was the accelerated death benefit concept.

Accelerated Death Benefits

The living benefits approach was based on the universal complaint of life insurance policyholders that those who suffered from a catastrophic or terminal injury or illness struggled physically and financially while a substantial death benefit was in force but inaccessible. While there was easy access to the cash value (if the policy wasn't term insurance), the amount wasn't nearly as high as the actual face amount of the policy.

An accelerated death benefit gave the policyholder access to at least a portion of the death benefit before he died. The money can be used for a variety of expenses before death actually occurs including expenses such as the cost of a nursing home stay or home health care.

The accelerated death benefit is a policy option first added to life insurance policies at an additional premium charge. Today, few, if any insurers charge for this benefit until the policyowner exercises his or her right to withdraw the money. At the time of payout, an administrative fee is assessed.

Initially, certain terminal or catastrophic illnesses such as a stroke, renal disease and heart failure qualified for accelerated death benefits.

However, many insurers today have broadened their categories to include a stay in a nursing facility or, in some cases, any type of long term care expense.

The popularity of accelerated death benefits has grown dramatically. By March 31, 1994, 18.1 million policyholders were covered by this type of living benefits rider, a stark contrast to the 1.1 million people who owned a living benefits rider in 1991. There are 215 insurers (representing 79 percent of the total life insurance in force in the country) now marketing this type of option with their life insurance products. Most insurers offer it to existing as well as new policyholders and may well have added the option to existing policies since there is no additional premium needed for this feature.[1]

Most insurers place a limitation on the amount of the withdrawal, varying from 25 to 50 percent. While a few companies will allow a higher amount (up to the entire face amount), the limits are more common.

The accelerated death benefit can be used, depending on the amount of benefit allowed, to fund long term care expenses. But at what cost to other income needs that life insurance was intended to satisfy? If the policy was purchased for example, to specifically pay estate taxes, a mortgage balance, and provide income for the family, there will be little or no money available to handle financial problems if the accelerated death benefit option is exercised to pay for long term care expenses. If long term care expenses were budgeted into the face amount calculation, then it is another way to meet one's long term care needs.

The chart below lists the number of products and the type of policies with the accelerated death benefit option:

Chart 1

Policies with Accelerated Death Benefits	1992	1994
Universal Life	80	70
Traditional Whole Life	52	68
Term	28	36
Single Premium	18	24
Other Permanent Life Policies	17	28

Source: American Council of Life Insurance & LIMRA International

The chart below indicates the number of products and conditions allowed and the portion of the policy face amount that can be withdrawn.

Chart 2

Conditions That Accelerate Death Benefit Payments	No. of products	%
Terminal illness	175	83
Dread disease	26	12
Long-term care	24	11
Permanent confinement	22	10

Source: American Council of Life Insurance & LIMRA International

The trend of offering accelerated benefits and expanding the list of conditions is increasing. As consumers consider life insurance programs, more and more they will see this feature included automatically in many of the plans.

This should not necessarily be considered a substitute for long term care insurance. Read the accelerated benefits feature carefully to ascertain the flexibility involved in using the death benefit to cover long term care expenses. If the accelerated death benefit feature is adequate, increase the death benefit by a substantial amount. This can be done by calculating the annual long term care costs and multiplying this amount by at least two (for the average length of stay of two years) and five (five year length of stay based on the *New England Journal of Medicine* report).

Long Term Care Riders

Accelerated death benefits were originally intended for terminal or catastrophic illnesses. Today, there are a number of long term care riders that are being offered as living benefits on a life insurance policy. Since many people are now considering long term care coverage in their estate planning review, it makes sense to combine the estate planning need satisfied by life insurance with an additional benefit that would solve the need for long term care.[2]

Historically, consumers do not consider buying long term care coverage before age 65. They typically associate the long term care need with retirement. By the time the coverage is sought, the premiums may be too high or the coverage unattainable due to health conditions. As noted earlier, buying long term care coverage before age 65 would result in a lower cost. Consideration of a long term care rider added to a life policy would accomplish this early purchase objective.

The need for a larger face amount in a life insurance policy usually diminishes with time — children grow up and move on, the mortgage is almost paid off and other debt is reduced. With a potential long term care need looming, the use of the larger death benefit can be applied to long term care expenses. If forced to rely on cash value, the money available may not be adequate to pay the cost of long term care services.

Some long term care riders allow direct access to the policy face amount at a stipulated percentage each year. Typically, the rider pays two percent of the face amount of the policy each month for long term care expenses. For example, a $100,000 policy would yield a $2,000 monthly payout for long term care expenses, or approximately $66 a day. Payments would continue until a policy payout limit is reached (50-75 percent of the total face amount) or the entire face amount is paid, which would take 50 months at two percent.

Initially, this type of rider paid the flat percentage of face amount out each month for a nursing home stay only, but now more and more of the long term care services previously described are eligible for this type of funding. A policy might offer a different percentage of monthly payout depending upon the type of long term care service needed. For example, a nursing home confinement yields four percent of the policy face amount each month up to 25 months, while the standard two percent payout is made for home health care or adult day care expenses. Using the example of the $100,000 policy, the nursing home monthly payout would be $4,000 per month or $133 a day, paying a major portion of the cost, while the $2,000 per month or $66 a day is better suited to the lower costs of home health care or adult day care.[3]

This option can also be enhanced by allowing an extension of benefits. In one insurer's version, after the 50 month period of paying two percent of the face amount exhausts the policy death benefit, an extension of benefits creates a continuing monthly flow of the same benefit amount for another 50 months or as long as needed. In effect, this option creates a second face amount to be similarly paid out at the conclusion of the first payout. While there is an additional cost for this benefit, it's not that high since there is, in effect, a 50 month deductible, reducing the number of people who will survive to claim this additional extension.[4] Still, with more and more people able to function (although not independently) due to advances in medical science, this option reduces or eliminates the likelihood of outliving the benefits.

A second version of this rider functions similarly to a stand-alone individual long term care policy, paying a separate daily benefit with an elimination period and benefit period. This option has its own pool of benefits and the face amount of the life policy remains untouched. The cost is much higher than the version which reduces the face amount, but it allows both coverages — life insurance and long term care — to be independent of each other while encompassing all benefits under one policy.

Tax treatment of this early payout of life insurance benefits is not entirely clear. While some private letter rulings appear favorable, no universal tax law exists governing long term care benefit payments. See Chapter 15, Taxation and Legislation Issues, for more details.

A convenient way to obtain long term care insurance and at the same time incorporate it into one's financial plan is a long term care rider in a life insurance policy. Young buyers are targeted for this type of insurance because it allows insurers to effectively spread the risk since it is more likely that the elderly will utilize this coverage in greater numbers. The ease of purchase, low cost, and better chance of eligibility make this option potentially attractive to future long term care insurance buyers.

Annuities

The growth in annuity sales for the past several years has been phenomenal. Many deferred annuity policies now contain a provision that allows the annuitant to withdraw funds, avoiding any applicable surrender charges or penalties, to pay long term care expenses.[5] Access to this money, which could represent a significant amount of retirement assets, may meet most of the long term care costs on an immediate basis depending on the amount of the annuity. If the annuitant needs care in a nursing home and there is little chance of recovery or release from the facility, these proceeds might be more appropriately used to fund the long term care need rather than funding retirement needs, generally.

Many agents and financial planners recommend variable annuities because of the product's tax deferral and potentially substantial interest rate. The interest earned may be withdrawn to pay the premium for a long term care policy. This alternative preserves the original asset, creates an alternate funding vehicle for a long term care policy and still results in a large asset that can be used to meet a variety of other needs, including retirement funding.

Since discussions about annuities often focus on retirement, what better time to talk about the serious threat of long term care that can affect retirement?

Single Premium Long Term Care

Consumers considering long term care insurance in their mid-50's to mid-60's may be in a financial position to place a large sum of money in an insurance vehicle that can serve as both a death benefit and a long term care benefit. This is the premise of single premium long term care where health coverage is wrapped in a single premium whole life policy.

The single premium whole life product lost much of its marketing edge in 1988 when the federal government introduced the concept of the modified endowment contract. Policies issued after June 20, 1988 must meet a test, termed the "seven pay" test, in order to not be labeled as a modified endowment contract. The seven pay test requires a certain level of premium be paid for a certain level of policy death benefit. A policy that does not pass the seven pay test is subject to less favorable taxation on policy distributions than a policy that does pass the test. One aspect of this less favorable taxation is that policy withdrawals made before age 59$\frac{1}{2}$ are subject to a ten percent premature distribution penalty tax.

A single premium policy will often fail the seven pay test and any policy loans and withdrawals are subject to the ten percent penalty tax. However, with the need for long term care benefits most often arising after age 59$\frac{1}{2}$, this vehicle still represents a viable financing option for long term care needs. A single premium will buy a life insurance policy that will fund both a death benefit and long term care needs. Depending upon the type of need —death or long term care — the policy will reimburse accordingly.

One insurer has a joint version of this policy where both husband and wife are insured under the program. A lump sum, usually $50,000 or more, is deposited purchasing a face amount which continues to grow as the policy earns interest. Death proceeds are paid on the second death, but the long term care benefit is paid to the first insured needing this type of service. The long term care benefit payout directly reduces the face amount of the policy, typically paying on a two percent per month basis.

Long term care benefits are an essential part of living benefits as their inclusion in a variety of life insurance and annuity policies shows. Many agents and financial planners are enjoying success in helping consumers to fund their long term care needs through life insurance rather than with individual long term care policies.

STATE PARTNERSHIPS

In the May, 1991 issue of *The Disability Newsletter*, the following statement appeared at the conclusion of an article on long term care insurance:

Many people believe that the private sector will not be able to fill the entire void (for long term care), and that the only means to address all consumer needs is some sharing of coverage between the public and private sectors. As such, the most popular scenario for the long term care market is that sometime in the late 1990s, the public sector will become more active in providing long term care coverage to our society.

The ill-fated, sweeping overhaul of the nation's health care system led by Hillary Rodham Clinton's task force was "faced down". The reality of long term care costs and coverage for this need all but eliminated the final proposed version. Current Medicare and Medicaid budget talks are almost certain to result in less long term care coverage not more.

These aforementioned statements may yet be prophetic as public and private sector cooperation has been reaching new heights with programs designed to encourage consumers to purchase long term care coverage rather than rely on Medicaid funds after assets are either spent or transferred. In 1987, the Robert Wood Johnson Foundation funded a study done by the state of Connecticut to assess the chances of a collaboration between insurers, consumers and the state to solve both the financing of long term care and the preservation of a Medicaid program, teetering on the edge of distinction. The result was the creation of the Connecticut Partnership for Long Term Care.

This partnership resulted from efforts put forth following a conclusion that the chances of the insurance industry or the government shouldering the burden of providing long term care coverage for a continually aging U.S. population was unrealistic. Private insurance would be appropriate and affordable for some, the study concluded, but would not ease the strain on the Medicaid budget created by the growing need for long term care funding for poor Americans.

Connecticut's purpose, as stated by Kevin J. Mahoney, project director for the Connecticut partnership, was to provide people with the chance to plan ahead to meet long term care needs without impoverishment and to rein in Medicaid expenditures. Connecticut estimated long term care payouts under Medicaid would reach $1.4 billion by the year 2000.

On August 28, 1991 Connecticut received formal approval from the federal government of its Long Term Care Partnership program. This was a much needed endorsement since the partnership would affect Medicaid rules. The program involved the sale of a specified state approved policy form sold by insurers, which provided long term care coverage in a lump sum amount. Upon entry into a nursing home, costs would be reimbursed from this lump sum amount until the individual recovered or the funds were exhausted. The key point here is that for every dollar of coverage paid under the policy, the insured could protect a similar dollar amount in assets that would not have to be spent or transferred to become eligible for Medicaid.

For example, a $50,000 policy paying benefits in full would enable the individual to shield an additional $50,000 of assets from Connecticut's current Medicaid rules (assets of $2,000 are allowable) without divesting assets in other ways — an obvious advantage for residents of Connecticut. The state benefits, too, since the $50,000 policy benefits must be exhausted first (including any assets over and above $50,000) before any Medicaid funding is needed. Some people will not outlive the policy benefits and thus will not file for Medicaid. Here are examples of asset sheltering:

	Personal Assets	Long Term Care Insurance Payouts	Medicaid Countable Assets
Person #1	$ 65,000	$ 65,000	-0-
Person #2	250,000	250,000	-0-
Person #3	500,000	250,000	$250,000
Person #4	500,000	-0-	500,000

Each of these individuals represent a different scenario.

- Person #1 has used the entire policy benefit and completely preserved the $65,000 assets owned without transfer. Without the partnership allowing a dollar for dollar exclusion, the assets would have had to be exhausted.

- Person #2 also accomplished the same goal but with a greater benefit need and a matching policy benefit.

- Person #3 purchased a lump sum amount below the fully countable assets. If the entire $250,000 lump sum is spent and a need for benefits still exists, $250,000 of assets are preserved and $250,000 is subjected to payout (unless already transferred) before application for Medicaid can be made.

- Person #4 chose not to participate in the partnership, leaving the full $500,000 asset base potentially exposed to Medicaid countable assets.

Since the start of Connecticut's private cooperative effort, more than 2,000 of these policies have been sold. In the first version of the policy, a 65-year-old buying a $50,000 policy would pay a premium of approximately $960 a year. Currently, there are eight insurers participating in the Connecticut Partnership program offering residents a variety of carriers to choose from. The average age of the person purchasing the coverage is 59 versus 67.5 nationwide.[6] A variety of long term care services are covered in the current policy version available.

The partnership allows for preservation of wealth — and the Medicaid program. Three other states have received funding and have started their own partnerships — Indiana, New York, and California. Five additional states — Colorado, Florida, New Hampshire, Oklahoma and Vermont — were awarded grants through the Robert Wood Johnson

Foundation to improve the financing and delivery of long term care services.[7]

VIATICAL SETTLEMENTS

A number of long term care policies contain benefits payable while receiving hospice care. Hospice care is provided for those with terminal illness. Medicare provides substantial coverage for hospice care.

Terminal illness can also necessitate the need for long term care services as part of treatment. As mentioned earlier, accelerated death benefits can be used to fund some of these expenses in the last days and months of life.

Viatical settlements is a new method used to obtain funding to pay long term costs. Derived from the word viaticum, meaning communion given to Christians who are dying, a viatical settlement arrangement calls for an exchange.[8] The terminally ill patient transfers ownership in a life insurance policy in return for a smaller amount of cash. The individual receives the much needed cash and the company bestowing the dollars receives the policy death benefit upon the death of the insured at a substantial high rate of return. Typically, the individual receives 60 to 80 cents on the dollar for the policy.

Most commonly, people with AIDS have sought viatical settlements to help fund their final months and expenses. Cancer and Alzheimer's patients have also received dollars under this type of program.

State regulators, while acknowledging that this source of funding of medical costs has been beneficial to many, are trying to find a balance between desperation and greed. Too often, these policies are exchanged for far below their value, simply because the patient sees no other way to obtain money needed for living and health care expenses. Both Washington and Texas have passed regulations concerning the registration of viatical companies and their agents.[9]

The viatical market continues to grow — over $300 million and climbing. Even an insurance carrier has an affiliation with a viatical partner. Viaticals have been seeking investors, with one recently offering 2.3 million shares for sale at an expected value of $15 per share for the purpose of raising a total of $34.5 million.[10] Those investing, however, should be cautious since a number of viatical firms have folded in recent years.

As a means of funding long term care services, viaticals may have some merit. There are a number of competent viatical firms today and, without a long term care insurance policy, the financial alternatives available to individuals who need long term care services are few. While disposal of the life insurance policy may defeat other financial objectives originally intended, a viatical settlement will mean cash when it's needed.

A person must apply for a viatical settlement (some applications are quite lengthy) and answer questions in regard to one's medical history. Obviously, the more advanced the illness, the more likely a settlement. Viatical companies don't need the money right away, but the longer the wait, the lower the investment return.

Viatical settlements are another financing alternative for long term care services. Any one of the arrangements mentioned in this chapter may be a superior alternative to an individual long term care insurance policy. This is something for the agent and the client to determine.

CHAPTER NOTES

1. *Life Association News*, "Long Term Care or Short Term Life?", November, 1995, p. 120.
2. *Business Week*, "These Insurers Are In It For The Long Haul", July 24, 1995, p.80.
3. *The National Underwriter*, "Market Mix", November 6, 1995, p. 25.
4. *The National Underwriter*, "New LTC Rider Extends The LTC Benefit Period", November 27, 1995, p. 11.
5. *The National Underwriter*, "Want LTC Alternatives? Consider These Options", September 11, 1995, p. 13.
6. *The Hartford Courant*, "In Estate Planning, Many Prepare For Long Term Care", August 20, 1995, Business, p. 81.
7. *The National Underwriter*, "Johnson Foundation Awards LTC Grants to 5 More States", 1995, p. 20.
8. *Daytona Beach News Journal*, "Middlemen Profit Most On Death Deals", Jane Bryant Quinn column, 1995.
9. *The National Underwriter*, "Washington, Texas Set Rules For Viatical Firms", December 11, 1995, p. 18.
10. *Florida Agent Magazine*, "Viaticals", November, 1995, p. 5.

Chapter 14

THE EMPLOYER-PROVIDED THEME: TAKING CARE OF YOUR OWN FINANCES

The Human Resources Department of a medium to large business usually is considered the "pulse" for knowing what is going on with the average American. Each day, employees encounter situations which usually are referred to the Human Resources Department. If there is a emerging pattern or trend, this department is bound to spot it.

The recent "boomer-echo" phenomenon, where workers in their 30's and 40's are having children, has resulted in the need for many large firms to arrange some type of day care for their employees. In so doing, life for the employees is much more convenient and the employer receives a fair amount of productivity in return.

EMPLOYEES AS CAREGIVERS

The latest trend that employers are noticing is the employee as caregiver for an aging parent or relative. According to the National Council on Aging, nearly 12 percent of the nation's workforce is currently providing assistance to elderly individuals, spending around 15 hours per week furnishing this care. Further, a study conducted by the Families and Work Institute found that the responsibility of caring for an elderly family member is emotionally and physically draining, often hampering the quality of an employee's work. The study cites the fact that 91 percent of the employee-caregivers alter their work habits, usually in a negative way.[1]

Since this affects the employer's bottom line, this type of trend generally calls for a plan of action. On-site day care centers or child care allowances helped employees with children. But would the same type of arrangement assist the caregiver of an aging parent or relative? Could employers afford a similar program for employees that are caregivers?

Compounding the problem is the unpredictable nature of adult caregiving. For example, the adult requiring assistance may not necessarily be close by. While child-rearing often brings more pleasure to the employee, adult caregiving can be depressing as one watches a parent or family member deteriorate in front of his or her eyes.

Another factor to consider is the growing shift in responsibility from employer to employee in selecting and paying for health care benefits. Medium to larger size companies — the most likely to be affected by the demands on an employee's time for adult caregiving — have largely instituted a variety of managed care health plans from which to choose. These managed care health plans range in benefit flexibility, out-of-pocket expenses and cost. Flexible benefit cafeteria plans have further shifted the responsibility of benefit choice to the employee while employers have frozen their contribution level for benefits. Moreover, in the future, retired employees will see less and less benefits from their employer. Benefits will have to be accumulated during the employee's working years.

FLEX-TIME

One solution for employees has been flex-time. This allows employees to work on a schedule that keeps them productive but also allows them the time needed to care for an aging adult. An employee at a benefits consulting firm in New Jersey acknowledged that he was overwhelmed by the medical, financial and personal tasks necessary in his caregiving role. Even seemingly simple jobs, like having enough of the proper medical devices around the house for the aging adult's use was a major task. Flex-time allowed this individual to leave the office when he had to and make up the time later on.[2]

Flex time is critical. In the Families and Work Institute study mentioned earlier, 56 percent of workers said they worried about their elderly dependents while at the office or factory. Forty-eight percent used the telephone more than usual to check up on them. Thirty-seven percent of workers were tardy due to adult caregiving responsibilities.[3] This has to affect productivity.

According to benefit consultants Hewitt and Associates, 66 percent of Fortune 500 companies offered flex-time — up from 54 percent in 1990 when flex-time was related more to child-rearing.[4] Clearly, adult caregiving responsibilities are having an affect on the workplace.

The Family and Medical Leave Act, passed in 1993, requires employers of a certain size of company to allow as many as 12 weeks of unpaid leave for the care of a seriously ill family member.[5] However, the key word here is unpaid. Many individual employees can't afford to go without a paycheck for any length of time — not even one week, let alone twelve. Some companies are more understanding and in a better financial position to help finance some time off for an employee in a caregiving situation. But the majority of firms are not.

Employers realize that flex-time alone won't solve the problem. As such, employers have begun seeking out and offering long term care insurance for their employees — many on a group basis. While most of the discussion in this book to date has centered on individual policies, the emergence of group long term care is directly related to the decreasing productivity caused by employees' growing need to take care of adult family members.

TAKE CARE OF YOUR OWN FINANCES

There is a "catch" to the long term care insurance coverage offered on a group basis. Much of it is voluntary group — employees can choose whether they want the coverage or not. The employer makes it available (usually on a lower cost basis than if the employee purchased an individual plan) and may even contribute to a portion of its cost if the employee elects the coverage. The employee however, has to pay a substantial part of the premium.

Employers are simply saying to employees — take care of your own finances. We'll help, with salary and a generous amount offered for employee benefits to be spent as the employee sees fit. But employees must choose wisely and begin to invest in their own future, too, and not rely on their employer for financial matters.

Employees, for the most part, are stretched to the limit as it is. In 1994, the national personal savings rate had dipped to 4.1 percent, an all-time low according to *Fortune* magazine. Further, the National Institute on Aging reports that most married couples would rather give the little money they do have saved to their children, not their parents.

GROUP LONG TERM CARE

Historically, group coverage predated individual policies in the insurance marketplace. Both group life and group disability were forerunners of individual policies. This is not the case with group long term care.

The individual product for long term care surfaced first. After the introduction of Medicare, a few companies led by CNA introduced nursing home coverage for skilled care on a short-term basis. The year was 1965. The first group long term care plan would not be developed until 1987.

The reason it took so long to develop a group long term care product was the claims experience needed to price a product. Group plans carry a lower premium cost than individual policies do, yet if actuaries felt uncomfortable with the pricing of an individual policy, how easy could it be to lower the premium for a group plan?

Moreover, long term care was not a primary concern in the 1960s and 70s. It is only a recent trend as the population starts to age more rapidly and has forced employees to become caregivers for the aging adult. Thus, there was no employer motivation to offer this type of coverage — there was no market demand for group long term care.

It was employers that first realized the issue of group long term care was becoming a reality. A number of large corporations, including IBM and AT&T went to insurers offering this coverage and requested the design of a group long term care policy. The problem for insurers hadn't altered much since 1965. How do you price this type of policy when the data remains scarce?

Reluctant to pursue group long term care, the earlier group policies were developed specifically for larger firms. For example, John Hancock worked with IBM's benefits team to assemble a voluntary group product. A 16 page brochure announcing the program was mailed to all employees, including an offer to receive a free videotape about the new product. In addition, premiums were published for ages 20 to 95 and were divided into three program options: $50 a day, $100 a day, and $150 a day.

A further departure from the traditional group insurance product, this voluntary program gave access to coverage not only to employees but to employee's parents and relatives. Employees that were around 25 years old felt they had little need for this product but had parents in their 50's and even grandparents in their 70's and 80's that might have an interest in this type of program. Retirees of the company also had an opportunity to buy this coverage and many seized the opportunity to purchase long term care benefits.

In February of 1991, a *New York Times* article indicated that AT&T started mailing out long term care product announcements to 119,000 managers. By this time, companies like Ford Motors, American Express, Monsanto, Proctor & Gamble, and the states of Maryland and Nevada had already ventured into the group long term care product market.

Growth in this new group market was steady in the beginning. In 1988, group long term care represented 1.8 percent of all long term care policies sold. According to the Health Insurance Association of America, by mid-1990, there were 153 employer-sponsored plans. By that time, some 700,000 employees were offered the opportunity to purchase coverage as a voluntary employee benefit. At that time, 79,500 people were covered, 60 percent of them active employees, and the balance was retirees or family members. Thus, by 1991, group long term care was up to 8.7 percent of all long term care policies sold.[6]

The number of insurers offering coverage also increased. Of the insurance companies offering individual long term care in 1988, only six percent offered group long term care coverage. By 1991, the number of companies offering group long term care was 14 percent.[7]

In 1991, group long term care sales peaked. Since then, a steady decline in results has limited further progress of this type of insurance model. Outside analysts like the Life Insurance Marketing Research Association (LIMRA) have determined the reason for the decrease in the sale of group long term care based on a couple of factors. First was the lengthy Congressional debate surrounding the Clinton national health care program. Employers were not only concerned how long term care would be affected by a national health care program, but the uncertainty of the impact on an employer's overall health care costs brought employee benefit expansion to a grinding halt. Second, there has never been a clear status about the tax ramifications of long term care coverage at all — let alone the impact of the employer providing this benefit for employees. This not only made employers reluctant to consider this coverage, it relegated group long term care to a voluntary status, with premiums paid by the employee.

The result was a four percent sales decrease in 1993 followed by a 79 percent drop in 1994.[8] Obviously, the uncertainty documented above had much to do with this reversal in the growth of group long term care.

Group long term care coverage is not going to go away. Long term care is an insurance market for the future. Group coverage will likely take a larger role if and when tax clarification of long term care results in this product being favorably treated as other health insurance programs have been.

GROUP PREMIUMS

Employer-sponsored plans are usually paid for by the employer. This is not the case with the majority of group long term care programs to date. The employee selects the plan and premium amount that best fits his situation. If the employer contributes at all, it is generally in the form of a subsidy, covering only a portion of the employee's costs.

Tax clarification remains the primary reason for the lack of employer contribution. Employee benefit dollars remain lean despite some progress in reducing health care costs through managed care type programs. Additionally, the cost of group long term care, while less expensive than individual long term care, is still higher in relation to the premiums for individual plans than group life or disability is to their individual counterparts.

A comparison of group versus individual premiums is illustrated below:

Group Versus Individual Premiums

Age 50
$100/day coverage
5 year benefit period
Inflation option included

Elimination Period	Monthly Premium	
	Individual	Group
20 days	$86.89	$50.80
60 days	82.40	49.00
100 days	77.82	47.50

While group long term care is less than individual coverage, the rate reduction borders on the 30-40 percent discount range rather than the 50-70 percent one might find in the disability income market.

Since many of the plans are voluntary, a step-by-step chart allows the employee to select the plan specifics and premium. Figure 14.1 is an example of one insurer's step-by-step guide:[9]

Figure 14.1

A GUIDE IN SELECTING A VOLUNTARY PLAN		
Steps	**Example**	**Your Premium**
Step 1: Find your current age in the following chart.	This person is age 30.	Your age: _____
Step 2: Determine the coverage you want and find the "Monthly Premium per $10 Daily Benefit".	This person wants a daily benefit of $100, a 60 day elimination period, $75 home health care option, inflation and return of premium benefits. The monthly premium per $10/day benefit is $1.98.	Your coverage: $____ daily benefit ____ elimination period ____ home health care ____ inflation ____ return of premium
Step 3. Figure your monthly premium by multiplying the amt. from Step 2 by the number of $10/day benefits you want. For example, someone who wants $40 in daily benefits would have 4 units of $10 daily benefit.	This person multiplies: $1.98 from Step 2 times 10 (for $100 in daily benefits) = $19.80 total monthly premium	$_____ (amount from Step 2) times _____ (for $_____ in daily benefits) = $_____ total monthly premium

As you can see, there is no mention of a benefit period. In this case, there was a fixed benefit period with no options to select a different period of time, shorter or longer. Group benefits are generally meant to be streamlined to a certain extent while individual products let you tailor your own program. Given the voluntary nature of group long term care it has remained more flexible than traditional group insurance — choosing an elimination period and a benefit level is not the norm in group coverage.

Since group health insurance products are allowing the employee to choose what type of coverage (HMO, PPO, POS, etc.) and how much to spend (varying co-payment and coinsurance choices) the employee benefit decision making responsibility has shifted from employers to employees.

Group long term care premiums vary dramatically with age. Since coverage is extended to retirees and employees' relatives, one can clearly see the premium relationship with age, as shown below:

Group LTC Premiums

Based on average annual premiums at selected age for varying group plans[10]

$80/day, 90 day elimination period, 5 year benefit period

AGE	ANNUAL PREMIUM
30	$ 125.00
40	176.00
50	328.00
65	1108.00
79-80	4438.00

Will the younger buyer be motivated to purchase this coverage based on the relatively few dollars that is needed? After all, younger people do utilize long term care services, even though it is on an infrequent basis.

Utilizing the benefits is of little concern to the 25-year-old. What might be more motivating is the knowledge that expenditures over a lifetime for this product, due to its low cost early on, are not as high as for those who choose to buy it at an older age.

"Buy Now" Motivation

$80/day, 60 day elimination period, 5 year benefit period

Age	Annual Premium	Years To Age 70	Total Premium Pd.	Total Benefits
25	$108.48	45	$4881.60	$219,000
35	$168.96	35	$5913.60	$219,000
45	$325.44	25	$8136.00	$219,000
55	$666.25	15	$9993.60	$219,000

Due to the lower premiums, the potential outlay over a period of time is still much lower than if one chose to wait, say, 20 years to purchase the coverage at age 45 when it seems more relevant. This chart does not factor in rate increases that may be made, but wouldn't alter the overall picture much since the rate increases at the younger ages will be made to lower premiums, lessening the impact.

The average age of the buyers for group long term care will continue to be in the age 40 to age 60 range. The policy is still an excellent buy at these ages and the sense of urgency is greater than for the younger individual early in a working career.

Rates will continue to be adjusted as insurers evaluate their group claims experience. Until more policies are sold, however, the validity of their results is still suspect. Efforts will continue to be made to attract the younger buyer, as evidenced by the long term care brochure distributed to IBM employees. Here are excerpts from the brochure on long term care:

"It seems only yesterday we looked toward adulthood as a time that was very distant, a time we could hardly imagine reaching. Yet many of us are now as old as our parents were when we were teenagers, and it doesn't seem so long ago."

"We grow, we change, we mature, and hopefully plan ahead. We build assets and investments. Then we strive to protect them against risks that could put them in jeopardy. One such risk is long term care."[11]

Insurers are clear in their message: long term care can be important irrespective of age. Protecting your income and assets is essentially what insurance is all about. Long term care is another cog in the protection wheel.

GROUP POLICY PROVISIONS

Traditionally, group coverage has maintained a streamlined approach to benefits.[12] Interviews to enroll employees into the program have typically been much shorter in length than the time one would spend with an individual for individual coverage. The employee enrollment is usually done on company time, while the individual appointment may be over a meal or the kitchen table.

As such, benefits must be easy to explain in a short period of time. Rather than give the employees a wide variety of choices that must be carefully explained, group plan parameters are often pre-set. In group life insurance, the amount is fixed at, for example, $15,000. In group disability income, the product may call for 60 percent coverage of salary, beginning on the 91st day and continuing to age 65.

Group insurance plans are not usually voluntary. Payment of premium can be made by either the employer paying the full premium, or a requirement of a certain level of participation.

Group long term care may also be streamlined, but generally the benefits are not unlike the typical individual program. Only one of the plan design choices may be pre-set. For example, the elimination period may be fixed at 30 days, but the employee can choose the daily benefit and the length of time benefits are payable. Or the benefit period is set at four years and the employee chooses the daily benefit amount and the elimination period.

Chapter 11, Today's Basic Long Term Care Policy, reviews the basic policy features found in individual policies. Many of these features also appear in group versions of the coverage, further explanation of the closer similarity in pricing between individual and group. But there are a few provisions that may be different.

Coordination of Benefits: One would be more apt to find a coordination of benefits provision in a group plan than in an individual plan. The same with long term care. Benefits in the policy are often offset by dollars received from Medicare or other group long term care plans. This primary coverage versus secondary coverage is typical of group plans.

As an example, an employee could be covered at work and also on a spouse's group long term care plan. At claim time, if the employee needed long term care, that policy at his or her place of employment would be the primary coverage and the spouse's coverage secondary, paying for costs not covered by the primary plan.

Portability: Group plans often offer a conversion privilege for employees to have the option of exercising if they should leave their place of employment. The conversion would be made to a different policy which normally is not as generous in benefits as the original plan. So far, however, group long term care plans are more likely to offer a portability rather than a conversion feature. This means the employee can elect to take the identical coverage when departing the firm and continue to pay for it on some basis other than payroll deduction.

This makes sense, especially since most of the premium is paid for by the employee. Thus, the employee in a sense already *owns* the coverage. Portability simply lets the employee keep the coverage.

COBRA requires employers to offer the continuation of health insurance coverage for terminated employees. This does not apply to long term care policies. The portability provision of many group long term care programs eliminates the need for any type of COBRA consideration.

Nonforfeiture: Since many of the larger group long term care plans are not off-the-shelf products, they contain features that a company may have specifically desired. For example, a nonforfeiture feature might allow an employee who has paid premiums for ten consecutive years and then ceases payment to retain 30 percent of the original daily benefit amount.

With the current NAIC focus on nonforfeiture benefits, this provision is likely to come up more and more in individual plans. With the group plans individually designed in the 1980's, some of them already have this consumer-oriented feature.

SUMMARY

A recent study by William Mercer revealed that 72 percent of employers regard long term care as an extension of their employee health care coverage. Ninety-three percent say protecting employee and retiree financial security is an important objective in offering group long term care benefits, while 80 percent believe it will encourage employees and retirees to plan their financial future.

Employers want employees and retirees to take control of their own finances. Combining a 401(k) plan with a group long term care plan is a significant step in shifting responsibility for financial security retirement to the employee. The 401(k) plan, a popular retirement program, allows the employees to build up substantial amounts of retirement income. Long

term care is the protection of the retirement income from the high cost of
health care services, most often needed during the retirement years.

CHAPTER NOTES

1. *Health Line*, American Political Network, Inc. "Elder Care", August 23, 1995.
2. *The New York Times*, "Need Extra Care For An Aging Parent? Maybe the Boss Can
    Help" August 20, 1995.
3. *Health Line*, American Political Network, Inc., "Elder Care", August 23, 1995.
4. *The New York Times*, "Need Extra Care For An Aging Parent? Maybe the Boss Can
    Help" August 20, 1995.
5. *The Dallas Morning News*, "As Parents Age, Policies Change", Workplace Issues,
    August 31, 1995.
6. Data from the Health Insurance Association of America's annual review of long term
    care insurance.
7. HIAA data.
8. *The National Underwriter*, "Group Long Term Care Sales And In-Force", June 5,
    1995, p. 7.
9. This guide is from the Principal Financial Group's long term care offering in the
    employer-employee market.
10. Health Insurance Association of America data.
11. From the IBM/John Hancock Long Term Care Insurance Program for Employees and
    Retirees, 1990.
12. *Life Association News*, "Group LTC Insurance Finally Comes of Age", July, 1995,
    p. 106.

Chapter 15

TAXATION AND LEGISLATION ISSUES

Aside from health insurance, long term care insurance, with its short history, has been the most heavily regulated product in the industry. Life insurance, annuities, disability income — none of these coverages has been scrutinized the way long term care insurance has been.

Much of the attention is due to the fallout from the industry's Medicare supplement fiasco. This disaster taught state insurance departments to be over-protective when it comes to any products that affect seniors. There is no sense in provoking a Congressional push to take over regulation of the insurance industry. The McCarran-Ferguson Act (state regulation) can easily be repealed by a Congress unified in its efforts.

The regulation, driven primarily by the National Association of Insurance Commissioners (NAIC) is product oriented. As outlined earlier in this book, attention focused on eliminating "gatekeepers" — caveats that can cut down on filed claims considerably. While this has been helpful in making products both useful and competitive, a key ingredient — tax clarification — is missing and prevents long term care from claiming a serious share of the insurance marketplace.

TAXES

To date, the Internal Revenue Code does not directly address the tax consequences of a long term care product. Health insurance and disability income have fairly clear guidelines. There are no guidelines for the issues concerning long term care insurance such as:

1. whether premiums would be deductible if the employer pays the costs of long term care insurance;

2. whether long term care insurance benefits would be taxable or received income tax free; and

3. whether long term care insurance could be incorporated in a Section 125 plan (flexible benefit cafeteria plan) allowing premiums paid by the employee to be paid a pre-tax basis.

This situation could easily be rectified by Congress who has the power to alter the Internal Revenue Code. There have been tax proposals circulating on this product for at least a decade. At various times, Congress has been considering these actions:

1. income tax credits to families caring for someone with long term care needs in the home;

2. allowing premiums for private long term care insurance to be tax deductible as a medical expense;

3. making long term care insurance benefits income tax free; and

4. allowing tax free distributions from Individual Retirement Arrangements (IRAs) and 401(k) retirement plans for people age 60 or older to buy long term care insurance.[1]

5. allowing long term care premiums to be deductible to self-employed persons up to a limit of 30 percent.

With a Republican controlled Congress currently debating these issues, there is a strong possibility some action will be taken. Given President Clinton's present position as a defender of seniors' benefits, he has his own incentives for seeing this type of legislation passed.

Early in 1995, the House Ways and Means Committee approved tax cuts that included a section providing favorable tax clarification for long term care insurance. (See also the Conference Committee Report on H.R. 2491, The Revenue Reconciliation Act of 1995.) It would cost the government an extra $5.3 billion at a time when balancing the budget is of primary importance. The clarification includes treating long term care insurance as health and accident insurance for purposes of the tax code, meaning employer provided long term care benefits would be received income tax free by employees subject to an overall limit. Benefits payable under a long term care policy, in general, would be income tax free and premiums subject to certain limitations paid could be deductible under Section 213 (as medical expenses to the extent they exceed 7.5 percent of adjusted gross income). The clarification however, would not allow long term care to be part of a Section 125 cafeteria plan.[2]

In the Senate, the Medicare Consumer Protection Act, the latest in a long line of bills concerning Medicare and long term care insurance, contained language clarifying the tax status of long term care. It also focused on non-duplication of benefits between private insurance and Medicare. This is in direct conflict with edicts from the Health Care Financing Administration (HCFA), Medicare's administrative arm. The HCFA interpreted a 1994 law as saying it was illegal to coordinate benefits with Medicare and any long term care insurance policy that does have a non-duplication provision is not valid.[3] HCFA has always supported legislation that makes Medicare secondary to private insurance. The non-duplication terminology appears in Chapter 11, Today's Basic Long Term Care Policy.

The only comments the Internal Revenue Service has formally delivered on the subject of long term care insurance came in Private Letter Ruling 9106050 issued in 1991 concerning the tax treatment of universal life policies that have a long term care rider attached (see Chapter 13, Alternate Financing Options Using Insurance, for more details on this type of benefit). The long term care rider cited in the private letter ruling was funded through a monthly charge to the policy cash value covering the cost of confinement in a convalescent facility and a period of home care.

The private letter ruling is laden with technical language as complicated as the code itself. Essentially, a policy will fail to qualify as life insurance for federal tax purposes if premiums are excessive relative to the level of death benefit protection afforded by the policy. In determining this, the IRS evaluates all future benefits of the policy including death and endowment benefits and certain qualified additional benefits like waiver of premium, AD&D, guaranteed insurability and other similar riders. This private letter ruling did not consider a long term care rider to be a qualified additional benefit.

This meant that the presence of a long term care rider on a universal life insurance policy did not have any effect on its evaluation as life insurance for federal income tax purposes. Further, this private letter ruling noted that any extra premium paid for a long term care insurance rider will increase the policyholder's investment in the contract for purposes of determining the taxation of distributions from a life insurance policy. When cash value is reduced to cover the cost of the rider, the payment will not be treated as a taxable distribution unless and until the amount paid exceeds the taxpayer's investment in the contract.[4]

A private letter ruling applies only to the individual or entity to whom the letter is addressed. It is not meant to be a broad interpretation of the IRS on a particular subject. To find out how the IRS views a specific policy, a request should be made for a private letter ruling.

Tax issues still remain cloudy as the clarification of taxation of long term care insurance premiums and proceeds is being discussed in current negotiations in Washington, D.C.

LEGISLATION

In 1990, the Pepper Commission (led by senior Claude Pepper of Florida), a bipartisan group formed to review access to health care and long term care for all Americans, published its findings and recommendations. One proposal that emerged from this study was to cover the first three months of a nursing home stay through a public entitlement fund without regard to income. While this was an improvement over Medicare's current coverage, this type of recommendation would not presently survive in the face of today's discussions over balancing the budget, some six years later.

A second recommendation was to cover the cost of care after the first two years of a nursing home stay. In effect, this was a government funded nursing home plan with a two year elimination period. While this proposal might receive more consideration, most new programs that involve disbursement of benefits are not likely to survive budget negotiations.

The future of both Medicare and Medicaid hangs in the balance on Capitol Hill today. Before 1996 is over, resolution should be reached and most likely it will take the form of a compromise. It seems unlikely the two sides will completely agree on the proposed packages being debated. The contrast in both side's arguments can be seen in the following comments:

Representative Henry Waxman — Democrat, California:

"Republican proposals to cutback Medicare payments will destroy Medicare in a few short years because many doctors will decide not to take Medicare patients at the lower payment rates."

Speaker of the House, Newt Gingrich — Republican, Georgia:

"Think about a party whose last stand is to frighten 85-year-olds and you'll understand how totally morally bankrupt the modern Democratic Party is."[5]

Congress is on the verge of landmark legislation concerning a balanced budget and it's unrealistic to expect it to pass both the House and the Senate and secure a presidential signature without a substantial amount of debate. There are a number of broad issues to be worked out in which both parties have historically taken opposite positions. There are decisions inside this bill that will affect Americans for decades and any changes considered should take time.

How will long term care issues fare in the face of this historic debate? Some Republicans' Medicare proposals include requiring a 20 percent co-payment on the part of the senior citizen for both nursing home and, more importantly, home health care benefits where Medicare has been more liberal in its reimbursements.[6] If a senior chose a Health Maintenance Organization instead of the typical indemnity Medicare plan, expanded nursing home and home health care benefits with little out-of-pocket costs involved could save seniors thousands of dollars — as long as they utilized the providers within the scope of the HMO. Traditionally, seniors have objected to having to select from a list of providers.

While both Republicans and Democrats have been unable to agree so far, there is plenty of expectation that the final budget compromise reached will finally include clarification of the tax treatment of long term care insurance and long term care expenses. There is broad bipartisan support for these regulations and both sides need issues they can agree on first before resolving some of the more tricky issues. While there is a price tag on these clarifications (the $5.3 billion in lost revenue earlier noted), the concern about the cost is tempered by the potential savings to Medicare brought about by a greater reliance on private long term care insurance.[7] The greater the presence of long term care insurance, the more likely future expenditures in both Medicare and Medicaid will be reduced. While the numbers cannot yet be quantified, both sides agree on this underlying principle.

Insurers know that tax clarification can only help with long term care sales, especially in the sagging employer-employee market.[8] If all long term care premiums are allowed as a deductible expense, sales would undoubtedly soar. While the future of long term care insurance isn't totally in the hands of Congress, the path will definitely be marked by legislative action.

CHAPTER NOTES

1. *The Bradenton Herald*, "Long Term Care Insurance", October 22, 1995, p. 1.
2. *Legislative Report*, Association of Health Insurance Agents, March 21, 1995, HLR 95-7.
3. *LTC Update*, published by the CNA Companies, September 1995, Issue 9.
4. *Washington Report*, Association for Advanced Life Underwriting, Bulletin No. 91-22, February 19, 1991.
5. *The New York Times*, "GOP Announces Plan To Overhaul Medicare System", September 15, 1995.
6. *The Wall Street Journal*, "Senate Republicans Overhaul Would Mean Higher Fees For Recipients", September 13, 1995.
7. Infax alert from William M. Mercer, Inc., releases December 1, 1995, entitled "Long Term Care Insurance Under the Budget Bill".
8. *The National Underwriter*, "LTC Companies Expecting Tax Changes To Fuel Sales", December 4, 1995, p. 7.

Chapter 16

SUMMARY: THE AGENT'S CHECKLIST

The long term care product is burdened with risk for the insurance agent. Despite rigid NAIC regulation, there can be significant differences within a policy's definitions, benefits and features. It is imperative for the agent and financial planner to carefully review the complete policy specifications before making any recommendations.

Don't get caught in the "premium trap". Selling low premiums can create several difficulties:

1. Benefits may not be as strong as claimed, which the client won't discover until filing for benefits.

2. The insurer may be forced to raise premiums significantly later on, turning the policy from a bargain to unaffordable — perhaps at the very time the client may need the policy benefits. This has already happened in the industry — be careful! To assist in the evaluation of specific policy features, Figure 16.1, a policy checklist, focuses on key policy issues.

In addition to evaluating the policy, it is important to evaluate the insurance company standing behind the product. How long has the insurer been selling long term care insurance? Does the company sell other health insurance products? What is its current experience with long term care claims? What are the company's financial ratings?

Financial ratings are available from several sources — A.M. Best, Standard & Poor's, Moody's, and Duff & Phelps. One of the problems in using all of these analysts' ratings is that they differ in identification. Figure 16.2 will assist in categorizing these ratings:

If a company has been assigned some type of "A" rating, there is a certain comfort level about its future ability to meet policyholder obliga-

Figure 16.1

POLICY CHECKLIST

Feature   Policy _____

1. Elimination Period

2. Benefit Period
        Years
        Pool of Money

3. Specified Daily Benefit
        Indemnity
        Actual Cost

4. Covered Services   Amount of each:
        Nursing Home   _____
        Home Health Care   _____
        Adult Day Care   _____
        Assisted Living Facility Care   _____
        Respite Care   _____
        Hospice Care   _____
        Bed Reservation Benefit   _____
        Medical Help Benefit   _____

Definitions
        Triple Trigger?
                Activities of Daily Living
                        Bathing included?
                        Dressing included?
                Cognitive Impairment
                Medical Necessity
        Renewability Provision
        Pre-existing conditions

Additional Benefits
        Waiver of Premium
                Commencement?
                Waived when receiving what care?
        Inflation
                Simple or compound?
                Interest percentage?
                Any limit on increases?
        Return of Premium
                When?
                Does policy continue?

Does the insurer make retroactive product enhancements?

Spouse Discount?

Restoration of Benefits?

Figure 16.2

QUALITY FINANCIAL RATINGS				
Description of Rating	**A.M. Best**	**Standard & Poor's**	**Moody's**	**Duff & Phelps**
Superior	A++, A+	AAA	Aaa	AAA
Excellent	A, A-	AA+, AA, AA-	Aa1, Aa2, Aa3	AA+, AA, AA-
Very Good	B++, B+	A+, A, A-	A1, A2, A3	A+, A, A-
Good	B, B-	BBB+, BBB BBB-	Baa1, Baa2, Baa3	BBB+, BBB BBB-
Fair	C++, C+	BB+, BB, BB-	Ba1, Ba2, Ba3	BB+, BB, BB-
Marginal	C, C-	B+, B, B-	B1, B2, B3	B+, B, B-
Highly Vulnerable		CCC, CC	Caa, Ca, C	CCC+, CCC CCC-
Below Minimum Standards	D	C, D		
Under State Supervision	E			
In Liquidation	F			

tions. The "A" ratings should be consistent, however, among the rating services. The "B" ratings with A.M. Best for example, should be evaluated carefully and companies carrying this rating should only be used, in my opinion, when there is an accompanying "A" rating from other services.

In addition to a policy evaluation, the consumer could request information from the insurance agent or financial planner regarding community resources and additional details on long term care providers and facilities. In addition to doing your own research in your local area, Figure 16.3 is a checklist of outside services and potential support systems within a community or state.

Adult caregivers may ask you for information relating to any of these subjects. Keeping a file of resource material will give you a value-added service that many agents and financial planners may not offer.

Figure 16.3

SERVICES CHECKLIST	
Service Needed	**Resources**
Elder social programs and volunteering	Senior centers, day care, nutrition sites, senior companions, YMCA/YWCA, AARP talent bank
Chore Services	Local aging social services, area churches or synagogues, fraternal orders, youth groups, neighborhood organizations
Elder Law	Elder law attorneys, local bar association, Legal Aid, banks
Bereavement support	Church and synagogue groups, AARP Widowed Persons Service, National Assoc. of Military Widows
Transportation	City elderly transportation services, handicapped transportation services, Red Cross, churches or synagogues
Housing	Retirement communities, public housing, foster homes, intermediate and skilled care facilities, nursing homes, house sharing, group homes, American Association of Homes For the Aged
Homemaker Services	Visiting Nurse Association, Social service agencies, private homemakers, Red Cross
Home Health/Personal Care	Home health care agencies, Visiting Nurses Association, Red Cross, private duty nurses, public health nurses
Nutrition	Meals on Wheels, Nutrition sites at senior centers, Home-delivered meals, Weekend meals programs
Adult-sitting	Adult day care centers, Live-in attendants, social service agencies, foster homes
Handicapped services	Disease-specific organizations (American Cancer Society, for example), local office administering Americans With Disabilities Act
Mental Health	City Mental Health Department, geriatric social workers, Alzheimer's association, crisis intervention units, psychiatric hospitals
Hospice	Hospice Association, Visiting Nurses Assoc., Cancer Society, local church or synagogue, local hospital social services department

Figure 16.4 lists national information hotlines that can assist you in building a resource library.

Figure 16.4

INFORMATION HOTLINES	
The U.S. Public Health Care Service in Maryland:	1-800-336-4797 1-301-565-4167
Elder Care Locator	1-800-677-1116
Family Caregiver Alliance	1-800-445-8106
Medicare	1-800-638-6833
National Health Information Center	1-800-336-4797
National Clearinghouse for Alcohol & Drug Info.	1-800-729-6686
National Institute on Aging	1-800-222-2225
Alzheimer's Association	1-800-272-3900
Alzheimer's Disease Education & Referral Ctr.	1-800-438-4380
Arthritis Foundation	1-800-283-7800
American Cancer Society Response Line	1-800-227-2345
Depression Awareness	1-800-421-4211
American Diabetes Association	1-800-232-3472
Well Spouse Foundation	1-800-838-0879

In addition to telephone resources and pamphlets that can be obtained from these organizations, there are a number of books available which address caregiving and elder care. Recently, former President Jimmy Carter's wife, Rosalyn, published a book about taking care of aging parents, giving a high profile to the long term care issue. Entitled "Helping Others", it was published in 1994 to some acclaim. Other titles which may be of interest:

> 1. 1994 — Weisheit, Eldon, *Aging Parents* (Lion), subtitle: When Mom and Dad Can't Live Alone Anymore.

2. 1993 — Heath, Angela, *Long-Distance Caregiving* from the Working Caregiver series published by (American Source), subtitle: A Survival Guide For Far Away Caregivers.

3. 1992 — Smith, Kerri S., *Caring For Your Aging Parents* from the Working Caregiver series published by (American Source), subtitle: A Sourcebook of Timesaving Techniques and Tips.

4. 1991 — Abel, Emily K., *Who Cares For the Elderly?* (Temple University Press), subtitle: Public Policy and the Experiences of Adult Daughters.

5. Moskowitz, Francine & Robert, *Parenting Your Aging Parents* (Key Publications), subtitle: Guidance Through the Family Nightmare of the 90's.

6. 1988 — Anderson-Ellis, Eugenia, *Aging Parents and You* (Master Media), Revised and updated in 1993.

Finally, one of the best resources for elder care information are the various state agencies on aging (see Appendix B). These departments maintain a lot of information from nursing home costs to ratings of long term care providers and can refer you to the appropriate local contacts.

Working in the long term care market can be a very productive and rewarding experience. You may be encountering some of the issues discussed in this book within your own family. Remember that the key to being successful in this market is to recognize both the emotional and technical aspects of the sale. Many situations are delicate at best and it will take a few sales interviews to understand the variety of potential circumstances that can surround the long term care issue. Continue to read and keep up with the latest information, both social and product. Finally, budget resolutions on Capitol Hill should bring good news concerning the tax status of long term care.

Developing clients in this market will keep you in good stead for some time to come. Unquestionably, long term care is an insurance market with a future.

CHAPTER NOTES:

Resource information used in this chapter derived from:

1. *Health Benefits Planning Guide For Seniors*, compiled by Phyllis R. Shelton.
2. *Miles Away and Still Caring*, An AARP Guide for Long Distance Caregivers.
3. *The Sandwich Generation*, Issue 1, 1995.

Appendix A

COMPANIES SELLING LONG-TERM CARE INSURANCE
(as of January 1995)

Reprinted with permission of the Health Insurance
Association of America

Company names that are italicized are affiliates or subsidiaries of the company above them. (Unless otherwise noted, all companies listed below provide an individual and/or group association plan.)

Aetna Life & Casualty[1]
Aid Association for Lutherans[2]
Allianz Life Insurance Company of North America[3]
Allied Life Insurance Company
American Family Life Assurance Company of Columbus
American Independent Insurance Company
American Physicians
American Republic Insurance Company
American Travellers Life Insurance Company
AMEX Life Assurance Company
American Centurion Life & Accident Assurance Co.
Bankers Life and Casualty Company
Banner Life Insurance Company[4]
Beneficial Life Insurance Company[4]
C.S.A. (subsidiary of Blue Cross and Blue Shield of Arizona)
Blue Cross and Blue Shield of Connecticut, Inc.[3]
Blue Cross and Blue Shield of Delaware
ALLNATION Life Insurance Company (subsidiary of Blue Cross and Blue Shield of Delaware)
Blue Cross and Blue Shield of Florida

Hawaii Medical Service Association[3]
Blue Cross and Blue Shield of Indiana
Blue Cross and Blue Shield of Iowa
Blue Cross and Blue Shield of Kansas, Inc.
Southeastern United Agency[3] (subsidiary of Blue Cross and Blue Shield of Kentucky)
Blue Cross and Blue Shield of Maryland, Inc.
MedAmerica Insurance Company[3]
Medical Life Insurance Company[3]
Blue Cross and Blue Shield of Minnesota[3]
Blue Cross and Blue Shield of Missouri
Blue Cross and Blue Shield of Montana
Blue Cross and Blue Shield of the National Capitol Area[3]
Corporate Diversified Services, Inc. (subsidiary of Blue Cross and Blue Shield of Nebraska)
Combined Services, Inc. (subsidiary of Blue Cross and Blue Shield of New Hampshire)
Finger Lakes Long Term Care Insurance Company[3] (subsidiary of Blue Cross and Blue Shield of Rochester, New York)

Group Insurance Services (subsidiary of
   Blue Cross and Blue Shield of North
   Carolina)
Blue Cross and Blue Shield of North
   Dakota
Consumer Services Casualty Insurance
   Company (subsidiary of Blue Cross of
   Western Pennsylvania)
Capital Blue Cross (Harrisburg, Pennsyl-
   vania)
Independence Blue Cross (Philadelphia,
   Pennsylvania)
Group Services, Inc. (subsidiary of Blue
   Cross and Blue Shield of Utah)
Blue Cross and Blue Shield of Virginia[3]
Blue Cross of Washington and Alaska
King County Medical Blue Shield
   (Seattle, Washington)
Mountain State Blue Cross and Blue
   Shield (West Virginia)
Blue Cross and Blue Shield of Wyoming
Business Men's Assurance Company[4]
Calfarm Life Insurance Company[4]
CIGNA Corporation[1]
Continental Casualty Company (CNA)[3]
Continental General Insurance Company[2]
Continental Western Life Insurance
   Company[4]
Country Life Insurance Company
Employers Modern Life Insurance
   Company[4]
Equitable Life and Casualty Company
Equitable Life Insurance Company of
   Iowa[4]
Executive Fund Life Insurance Company
*National Executive Fund Insurance
   Company*
Pennsylvania Life Insurance Company
Federal Home Life Insurance Company
Harvest Life Insurance Company
First Penn Pacific Life Insurance
   Company[4]
Golden Rule Life Insurance Company[4]
Grange Life Insurance Company[4]
Great Fidelity Life Insurance Company
Great Republic Insurance Company
Guarantee Trust
IDS Life Insurance Company

*IDS Life Insurance Company of New
   York*
Interstate Assurance Company[4]
ITT Hartford Life and Annuity Insurance
   Company[4]
John Alden Life Insurance Company
John Hancock Mutual Life Insurance
   Company[3]
Kansas City Life Insurance Company[4]
Life and Health Insurance Company of
   America
Life Insurance Company of Georgia
Life Investors Insurance Company of
   America
Bankers United Life Assurance Company
Monumental Life Insurance Company
PFL Life Insurance Company
Lincoln National Life Insurance
   Company[2]
Lutheran Brotherhood
Medico Life Insurance Company
Mutual Protective Insurance Company
Metropolitan Life Insurance Company[5]
Mutual of Omaha[3]
National States Life Insurance Company
National Travelers Life Company[4]
Nationwide Life Insurance Company[4]
New York Life Insurance Company
Penn Treaty Insurance Company
*Network American Life Insurance
   Company*
Physicians Mutual Insurance Company
Pioneer Life Insurance Company of
   Illinois
The Principal Financial Group
Provident Life and Accident Insurance
   Company
Prudential Insurance Company of
   America[3]
Pyramid Life Insurance Company
Reliance Standard
Security Mutual Life Insurance Company
   of Lincoln, Nebraska[4]
Sentry Life Insurance Company[3]
Shelter Life Insurance Company[4]
Standard Life & Accident Insurance
   Company
Sunset Life Insurance Company[4]

Teachers Insurance and Annuity Association[3]
Time Insurance Company[2]
Transamerica Assurance[4]
Transamerica Occidental Life Insurance Company
Transport Life Insurance
The Travelers Insurance Company
United American Insurance Company
Union Bankers Insurance Company

United Farm Bureau Family Insurance Company[4]
United Security Assurance Company of Pennsylvania
UNUM Life Insurance Company[6]
US Life Corporation[4]
All American Life Insurance Company[4]
Old Line Life Insurance Company[4]
Westfield Life Insurance Company[4]

---

1. Provides an employer-sponsored plan only.
2. Provides an individual plan and a plan offered as part of a life insurance policy.
3. Provides an individual and employer-sponsored plan.
4. Provides a plan offered as part of a life insurance policy only.
5. Provides an employer-sponsored plan and a plan offered as part of a life insurance policy.
6. Provides an individual plan, employer-sponsored plan, and coverage to members of a continuing care retirement community.

Sources: Health Insurance Association of America and Blue Cross and Blue Shield Association.

Appendix B

STATE AGENCIES ON AGING

Alabama
Commission on Aging
770 Washington Avenue, Suite 470
Montgomery, AL 36130
1-800-243-5463 (in state)
(205) 242-5743

Alaska
Older Alaskans Commission
P.O. Box C MS 0209
Juneau, AK 99811
(907) 465-3250

Arizona
Department of Economic Security
Aging and Adult Administration
1789 W. Jefferson Street
Phoenix, AZ 85007
(602) 542-4446

Arkansas
Division of Aging & Adult Services
Donaghey Plaza South Suite 1417
P.O. Box 1417/Slot 1412
Little Rock, AR 72203
(501) 682-2441

California
Department of Aging
1600 K Street
Sacramento, CA 95814
(916) 322-3887

Colorado
Aging and Adult Services
Department of Social Services
1575 Sherman St., 10th Floor
Denver, CO 80203-1714
(303) 866-3851

Connecticut
Department on Aging
175 Main Street
Hartford, CT 06106
(800) 443-9946 (in state)
(203) 566-7772

Delaware
Division of Aging
Dept. of Health & Social Services
11901 DuPont Highway
New Castle, DE 19720
(302) 577-4660

District of Columbia
Office on Aging
1424 K Street, NW, 2nd Floor
Washington, DC 20005
(202) 724-5626 or 5622

Florida
Office of Adult & Aging Services
1317 Winewood Boulevard
Building 2, Room 323
Tallahassee, FL 32399
(904) 488-8922

Georgia
Office of Aging
Department of Human Resources
878 Peachtree St. NE, Room 632
Atlanta, GA 30309
(404) 894-5333

Idaho
Office on Aging
Statehouse, Room 108
Boise, ID 83720
(208) 334-3833

Indiana
Department of Human Services
402 W. Washington St.
P.O. Box 7083
Indianapolis, IN 46207
(317) 232-7020

Kansas
Department on Aging
122-S Docking State Office Bldg.
915 SW Harrison
Topeka, KS 66612-1500
(913) 296-4986

Louisiana
Governor's Office of Elderly Affairs
4550 N. Boulevard
P.O. Box 80374
Baton Rouge, LA 70898
(504) 925-1700

Maryland
State Agency on Aging
301 W. Preston St., Room 104
Baltimore, MD 21201
(401) 225-1102

Michigan
Office of Services to the Aging
611 W. Ottawa St.
P.O. Box 30026
Lansing, MI 48909
(517) 373-8230

Hawaii
Executive Office on Aging
335 Merchant St., Room 241
Honolulu, HI 96813
(808) 586-0100

Illinois
Department on Aging
421 E. Capitol Avenue
Springfield, IL 62701
(217) 785-2870

Iowa
Department of Elder Affairs
Jewett Bldg., Suite 236
914 Grand Avenue
Des Moines, IA 50309
(515) 281-5187

Kentucky
Division of Aging Services
Department of Social Services
275 E. Main Street
Frankfort, KY 40621
(502) 564-6930

Maine
Bureau of Elder & Adult Services
35 Anthony Ave., Station 11
Augusta, ME 04333
(207) 624-5335

Massachusetts
Executive Office of Elder Affairs
1 Ashburton Place, 5th Floor
Boston, MA 02108
1-800-882-2003 (in state)
(617) 727-7750

Minnesota
Minnesota Board on Aging
Human Services Building 4th Floor
444 Lafayette Road
St. Paul, MN 55155-3843
(612) 296-2770

Mississippi
Council on Aging
455 N. Lamar Street
Jackson, MS 39202
1-800-345-6347 (in state)
(601) 359-6770

Montana
Governor's Office on Aging
State Capitol Bldg., Room 219
Helena, MT 59620
1-800-332-2272 (in state)
(406) 444-3111

Nevada
Department of Human Resources
Division for Aging Services
340 N. 11th St., Suite 114
Las Vegas, NV 89101
(702) 486-3545

New Jersey
Department of Community Affairs
Division on Aging
S. Broad and Front Sts., CN 807
Trenton, NJ 08625-0807
1-800-792-8820 (in state)
(609) 292-0920

New York
State Office for the Aging
2 Empire State Plaza
Albany, NY 12223-0001
1-800-342-9871 (in state)
(518) 474-5731

North Dakota
Department of Human Services
Aging Services Division
State Capitol Building
Bismarck, ND 58507-7070
(701) 224-2577

Missouri
Division on Aging
Department of Social Sciences
615 Howerton Court
P.O. Box 1337
Jefferson, MO 65102-1337
(314) 751-3082

Nebraska
Department on Aging
State Office Building
301 Centennial Mall South
Lincoln, NE 68509
(402) 471-2306

New Hampshire
Department of Health & Human
Services; Division of Elderly &
Adult Services
6 Hazen Street
Concord, NH 03301
(603) 271-4680

New Mexico
Agency on Aging
La Villa Rivera Bldg.,
224 E. Palace Avenue, 1st Floor
Santa Fe, NM 87501
1-800-432-2080 (in state)
(505) 827-7640

North Carolina
Department of Human Resources
Division of Aging
693 Palmer Drive
Raleigh, NC 27626-0531
(919) 733-3983

Ohio
Department of Aging
50 W. Broad Street, 8th Floor
Columbus, OH 43266-0501
(614) 466-1221

Oklahoma
Department of Human Services
Aging Services Division
312 NE 28th Street
Oklahoma City, OK 73125
(405) 521-2327

Pennsylvania
Department of Aging
231 State Street
Barto Building
Harrisburg, PA 17101
(717) 783-1550

Rhode Island
Department of Elderly Affairs
160 Pine Street
Providence, RI 02903
(401) 277-2858

South Dakota
Agency on Aging
Richard F. Kneip Bldg.
700 Governor's Drive
Pierre, SD 57501
(605) 773-3656

Texas
Department on Aging
Capitol Station
P.O. Box 12786
940 U.S. Rte. 35 South
Austin, TX 78741
(512) 444-2727

Vermont
Office on Aging
Waterbury Complex
103 S. Main Street
Waterbury, VT 05671-2301
(802) 241-2400

Oregon
Department of Human Resources
Senior Services Division
500 Summer St. NE, 2nd Floor
Salem, OR 97310
1-800-232-2020 (in state)
(503) 378-4728

Puerto Rico
Governor's Office of Elderly Affairs
Gericulture Commission
Box 11398
Santurce, PR 00910
(809) 722-2429

South Carolina
Commission on Aging
400 Arbor Lake Drive
Suite B-500
Columbia, SC 29223
(803) 735-0210

Tennessee
Commission on Aging
706 Church Street
Suite 201
Nashville, TN 37243-0860
(615) 741-2056

Utah
Division of Aging & Adult Services
120 North 200 West
P.O. Box 45500
Salt Lake City, UT 84103
(801) 538-3910

Virginia
Department for the Aging
700 Centre, 10th Floor
700 E. Franklin Street
Richmond, VA 23219-2327
1-800-552-4464 (in state)
(804) 225-2271

Washington
Aging & Adult Services Administration
Department of Social & Health Services
12th and Jefferson Sts.
Mail Stop OB-44-A
Olympia, WA 98504
(206) 586-3768

Wisconsin
Bureau on Aging
Department of Health & Social Services
P.O. Box 7851
217 S. Hamilton St., Suite 300
Madison, WI 53707
(608) 266-2536

West Virginia
Commission on Aging
State Capitol Complex
Holly Grove
Charleston, WV 25305
(304) 558-3317

Wyoming
Division on Aging
Hathaway Bldg.
2300 Capitol Ave., Room 139
Cheyenne, WY 82002
1-800-442-2766 (in state)
(307) 777-7986

Appendix C

SAMPLE OUTLINE
LONG TERM CARE COVERAGES

NOTE: This is a sample outline of the coverages offered under a typical long term care policy. It does not represent the coverage offered by any single company or policy and is intended for instructional purposes only.

1. This policy is an individual policy of insurance.

2. **PURPOSE OF OUTLINE OF COVERAGE -** This outline provides a brief description of the important features of the policy. You should compare this outline to other outlines of coverage for other policies which are available. This is not a contract of insurance, but only a summary of coverage. Only the actual policy contains governing contractual provisions. It is the actual policy which sets forth in detail the rights and obligations of both you and the insurance company. Therefore, if you purchase this coverage or any other coverage you should read your policy carefully.

3. **TERMS UNDER WHICH THE POLICY MAY BE RETURNED AND THE PREMIUM REFUNDED -** If, for any reason, you are not satisfied with your policy it can be returned within 30 days to either our Home Office or to the agent from whom it was purchased. You will receive a refund of any premium that you have paid. Except for a refund of any premium paid beyond your date of death, the policy does not provide for a refund of any unearned premium upon surrender of the policy.

4. **THIS IS NOT A MEDICARE SUPPLEMENT POLICY -** If you are eligible for Medicare, review the Medicare Supplement Buyer's Guide available from the insurance company.

Be advised that neither the insurance company nor its agents represent Medicare, the federal government, or any state government.

5. **LONG TERM CARE COVERAGE** - Policies of this type are designed to provide coverage for one or more necessary diagnostic, preventative, therapeutic, rehabilitative, maintenance, or personal care services provided in a setting other than an acute care unit of a hospital, such as in a nursing home, in the community, or in the home.

6. **BENEFITS PROVIDED BY THIS POLICY** -

   A. IMPORTANT TERMS DEFINITION

   1. *Activities of Daily Living (ADLs)*- The activities of daily living (ADLs) used to qualify for benefits under this policy are: (1)Bathing; (2)Dressing; (3)Eating; (4)Toileting; and (5)Transferring. Bathing is washing in a tub or shower and getting into and out of the tub or shower without assistance. Dressing is putting on and taking off all necessary items of clothing and prosthetic devices including getting these items out of and returning them to their usual storage places. Eating is moving prepared food from a container into the body. Toileting includes getting to and from the bathroom and taking care of one's bowel and bladder needs including transferring to and from the toilet, cleansing oneself and adjusting one's clothing. Transferring is defined as changing positions such as from the bed to a chair, from a chair to an upright position, and from an upright position to a chair or a bed.

   2. *Cognitive Impairment* - This is a deterioration in intellectual capacity to the extent that one requires regular supervision for one's own safety and the safety of others. Cognitive impairment must be determined by clinical diagnosis or tests.

   3. *Elimination Period* - This is the number of days in which you received covered care or services before benefits are payable. Such days do not need to be continuous but must

be accumulated with a continuous 730 day period. The elimination period must be satisfied only one time.

4. *Inability to Perform Activities of Daily Living (ADLs)* - Dependence upon another because of the need, which is due to injury or sickness or frailty, for regular human assistance or supervision in performing normal activities of daily living.

5. *Long Term Care Facility* - A long term care facility is one which is licensed by the state as either a skilled nursing facility, an intermediate nursing facility or a custodial care facility. It must have 24-hour nursing services which are provided under the supervision of an R.N., L.V.N. or L.P.N. and it must keep a daily record on each patient.

6. *Medical Necessity* - This is defined as care or services which are consistent with accepted medical standards for the condition and are provided for acute or chronic conditions. It must be recommended by a physician and may not be designed primarily for your or your family's convenience.

7. *Pre-Existing Condition* - Any condition for which you received medical advice or treatment in the six months before the effective day of the policy.

B. BENEFIT LIMITS

1. The maximum daily facility benefit is equal to $_____.

2. The maximum daily home and adult day care benefit is equal to $_____.

3. The maximum lifetime benefit, or total amount the policy will pay during your lifetime for all benefits, is equal to $_____.

4. The elimination period is _____ days.

C. HOME AND COMMUNITY-BASED CARE BENEFITS

To receive home and community-based care benefits, you must require covered services while the policy is in force due to medical necessity or your inability to perform at least two activities of daily living or cognitive impairment.

1. *Caregiving Training Benefit* - The policy will pay the expenses incurred for caregiving training if you require a long term care facility stay or home or community-based care. The expenses cannot exceed three times the maximum daily home and adult day care benefit.

2. *Home and Adult Day Care Benefit* - For every day that you receive home and community-based care in your home or in an adult day care center, the policy will pay the lesser of: (1) the maximum daily home and adult day care benefit or (2) the total of (a) expenses incurred for adult day care; (b) expenses incurred for services provided by a medical social worker, home health aide, or homemaker; and (c) expenses incurred for occupational, physical, respiratory or speech therapy or nursing care services provided by a registered nurse, licensed practical nurse or a vocational nurse.

3. *Respite Care Benefit* - The policy will pay the lesser of the maximum daily home and adult day care benefit or the expenses incurred each day for respite care for up to 21 days each calender year.

D. LONG TERM CARE FACILITY BENEFITS

To be eligible for long term care facility benefits you must require a stay in a long term care facility that begins while the policy is in force and the stay must be due to medical necessity or the inability to perform at least two of the ADLs or cognitive impairment.

The long term care benefit is equal to the lesser of the maximum daily facility benefit or the charges made by the facility for the care, including room and board. The long term care benefit will be paid when you are charged for your room in the long term care facility while you are temporarily hospitalized. This benefit is limited to 21 days in each calendar year.

E. ALTERNATE PLAN OF CARE BENEFIT

If you require a stay in a long term care facility the policy will pay for alternate services, devices, or types of care under a written alternate care plan. This plan must be developed by health care professionals and must be agreed to by you, your doctor, and the insurance company. The plan must be medically acceptable. Benefits paid under the alternate care plan count against the policy's lifetime maximum benefit.

F. AMBULANCE BENEFIT

The policy will pay up to $75 per trip by ambulance to or from a long term care facility for up to five trips in each calendar year.

G. OPTIONAL BENEFITS

1. *Inflation Protection Rider - Automatic Equal Increases Option* - The maximum daily facility benefit and the maximum home and adult day care benefit will be increased by 5 percent of the amounts shown on the schedule of benefits. The increase will take place on the policy anniversary. The maximum lifetime benefit will be increased proportionately.

2. *Inflation Protection Rider - Automatic Compound Increases Option* - The maximum daily facility benefit and the maximum home and adult day care benefit and the remaining maximum lifetime benefit will be increased by 5 percent of the benefit in effect on the previous anniversary of your policy.

7. EXCEPTIONS, LIMITATIONS AND REDUCTIONS

This policy does not cover losses due to (1) war or an act of war; (2) intentionally self-inflicted injury, whether inflicted while sane or insane; (3) to the extent covered under Medicare or any other government program except Medicaid; (4) to the extent provided by a family member or person who ordinarily lives in the family home; (5) a mental illness or nervous disorder without evidence of organic disease. (Loss due to Parkinson's disease, Alzheimer's disease and senile dementia are covered.); (6) a stay in a hospital, a hospice, or a care facility that treats primarily the mentally ill, drug addicts, or alcoholics.

This policy will not pay benefits for a loss due to a pre-existing condition which is not disclosed in the application unless the loss begins more than six months after the policy is in force. Losses due to a pre-existing condition shown on the application are covered immediately.

NOTE: THIS POLICY MAY NOT COVER ALL OF THE EXPENSES ASSOCIATED WITH YOUR LONG TERM CARE NEEDS.

8. RELATIONSHIP OF COST OF CARE AND BENEFITS

Because the cost of long term care services is likely to increase over time, you should consider whether and how the benefits of this policy may be adjusted. Unless you elect one of the options listed below, the benefits under your policy will not increase over time.

Your benefits may increase over time if you select one of the following optional riders: (1) the Inflation Protection Rider - Automatic Equal Increases Option; or (2) the Inflation Protection Rider - Automatic Compound Increases Option.

If you select the Inflation Protection Rider - Automatic Equal Increases Option the maximum daily facility benefit and the maximum home and adult day care benefit will be increased by 5 percent of the amounts shown on the schedule of benefits. The maximum lifetime benefit will be increased proportionately. If you select the Inflation Protection Rider - Automatic Compound Increases Option the maximum daily facility benefit and the maximum home and adult day care benefit and the remaining maximum lifetime benefit will be increased by 5 percent of the benefit in effect on the previous anniversary of your policy.

If you do not select one of these optional benefits, you may request increases to your daily benefits on any policy anniversary date subject to health underwriting and the payment of an additional premium.

9. TERMS UNDER WHICH THE POLICY MAY BE CONTINUED IN FORCE OR DISCONTINUED

1. *Renewal* - This policy is guaranteed renewable. This means that your coverage will continue for life as long as you pay the policy premium in a timely fashion. We cannot change the coverage or benefits without your consent. We can change the premium rate but only if we give you 31 days prior written notice and we change the premium rate for everyone who has this policy form in your policy rating group in your state.

2. *Waiver of Premium* - After you receive fifteen days of covered care or services including any days that you are hospitalized or the days used to satisfy the elimination period, we will waive or refund premium on this policy each quarter as long as you received at least fifteen days of covered care or services in the prior quarter. You will be responsible for premium payments starting with the first premium due date on or after the date that payment of benefits ceases.

10. ALZHEIMER'S DISEASE AND OTHER ORGANIC BRAIN DISORDERS

This policy covers loss due to Alzheimer's disease, Parkinson's disease, senile dementia or other organic brain disorders.

11. PREMIUM

The total premium for this policy is $_____.

The portion of the premium for the Inflation Protection Rider - Automatic Equal Increases Option, if selected, is $_____.

The portion of the premium for the Inflation Protection Rider - Automatic Compound Increases Option, if selected, is $_____.

12. ADDITIONAL FEATURES

1. *Medical Underwriting* - Medical underwriting is used for this policy. Your eligibility for coverage is based on the answers to the medical questions in the policy application and any additional information that may be needed to complete our evaluation of your application.

2. *Unintentional Lapse Protection* - Under this policy, you have the right to name an individual to receive notification when your policy will lapse due to non-payment of premium. The notice will be sent no earlier than 30 days after the premium due date. The policy will not be terminated until 30 days after this notice is sent.

GLOSSARY OF TERMS

Accelerated Death Benefit. An option in a life insurance policy that will pay all or part of the policy face amount prior to death. This benefit can pay the cost associated with catastrophic medical conditions which can include the need for nursing home confinement.

Activities of Daily Living. Functional routines that relate to one's ability to live independently. These activities consist of bathing, dressing, feeding, toileting, continence, mobility and taking medicine.

Adult Congregate Living Facility. Residential or apartment housing for people which can include a minimum amount of assistance with the activities of daily living.

Adult Day Care. Services provided to individuals who cannot remain alone, including health and custodial care and other related support. This care is rendered in specified centers on a less than 24 hour basis.

Adult Day Care Facility. An institution designated to provide custodial and/or minimum health care assistance to individuals unable to remain alone, usually during working hours when the caregiver is employed.

Alternate Plan of Care. A long term care insurance policy feature which allows for substantial flexibility in designing a recovery and/or maintenance program for a claimant, using as many types of long term care assistance as needed on a reasonable cost basis.

Asset Spend-down. Procedure where an individual's income and assets are diminished in order to attain the minimum required levels of the various state's eligibility requirements for Medicaid assistance.

Assisted Living Facility. Residence for long term care patients on a less expensive basis and receives some long term care services.

Benefit Period. The length of time for which benefits under a long term care insurance contract will be paid (ie; four years or lifetime).

Bereavement Counseling. A support service designed to assist family members of terminally ill patients to cope with their grief. This service is often available under a hospice care program and a benefit may be payable under a long term care insurance policy.

Caregiver. A person providing assistance to a dependent person due to medical reasons or the inability to conduct routine activities of daily living.

Cognitive Impairment. One of the measurements used to determine eligibility for long term care benefits in a policy, it is the deterioration or loss of one's intellectual capacity, confirmed by clinical evidence and standardized tests, in the areas of: (1) short and long term memory; (2) orientation as to person, place and time; and (3) deductive or abstract reasoning.

Cohorts. A grouping of individuals based on their values and characteristics formed by the period of time they came of age. Understanding this orientation is important in relationship selling.

Comprehensive Benefits. A long term care insurance plan that offers a wide variety of coverage for long term care insurance services. This plan was modeled after the NAIC model policy in 1988.

Continuing Care Retirement Communities. This campus-type environment offers houses, apartments, communal dining facilities, a nursing facility, recreation, a library and other services. An entry fee and a stipulated monthly payment is required.

Custodial Care. The most common type of long term care service rendered, it provides assistance with activities of daily living and generally performed by a trained aide in a variety of settings, most often in the home.

Custodial Care Facility. Licensed by the state to provide custodial care and assistance with activities of daily living and a nursing staff to oversee the administering of medication.

Daily Benefit Amount. The specified amount of benefit payable for long term care services. The dollar amount may vary by service such as $100 a day payable for a nursing home confinement and $75 a day payable for home health care.

Diagnostic Related Grouping. Medicare uses this grouping as a guide for the treatment of Medicare recipients and payment to providers. This guide governs the length of hospital stay for each illness or injury. Hospital discharges often force individuals not well enough to go home to be admitted into a skilled nursing facility.

Elimination Period. In a long term care insurance policy, this is a period of time during which no benefits are payable and is sometimes referred to as a deductible. Examples of elimination periods are 15 and 100 days.

Employer-Sponsored plans. This is group long term care insurance first introduced in 1987. The earlier plans were voluntary, portable products with benefits and premiums similar to individual long term care coverage.

Gatekeepers. Also called "safety nets", these specific qualifications, must be met before becoming eligible for any specific benefit payment under a long term care insurance policy. These qualifications set by insurance company have largely been eliminated through NAIC's model policy and state regulation.

Geriatric Case Manager. An individual assigned to handle the various needs of a person unable to do for themselves. This qualified individual can coordinate every aspect of an aging adult's care from interviewing and hiring household help to paying bills and often serve as the eyes and ears of other family members not located in the immediate area.

Guaranteed Renewable. The renewal provision of a long term care insurance policy, ensuring that the policy cannot be canceled by the insurer nor can policy provisions be changed without the insured's consent. Policy premiums, however, may be adjusted upward based on the company's experience for an entire class of business.

Health Care Financing Administration. This is the administrative arm of Medicare and other programs.

Health Care Surrogate. An individual designated as a medical durable power of attorney to make medical decisions on behalf of another person.

Home Care. This is a type of long term care service, provided in the home, generally consists of activities of daily living assistance and are rendered by a trained aide.

Home Health Care. A program of professional, paraprofessional and skilled care usually provided through a home health care agency to a person at home. This care is often prescribed by a physician as medically necessary and can include nursing services, physical, speech, respiratory and occupational therapy.

Home Health Care Agency. An organization providing home health care or home care, state licensed or accredited as required, keeps clinical records of all patients, and is supervised by a qualified physician or registered nurse.

Hospice Care. A coordinated program for control of pain and symptoms for the terminally ill which may also provide support services to family members.

Inflation Protection Benefit. This optional benefit is designed to help preserve the value of the daily benefit amount. It automatically increases the daily benefit annually on a simple or compounded basis either by a stipulated percentage amount or an index measurement.

Intermediate Care. Occasional nursing services, preventive or rehabilitative, performed under the supervision of skilled medical personnel.

Intermediate Care Facility. An institution licensed by the state to provide patient care for those requiring constant availability and support, but very little in the way of skilled care. This facility may also provide custodial care services.

Long distance caregiving. A difficult position in caring for a family member while located in another area and not available for day to day assistance.

Long Term Care Insurance. A specific type of insurance policy designed to offer financial support in paying for necessary long term care services rendered in a variety of settings.

Long Term Care Rider. This is an optional benefit that can be added to a life insurance, annuity or disability income policy to provide benefits for long term care.

Managed Care. A type of claims management system for long term care insurance policies using pre-selected providers who have agreed to treat insurance company claimants on a reduced cost basis.

Medicaid. The joint federal and state welfare program administered by the states to provide payment for health care services, including long term care, for those meeting minimum asset and income requirements.

Medicare. Federal program organized under the Health Insurance for the Aged Act, Title XVIII of the Social Security Amendments of 1965, it provides hospital and medical expense benefits, including long term care services, for those individuals over age 65 or those meeting specific disability standards.

Medicare Catastrophic Act. Federal legislation enacted January 1, 1989, it expanded long term care benefit payments provided under Medicaid and also changed some Medicaid requirements. The Medicare changes in the Act were repealed that same year effective January 1, 1990. The Medicaid changes stayed intact.

NAIC Model Policy. Recommended minimum policy standards as designated by the insurance industry watchdog, the National Association of Insurance Commissioners (NAIC), originally established in 1988 and amended thereafter, states have the choice to adopt part, all or none of the standards for their own regulation.

Nonforfeiture Benefits. This long term care insurance policy feature enables the insured to continue long term care coverage in some form after the insured has ceased making premium payments. A cash return, a paid-up policy or an extended term feature are typical nonforfeiture benefits.

Partnerships. A joint public and private sector program that allows residents of a state to buy an approved long term care insurance policy that would pay benefits during a long term care claim and enable these residents to conserve some assets that would otherwise have to be spent down to access Medicaid. States introducing partnerships so far are

Connecticut, New York, Indiana and California, but several other states are expected to introduce their versions in the near future.

Pool of Money. Under a long term care insurance program, this is a variation on the typical benefit period. Rather than designate a period of time over which benefits can be payable, this concept creates a lump sum of money to be used as needed during a long term care claim. The claim ceases when services are no longer needed or the lump sum of money runs out.

Pre-existing condition. A diagnosed injury or sickness for which medical advice or treatment was sought prior to the effective date of the long term care insurance contract.

Prospective Payment System. Introduced to Medicare in 1983, this is the program that payments are calculated and made to providers of medical services for Medicare eligible individuals and includes diagnostic related groupings.

Respite Care. Services provided for caregivers to permit temporary periods of relief or rest in caring for a person. These services can be provided by a home health care agency or other state licensed facility and may be reimbursable under a long term care insurance policy.

Return of Premium. An optional benefit under a long term care insurance policy that provides a return of all or a portion of premiums paid less claims paid, either on a specified policy anniversary or, at policy surrender or, death of the insured.

Sandwich Generation. This term was coined when describing individuals caring for both a dependent children and an aging parent or relative.

Single Premium Long Term Care Insurance. This version of a long term care insurance policy calls for a single deposit by the insured. For example, $100,000 buys both life insurance and long term care protection.

Skilled Care. A professional type of nursing assistance performed by trained medical personnel under the supervision of a physician or other qualified medical personnel. It is the only type of care eligible for reimbursement in a skilled nursing facility under Medicare.

Spousal Impoverishment Protection. Medicaid changes made as part of the Medicare Catastrophic Act of 1988 provided an income and shelter allowance for the at home spouse whose partner is institutionally confined.

Subacute Care. Assistance provided by nursing homes for health services such as stroke rehabilitation and cardiac care for post-surgery that offers a lower cost alternative to hospital treatment of the same kind.

Swing beds. Hospital beds that may be designated as either acute care or skilled nursing, changing from one to the other to continue care to the individual without having to switch rooms or facilities.

Transfers. In qualifying for Medicaid, transfers are moving assets to someone other than a spouse or to a trust for the purposes of qualifying for Medicaid. Transfers must be made 36 months before Medicaid application (or 60 months if a trust is involved).

Triple Trigger. This is the designation for the three ways to be eligible for benefits under a long term care insurance policy including assistance with activities of daily living, cognitive impairment or medical necessity.

Viatical Settlements. The purchase, on a reduced basis, a life insurance policy owned by a terminally ill person.

Waiver of Premium. A policy provision of a long term care insurance contract that suspends premium payment after a specified period of time during which the insured is receiving policy benefits for long term care services. The suspension continues until recovery at which resumption of premium payment is expected.

INDEX

THE LONG TERM CARE HANDBOOK SUPPLEMENT

The Health Insurance Portability and Accountability Act of 1996

When The Long Term Care Handbook was published in June of 1996 the rules concerning the income taxation of long term care premiums and benefits were uncertain, as discussed in Chapter 15. Approximately two months later, in August of 1996, Congress passed legislation which directly addresses these issues.

The following is a summary of the changes made by The Health Insurance Portability and Accountability Act of 1996 which was signed by the President on August 21, 1996. The Act sets forth the income tax treatment of long term care premiums and benefits by adding Section 7702B to the Internal Revenue Code and amending several existing Code sections. This material updates primarily Chapter 15, "Taxation and Legislation Issues." The outline of the newly-created definition of a qualified long term care insurance contract supplements the discussion of today's basic policy found in Chapter 11. Further, the summary of the changes concerning accelerated death benefits and viatical settlements supplements the discussion of these topics found in Chapter 13.

Long Term Care Insurance Premiums

By amending the definition of "medical care" in Code section 213(d), the Act makes premiums paid for any qualified long term care insurance contract eligible for income tax deduction subject to the 7.5 percent adjusted gross income floor and a specific dollar limitation. The amount of this limitation increases with the age of the insured individual. For persons age 40 or less before the end of the taxable year, the limitation amount is $200. For those between 40 and 50, the limitation amount is $375; for those between 50 and 60, the limitation amount is $750; for those between 60 and 70, the limitation amount is $2,000 and for those over 70, the limitation amount is $2,500. This change is effective for taxable years beginning after December 31, 1996.

These limitation amounts will be indexed for inflation beginning after 1997. The increase will be linked to the increase in the medical care component of the Consumer Price Index and will be made in increments of $10. The Act directs the Secretary of the Treasury to prescribe a more appropriate adjustment to replace this adjustment.

Long Term Care Insurance Benefits

Generally, the Act provides that for contracts issued after December 31, 1996, a "qualified long-term care insurance contract" is treated as an accident and health insurance contract. Thus, amounts received from such a contract are treated as amounts received for sickness and personal injuries which are generally excludable from income. The new Code section takes this analogy a step further in providing that an employer plan providing coverage under a qualified long term care insurance contract will also be treated as an accident and health insurance plan.

However, newly-created Code section 7702B places a limit or "cap" on the amount of qualified long term care benefits that may be excluded from income. Generally, if the total periodic long term care payments received from all policies and any periodic payments received that are treated as paid by reason of the death of the insured (under another newly-added provision, Code section 101(g)) exceed a per diem limitation, the excess must be included in income.

The per diem limitation is equal to the excess of the greater of the $175 per day limitation or the costs incurred for qualified long term care services provided for the insured over the total payments received as reimbursement for qualified long term care services for the insured. The amount of the limitation, $175 per day ($63,875 per year), applies in 1997 and will be adjusted for inflation in later years.

Long Term Care Services Considered to be "Medical Care"

The Act amended Code section 213(d) which defines what is considered to be "medical care" for purposes of the income tax deduction to include "... amounts paid – for qualified long-term care services...". Thus, amounts paid for long term care services may be deducted from income, provided that the 7.5 percent of adjusted gross income floor is met.

However, an amount paid for qualified long term care services will not be treated as paid for medical care if the service is provided by the individual's spouse or a relative unless the service is provided by a licensed professional. A "relative" is generally any individual who could be considered a dependent under the Code (see Code section 152(a)(1) through (8)). Also, the service may not be provided by a corporation or partnership which is related to the individual (within the meaning of Code sections 267(b) or 707(b)).

Definition of a "Qualified Long Term Care Insurance Contract"

As is to be expected with any new tax provision, Code section 7702B abounds with definitions. The definition of a "qualified long-term care insurance contract," one of the most important to consider, is complex. An insurance contract meets this definition if:

1. the only insurance protection provided under the contract is coverage of qualified long term care services;

2

2. the contract does not pay or reimburse expenses incurred for services that are reimbursable under Title XVIII of the Social Security Act (or would be reimbursable but for the application of a deductible or coinsurance amount);

3. the contract is guaranteed renewable;

4. the contract does not provide for a cash surrender value or other money that can be paid, assigned or pledged as collateral for a loan or borrowed;

5. all premium refunds and dividends under the contract are to be applied as a reduction in future premiums or to increase future benefits; and

6. the contract satisfies certain consumer protection provisions concerning model regulation and model act provisions, disclosure, and nonforfeitability. (These provisions are discussed below under "Consumer Protection Provisions Applicable to Long Term Care Insurance Contracts".)

An exception to the rule concerning refunds and dividends (number 5 above) is for a refund made on the death of the insured or upon a complete surrender or cancellation of the contract which cannot exceed the aggregate premiums paid. Any refund given upon cancellation or complete surrender of the policy will be includable in income to the extent that any deduction or exclusion was allowable with respect to the premiums.

The Act states that the portion of a life insurance policy (i.e., a rider) that provides long term care coverage will be treated as a separate contract under the new rules. The Act also provides further instruction concerning the application of Code section 7702. Generally, the guideline premium limitation will be increased by the sum of any charges (not premium payments) against the life insurance contract's cash surrender value for such coverage less any such charges which reduce the premiums paid for the contact.

Further, there is no deduction permitted under Code section 213(d) for charges against the life insurance contract's cash surrender value unless the charges are includable in income as a result of the application of Section 72(e)(10) (which deals with modified endowment contracts) and the rider is a qualified long term care insurance contract.

"Qualified long-term care services" are defined as ".. necessary diagnostic, preventive, therapeutic, curing, treating, mitigating, and rehabilitative services and maintenance or personal care services which..." are required by a chronically ill individual and are provided under a plan of care

3

set forth by a licensed health care practitioner. A "chronically ill individual" is a person who has been certified as being unable to perform, without substantial assistance, at least two activities of daily living (ADLs) for at least 90 days or a person with a similar level of disability. Further, a person may be considered chronically ill if he requires substantial supervision to protect himself from threats to his health and safety due to severe cognitive impairment and this condition has been certified by a health care practitioner within the previous 12 months. Thus, the Act provides a separate "benefit trigger" for cognitive impairment. However, it apparently does not provide that benefits may be triggered by medical necessity.

The activities of daily living are: (1) eating; (2) toileting; (3) transferring; (4) bathing; (5) dressing; and (6) continence. To be considered a qualified long term care insurance contract a policy must take into account at least five of these ADLs in determining whether a person is chronically ill.

Existing Long Term Care Policies

The Act provides that any contract issued before January 1, 1997, which met the long term care requirements of the state in which the contract was "sitused" at the time it was issued, will be treated for tax purposes as a qualified long term care insurance contract and services provided under the contract or reimbursed by the contract will be treated as qualified long term care services.

If a contract which provides for long term care insurance coverage is exchanged after the date of the Act's enactment and before January 1, 1998, solely for a qualified long term care insurance contract as defined in Code section 7702B(b), no gain or loss will be recognized on the exchange. For purposes of this rule, if a contract providing for long term care coverage is canceled and the proceeds are reinvested in a qualified long term care insurance contact within 60 days, the transaction will qualify as an exchange.

Reporting Requirements for Long Term Care Benefits

The Act also adds several reporting requirements applicable to long term care benefits. Any person paying long term care benefits must file a return which sets forth: (1) the aggregate amount of long term care benefits paid by the person to any individual during any calendar year; (2) whether or not such benefits are paid, either fully or partially, on a per diem or other periodic basis without regard to the expenses incurred during the period; (3) the name, address, and taxpayer identification number (TIN) of such individual; and (4) the name, address, and TIN of the chronically ill or terminally ill individual for whom the benefits are paid.

Additionally, any person paying long term care benefits must provide a written statement to each individual whose name is reported under the above

4

requirement. The statement must show the name of the person making the payments and the aggregate amount of long term care benefits paid to the individual that is required to be shown on the above-mentioned form. This written statement must reach the individual on or before January 31 of the year following the calendar year for which the return was required.

For purposes of these reporting requirements "long term care benefits" are any payment under a product which is advertised, marketed or offered as long term care insurance and any payment which is excludable from gross income under Section 101(g). Although, newly-added Code section 6050Q which contains these reporting requirements does not specify, presumably the term "person" is used to encompass not only individuals but also companies paying long term care benefits.

Consumer Protection Provisions Applicable to Long Term Care Insurance Contracts

The Act contains certain provisions designed to protect consumers purchasing long term care insurance contracts. In order to be considered a qualified long term care insurance contract, a contract must:

1. meet certain provisions of the NAIC long term care insurance model regulation dealing with such issues as guaranteed renewal or noncancellability, prohibitions on limitations and exclusions, extension of benefits, continuation or conversion of coverage, replacement of policies, unintentional lapse, disclosure, post-claims underwriting, minimum standards, the requirement to offer inflation protection, and the prohibition against preexisting conditions and probationary periods in replacement policies;

2. meet certain provisions of the NAIC long term care insurance model act relating to preexisting conditions and prior hospitalization;

3. meet certain nonforfeiture provisions; and

4. comply with the newly-created disclosure requirement of Section 4980C(d).

The nonforfeiture requirement is met for a level premium policy if the contract offers the policyholder (including a group policyholder) a nonforfeiture provision which:

1. is properly captioned;

2. provides for a benefit available in the event of a default in the payment of premiums and the amount of the benefit may be adjusted only as necessary to reflect changes in claims, persistency and interest as reflected in changes in rates for premium paying contracts approved for the same contract form; and

3. provides for at least one of the following options: (a) reduced paid-up insurance; (b) extended term insurance; (c) shortened benefit period; or (d) other similar approved offerings.

The newly-added disclosure requirements of Code section 4980C provide that a policy must meet certain requirements of the NAIC long term care insurance model regulations pertaining to application forms and replacement coverage, reporting requirements, marketing filing requirements, marketing standards, the appropriateness of the recommended purchase, the standard format outline of coverages, requirements for certificates under group plans, policy summary, monthly reports on accelerated death benefits and the incontestability period. In addition, a long term care insurance policy that is approved must be delivered to the policyholder within 30 days of the approval date. Further, if a claim under a long term care insurance policy is denied, the issuer must provide a written explanation of the reasons for the denial and make available all information relating to the denial within 60 days of a written request from the policyholder.

To meet the disclosure requirements, the policy must state that it is intended to be a qualified long term care insurance contract under Code section 7702B(b).

The penalty for not meeting these requirements is a tax equal to $100 per insured for each day that these requirements are not met for each qualified long term care insurance contract.

These rules are effective for actions taken after December 31, 1996.

Long Term Care Insurance for Self-Employed Persons

Because the Act treats premiums paid for qualified long term care insurance contracts the same as medical insurance premiums, long term care insurance premiums are now eligible for deduction from income by self-employed persons.

The Act also increased the amount of health insurance (and long term care insurance) premiums that may be deducted from income by self-employed persons. Prior to this change, a self-employed individual could deduct 30 percent of amounts paid during a taxable year for insurance which provides medical care for the individual, his spouse and dependents. The Act gradually increases the percentage of health insurance premiums that may be deducted, ultimately reaching an 80 percent deduction in 2006.

A self-employed individual will be able to deduct 40 percent in 1997, 45 percent in 1998 through 2002, 50 percent in 2003, 60 percent in 2004, 70 percent in 2005 and 80 percent in 2006 and later years. Generally, sole proprietors, partners and S corporation shareholders owning more than two percent of the S corporation's shares may take advantage of this deduction.

Other Long Term Care Provisions

Additionally, the Act provides that long term care insurance may not be offered as a qualified benefit under a cafeteria plan. Further, beginning on January 1, 1997, employer-provided coverage for long term care services provided through a flexible spending arrangement (FSA) will be included in the employee's gross income.

Also, the COBRA continuation coverage requirements applicable to group health plans will not apply to plans under which substantially all of the coverage is for long term care services.

Accelerated Death Benefits and Viatical Settlements

The Act addresses the taxation of accelerated death benefits as well as amounts received for the sale or assignment of a policy to a viatical settlement provider by adding Code section 101(g). Generally, this new provision states that any amount received under a life insurance contract on the life of a terminally ill insured or a chronically ill insured will be treated as an amount paid by reason of the death of the insured. Section 101(a) of the Code states that amounts received under a life insurance contract by reason of the death of the insured are not includable in gross income.

However, amounts paid to a chronically ill individual are subject to the same limitations that apply to long term care benefits. Generally, this is the $175 per day limitation discussed above. Accelerated death benefits paid to terminally ill individuals are not subject to this limit.

Newly-added Section 101(g) also provides that if any portion of the death benefit under a life insurance contract on the life of a terminally or chronically ill insured is sold or assigned to a viatical settlement provider the amount paid for the sale or assignment will be treated as an amount paid under the life insurance contract by reason of the insured's death. In other words, such an amount will not be included in income. The Code now defines a viatical settlement provider as "any person regularly engaged in the trade or business of purchasing, or taking assignments of, life insurance contracts on the lives of insureds…" provided that certain licensing and other requirements are met.

There are several special rules that apply to chronically ill insureds. Generally, the tax treatment outlined above will not apply to any payment received for any period unless such payment is for costs incurred by the payee (who has not been compensated by insurance or otherwise) for qualified long term care services provided to the insured for the period. Additionally, the terms of the contract under which such payments are made must comply with the requirements of newly-added Code section 7702B plus several other requirements.

A terminally ill individual is a person who has been certified by a physician as having an illness or physical condition which can reasonably be expected to result in death within 24 months following the certification. A chronically ill individual is a person who is not terminally ill and meets the definition set forth above.

There is one exception to this new general rule of non-includability for accelerated death benefits and viatical settlements. The rules outlined above do not apply to any amount paid to any taxpayer other than the insured if the taxpayer has an insurable interest in the life of the insured because the insured is a director, officer or employee of the taxpayer or if the insured is financially interested in any trade or business of the taxpayer.

These provisions are effective for amounts received after December 31, 1996.

Group Health Plan Portability, Access, and Renewability Requirements

The Act also added Code sections 9801 through 9806 which set forth several requirements applicable to group health plans. These requirements deal with such issues as limitations on preexisting conditions, discrimination based on health status, and guaranteed renewability on multi-employer plans. Code section 9805(c)(2) states that, if offered separately, benefits for long term care, nursing home care, home health care, and community-based care are not subject to these requirements.

The materials discussed in this supplement are contained primarily in Act sections 311, 321, 322, 323, 325, 326, 331, and 401 which amended or added Internal Revenue Code sections 101(g), 106, 162(l), 125(f), 213(d), 4980B, 4980C and 7702B.

Need Additional Copies?

To order additional copies of *The Long Term Care Handbook* or to order copies of the other books in the handbook series, *The Mutual Fund Handbook* and *The Annuity Handbook,* use these handy postage-paid forms or, call **1-800-543-0874** and ask for **Operator NF** or **FAX** this form to **1-800-874-1916.**

Single copy $26.95	25 copies, ea....... 22.95	250 copies, ea. 18.95
5 copies, ea 25.60	50 copies, ea....... 21.50	500 copies, ea....... 17.50
10 copies, ea 24.25	100 copies, ea...... 20.50	1,000 copies, ea. 16.20

PACKAGE PRICES Any 2 titles - $44 (Save $9.90) All 3 titles - $63 (Save $17.85)

PAYMENT INFORMATION

*Add shipping & handling charges to all orders as indicated. If your order exceeds total amount listed in chart, call 1-800-543-0874 for shipping & handling charge. Any order of 10 or more or over $250.00 will be billed for shipping by actual weight, plus a handling fee. Unconditional 30 day guarantee.

SHIPPING & HANDLING (Additional)

Order Total	Shipping & Handling
$20.00 - $39.99	$6.00
40.00 - 59.99	7.00
60.00 - 79.99	9.00
80.00 - 109.99	10.00
110.00 - 149.99	12.00
150.00 - 199.99	13.00
200.00 - 249.99	15.50

SALES TAX (Additional)

Sales tax is required for residents of the following states: CA, DC, FL, GA, IL, NJ, NY, OH, PA.

■**NATIONAL UNDERWRITER.**

The National Underwriter Co.
Customer Service Dept #2-NF
505 Gest Street
Cincinnati, OH 45203-1716

2-NF

Please send me ____copies of *The Long Term Care Handbook* (#247)

____copies of *The Annuity Handbook* (#202)

____copies of *The Mutual Fund Handbook* (#207)

❑ Check enclosed*   ❑ Charge my VISA/MC/AmEx (circle one)   ❑ Bill me

Card #_____ Exp. Date_____

Signature_____

Name_____ Title_____

Company_____

Street Address_____

City_____State _____Zip+4_____

Business Phone (_____)_____

*Make check payable to The National Underwriter Company. Please include the appropriate shipping & handling charges and any applicable sales tax.

Offer expires 12/31/97

■**NATIONAL UNDERWRITER.**

The National Underwriter Co.
Customer Service Dept #2-NF
505 Gest Street
Cincinnati, OH 45203-1716

2-NF

Please send me ____copies of *The Long Term Care Handbook* (#247)

____copies of *The Annuity Handbook* (#202)

____copies of *The Mutual Fund Handbook* (#207)

❑ Check enclosed*   ❑ Charge my VISA/MC/AmEx (circle one)   ❑ Bill me

Card #_____ Exp. Date_____

Signature_____

Name_____ Title_____

Company_____

Street Address_____

City_____State _____Zip+4_____

Business Phone (_____)_____

*Make check payable to The National Underwriter Company. Please include the appropriate shipping & handling charges and any applicable sales tax.

Offer expires 12/31/97

BUSINESS REPLY MAIL

FIRST CLASS MAIL   PERMIT NO. 68   CINCINNATI, OH

POSTAGE WILL BE PAID BY ADDRESSEE

The National Underwriter Co.
Customer Service Dept. #2-NF
505 Gest Street
Cincinnati, OH 45203-9928

NO POSTAGE
NECESSARY
IF MAILED
IN THE
UNITED STATES

BUSINESS REPLY MAIL

FIRST CLASS MAIL   PERMIT NO. 68   CINCINNATI, OH

POSTAGE WILL BE PAID BY ADDRESSEE

The National Underwriter Co.
Customer Service Dept. #2-NF
505 Gest Street
Cincinnati, OH 45203-9928